The Leib Glantz Project

Forty-three New Arrangements of the Compositions of Cantor and Composer Leib Glantz

In Honor and in Memory of the Great Cantor Yonia Glantz

edited by
Jerry Glantz

published by
The Tel Aviv Institute for Jewish Liturgical Music

Visit the book's website at www.LeibGlantzProject.com

Page Layout: Words Plus Design, Tecumseh, Michigan, www.wordsplusdesign.com

Compact Disc musical editor & photography editor: Noam Brown, Bangkok, Thailand.

Musical notes editor on "Finale" software: Cantor Evan Cohen, Jerusalem, Israel.

End pages design, based on 1988 poster for Leib Glantz concert in Tel Aviv by Eliezer Weishoff.

Portrait of Leib Glantz by Saul Raskin.

Printed in Shanghai, China.

First Edition: 2013

Library of Congress Control Number: 2013945947

Glantz, Jerry
The Leib Glantz Project

Summary: Leib Glantz – Cantor and composer; forty three new musical arrangements of his famous compositions, including excerpts of his writings, lectures and research, and excerpts from academic essays by writers, philosophers, cantors, conductors, composers and musicologists defining his historical importance as an icon of Jewish music. Including three compact disks with Leib Glantz singing his most important compositions.

ISBN - 978-0-615-82939-5

1. Music. 2. Jewish music. 3. Musicology. 4. Cantorial = *Chazzanut.*
5. Cantor = *Chazan (Hazzan).* 6. Synagogue music. 7. Ashkenazic prayer modes.
8. Chasidism. 9. Chasidic music. 10. Zionism. 11. Israel.

Leib Glantz, with brother Cantor Yonah (Yonia) Glantz and Yonah's wife Sarah, in Portland, Oregon.

THIS BOOK IS DEDICATED IN HONOR OF

Cantor Yonia Glantz (1903-1962)

The Leib Glantz Project is dedicated in honor of the great Cantor Yonia Glantz *z'l*, brother of Cantor Leib Glantz.

Yonia was born in Kiev, Ukraine in 1903, where he eventually officiated as cantor in his father's Tolner Chassidim Synagogue.

He emigrated to the United States in 1930, and officiated as Chief Cantor in Congregation *Shaarie Torah* in Portland, Oregon, for 32 years. In 1933 he married Sarah Pomerantz, and they had a daughter, Devorah Weinstein, and a son, Kalman.

Yonia Glantz was greatly admired. His mastering of the Jewish Prayer Modes, the *Nusach,* was impeccable, and his beautiful lyric tenor enjoyed a wide and flexible range.

As a master of the art of the cantor, Yonia Glantz was a much loved and well-respected leader of the Portland Jewish community until his untimely passing in 1962.

Table of Contents

List of Composition Arrangements

continued on next page

Abbreviations:

C = Cantor

VSC = Vocal score (cantor + piano)

TTBB = Male choir

SATB = Mixed choir

NY=New York, NY; **LA**=Los Angeles, CA; **TA**=Tel Aviv, Israel; **Kish**=Kishinev, Bessarabia; **Kiev**=Kiev, Ukraine.

Musicrft=Musicraft Recording Corp; **Famous**=Famous Records Inc; **IMF**=Israel Music Foundation; **RCA**=Radio Corporation of America; **Besa**=Besa Record Company; **Reena**=Reena Record Corp; **Asch**=Asch Recordings. **LG Book**=The Man Who Spoke To God.

The Sponsors of The Leib Glantz Project

Cantor Roslyn Barak	Congregation Emanu-El, San Francisco, CA
Professor Alan & Dr. Naomi Berger	Boca Raton, Florida
Noam Brown	Bangkok, Thailand
Cantor Joel Caplan	Congregation Agudath Israel, Caldwell, NJ
Udi & Aviva Hermon Chersonsky	Herzliya, Israel
Harlan Cohen	Boca Raton, Florida
Katty Cohen & Jerry Glantz	Boca Raton, Florida
Cantor Sid Dworkin	Congregation Shaar Hashomayim, Montreal, Canada
Katrin Farkas	Mississauga, Canada
Eviatar Feldman	Nairobi, Kenya
Cantor Raphael Frieder	Temple Israel, Great Neck, NY
Cantor Morris Glazman	Congregation Kol Ami, White Plains, NY
Bill & Monika Glied	Toronto, Canada
Cantor Moshe Haschel	St. John's Wood Synagogue, London, England
Cantor Dov Keren	Sutton Place Synagogue, New York, NY
Cantor Nate Lam	Stephen S. Wise Temple, Los Angeles, CA
Cantor Yanky Lemer	Congregation Anshe Sholom, New Rochelle, NY
Cantor David Lipp	Congregation Adat Jeshurun, Louisville, Kentucky
Cantor Leon & Judge Meryl Lissek	Teanek, New Jersey
Cantor Abe Lubin	Congregation Beth El, Bathesda, MD
Cantor Beny Maissner	Holy Blossom Temple, Toronto, Canada
Cantor Mikhail Manevich	Washington Hebrew Congregation, Washington, DC
Rabbi Moshe Meirovich	Lodzer Centre Congregation, Downsview, Canada
Cantor Jacob Mendelson	Temple Israel Center, White Plains, NY
Cantor Neil Michaels	Temple Israel, West Bloomfield, MI
Cantor Alberto Mizrahi	Anshe Emet Synagogue, Chicago, IL
Canter Eric Moses	Beth Sholom Synagogue, Toronto, Canada
Cantor Penny Myers	Temple Beit Zion, Buffalo, NY
Cantor Emanuel Perlman	Congregation Chizuk Amuno, Baltimore, MD
Cantor Lindi Rivers	Holy Blossom Temple, Toronto, Canada
Cantor Efraim Sapir	Temple Anshei Shalom, Delray Beach, Florida
Cantor Azi Schwartz	Park Avenue Synagogue, New York, NY
Cantor Michael Smolash	Temple Israel, West Bloomfield, MI
Cantor Udi Spielman	B'nai Torah Congregation, Boca Raton, Florida
Claude Szwimer	JuMU = Nu Juwish Music, Paris, France
Ron & Deborah Weinstein	Seattle, WA
Haim & Gila Wiener	Miami Beach, Florida
Cantor Gideon Zelermyer	Congregation Shaar Hashomayim, Montreal, Canada
Cantor Avshalom & Roni Zfira	Boca Raton, Florida
Council of Hazzanim of Greater Montreal	Montreal, Canada
Toronto Council of Cantors	Toronto, Canada
Congregation Shaarei Tefila	Los Angeles, CA
Sinai Temple	Los Angeles, CA

"Music was created not only for pleasing the ear. It must have a meaning, express an activity, a natural or supernatural force, a feeling. Without meaning, it loses its reason for being."

Yaya Diallo
A drummer from Mali, Africa

Quoted from *Work Songs,* by Ted Gioia, Duke University Press, 2006.

Preface

JERRY GLANTZ

During his illustrious 65-year lifespan, Leib Glantz wrote two hundred and sixteen compositions. They encompassed Cantorial music, Chassidic music, as well as Hebrew and Yiddish art songs.

As a performing artist who mainly sang his own compositions, Glantz wrote the music the way he wanted to sing it *himself.* He was a lyric tenor with a vast vocal range and unique vocal capabilities.

Following his untimely passing in Tel Aviv in 1964, the Board of Directors of the **Tel Aviv Institute for Jewish Liturgical Music** (founded by Glantz in 1959), decided to terminate the institute's **Cantors Academy,** and transform it into the publishing organ of Leib Glantz's lectures, essays, articles and musical compositions.

In addition to the Hebrew book ***Zeharim* – In Memory of Leib Glantz,** seven volumes were published in the ***Rinat Ha'Kodesh* Series** – a collection of most of Glantz's important compositions. Cantor Israel Alter and Yehoshua Zohar, Glantz's long-time choir conductor, oversaw the project and David Loeb performed the editing. The series was co-published in the 1960s by the **Israel Music Institute**.

In the process of writing the book about my father – **The Man Who Spoke To God** (2008) – I discussed the ***Rinat Ha'Kodesh* Series** with composer, arranger and accompanist Raymond Goldstein, who maintained that the compositions in those volumes were not functional for contemporary cantors and performers.

In response, I invited Raymond to write an essay on this topic, which I included in **The Man Who Spoke To God**.

His comments troubled me. A year ago I invited him to compose a series of new arrangements to Leib Glantz's compositions, in what developed into **The Leib Glantz Project.**

Soon thereafter, Raymond and I scheduled a meeting in Florida, and Cantor Benjamin Maissner and Cantor Naftali Herstik joined us.

Cantor Herstik, who, as a teenager, had several meetings with Glantz, fondly recalls their discussions about *Chazzanut.* He also witnessed Glantz's *Davening* at the *Tiferet Zvi* Synagogue in Tel Aviv. Cantor Herstik was very enthusiastic about the idea of composing new arrangements, but made an important observation: "It is not sufficient to try to perform Leib Glantz's compositions, even with new arrangements, unless the potential performer thoroughly understands what Glantz was thinking when he composed a particular work and where he was coming from. In other words, what was Glantz's thought process when he was applying his musical interpretations to the prayer texts?"

I invited Cantor Herstik to write an introduction to each new arrangement, explaining his understanding of Glantz's creative process, and they are included in this book.

Herstik, the Director of **TACI (Tel Aviv Cantorial Institute)** and Raymond Goldstein, a senior faculty member at TACI, worked hand in hand in composing the new arrangements.

Cantor Benjamin Maissner of Toronto provided essential critical editing and encouraged many of his fellow cantors around the world to support this original Project. Maissner felt blessed to have participated in Glantz's services at the *Tiferet Zvi* synagogue for almost a decade, beginning at age ten.

Cantor Evan Cohen of Jerusalem performed wonders in the process of putting the countless pages of musical notes onto "Finale" software and preparing the material for publication.

The purpose of the **Leib Glantz Project** is to make his music both accessible and easily performable by current day musicians. I believe it is very important for potential performers to be able to listen to the way Glantz himself sang his compositions. This will enable them to experience the drama and the fervor that Glantz intended and succeeded in transmitting to his listeners.

As a companion to this book, the Leib Glantz Project includes a special website.

www.TheLeibGlantzProject.com enhances the scope of the Project by offering, in addition to the Glantz recordings, the introduction texts, and the original arrangements. Moreover, the same new arrangements appear in several other keys, which will enable performers with different vocal ranges to perform these arrangements with ease.

The website enables anyone to log on, print out the chosen musical notes and download the recordings **free of charge**.

Finally, it was heartwarming to receive the financial support for this endeavor from so many who recognize the importance and the uniqueness of Leib Glantz. I want to particularly acknowledge Ron and Devorah Weinstein, whose generosity made this Project feasible.

For me personally – the Leib Glantz Project was a labor of love.

Introduction

RAYMOND GOLDSTEIN[1]

MUSICAL ARRANGER AND CHIEF EDITOR OF THE LEIB GLANTZ PROJECT

Having had the privilege of being Musical Director to two international "Glantz" concerts given at the Tel Aviv Mann Auditorium over the years, in addition to a host of recordings with various cantors, I occasionally found myself having to work from scratch in reconstructing concert settings suitable for performance of Leib Glantz's compositions.

It wasn't that material didn't exist, either in manuscript or in publication, before and after his death. However, more often than not, settings were based on what was notated and not on what was actually sung by Glantz himself on his various recordings. The situation was compounded by the fact that various recordings of the same work were recorded by Glantz at different times with different ensembles as well as in different keys.

As a cantor, Glantz was primarily a melodist with much ingenuity, originality and inventiveness in his use of the ascending and descending fourth and fifth intervals, as well as placing an emphasis on accented nonessential notes to a given chord, thus exhibiting his own unique brand of *Nusach*. Like any great composer, two bars of Glantz immediately inform us as to the composer of the piece.

Glantz's music is not for the fainthearted. His main concern was for *Perush Ha'Milah* – interpretation of the text, showing the inner meaning of the particular prayer at hand.

Glantz's harmonic palate was based on traditional classical harmony, which can be inadequate when harmonic difficulties are caused, by the innate twists and turns of classical Hebrew modes, thus showing a frequent reliance on the use of the diminished chord as a panacea to any harmonic problem.

Today's liturgical singers have unfortunately become what I would call "gramophone cantors." If a recitative already notated is not the same as the recorded version, the performer will usually refrain from singing it in concert or at the synagogue service. The cantorial art is of course an extemporizing one and often no two performances are identical.

1. Raymond Goldstein is the associate conductor and resident arranger for the Jerusalem Great Synagogue choir and arranger/accompanist to the Tel Aviv Cantorial Institute (TACI). Born in Cape Town, South Africa in 1953, he has served since 1978 on the faculty of the Jerusalem Academy of Music, and since 1991 on the faculty of the Tel Aviv Cantorial Institute. His works include inter alia an opera, cantatas, and numerous sacred and secular arrangements.

In preparation of this edition, I greatly benefited from the invaluable guidance of Cantor Naftali Herstik. Together we delved into the various manuscripts and recordings at hand that enabled us to publish this practical and artistic collection of the best of Leib Glantz's great compositions.

Not all the settings are for vocal scores. Some are for TTBB (male) or SATB (mixed) choirs. The keys in the printed edition represent in most cases the keys that Glantz used in his own performances. In the manuscript collection of his works that are housed at the Tel Aviv Cantorial Institute, works were often transcribed into various other keys as well. Taking into account that not all future performers would be tenors with Glantz's unique tessitura, therefore, in addition to the printed publication, a special Leib Glantz Project website is available – with the arrangements presented in medium and lower keys.

My colleague, Cantor Evan Cohen, brilliantly executed the difficult task of computerizing the musical notations and the meticulous proofreading of this publication. It is my fervent hope that with this publication, future generations will have the opportunity to perform and promote the unique art of Leib Glantz — "The Man Who Spoke To God."

Biography of Leib Glantz

Leib Glantz was born in 1898 in Kiev, Ukraine. His father, paternal grandfather, and father-in-law were famous cantors.

As a child he studied in a religious Chassidic *Cheder* and later in a *Yeshiva.*

Leibele, as he was fondly nicknamed, was eight years old when he first appeared as cantor in his grandfather's synagogue. Word of the child prodigy spread swiftly, and he was invited to chant in several cities in the region. Soon after, Glantz, accompanied by his father, was invited to appear in several European countries.

In 1917, the year of the Bolshevik Revolution, Glantz completed his secular education, earned his high school graduation certificate and enrolled in the University of Kiev, while studying piano at the music school of the Ukrainian pianist and composer, Nikolai Tutkovski (1857-1930), composer of the Russian opera *"Boyni Viatar."* Upon graduation, Glantz enhanced his musical education, at the Kiev Music Conservatory under Reinhold Gliere (1875-1956), composer of some of the most important Russian symphonies, operas and ballets, such as *"The Red Poppy."* Influenced by these studies, Glantz applied his classical music tools towards composing Jewish liturgical music as well as Hebrew and Yiddish art songs.

Glantz planned to emigrate to Palestine in 1923, however the sudden death of his father necessitated a change in plans as his family became desperately dependent on his financial support.

Due to his intensive Zionist activism, and the Romanian communist regime's growing antagonism towards the Jews, in 1926 Glantz fled Eastern Europe for the United States.

Upon his arrival in New York in August, 1926, he was invited to appear in a major cantorial concert. His singing was received with great enthusiasm and he was offered the prestigious position of chief cantor at the famous *O'hev Sha'lom* synagogue in New York.

By 1928, Glantz was engaged as a recording artist with RCA Victor, and appeared on their prestigious "Red Label" record series. The first 78 RPM recordings appeared in 1929 and included twelve of his original compositions: *She'ma*

Yis'ra'el, Te'fi'lat Tal, Sho'mer Yis'ra'el, Kol A'do'nai, Le'chu Ne'ra'ne'na, Bir'kat Ko'ha'nim, Ki Ke'Shim'cha, Ki Hi'neh Ka'Cho'mer, Ein Ke'Er'ke'cha, D'voi're'le and *A'cha'rei Mo'ti.* These recordings established Glantz as one of the leading cantors of so-called *"Golden Age of Cantorial Music."*

At the same time, Glantz established himself as one of the leaders of the Labor Zionist movement in the United States. His first Palestine visit took place in May 1930, where he received a hero's welcome. The reaction to his concerts was inspiring.

In following years, Glantz appeared in concerts and synagogues throughout the United States, Canada, Mexico, South America, Western and Eastern Europe, South Africa, and Palestine.

In 1941, the Glantz family moved from New York to Los Angeles, California, where he served as chief cantor of *Sinai Temple* (1941-1946), and *Shaarei Tefila* Synagogue (1949-1954).

In 1946, following the Second World War Holocaust, Glantz embarked on an extensive concert tour throughout Europe, singing in numerous Jewish refugee camps. After attending the 1946 World Zionist Congress in Basle, he continued to Palestine for his second visit, followed by a third in 1947, appearing in concerts and prayer services in Tel Aviv, Haifa and Jerusalem. On his return journey to Los Angeles, he appeared in three concerts in London, and a gala concert at the New York Metropolitan Opera.

Leib Glantz, as musicologist, articulated his musical theories in a monumental 1952 keynote lecture before the delegates of the Fifth Annual Convention of the Cantors Assembly of America. His lecture, based on extensive musicological research, was considered a new path toward the analysis and understanding of the concealed secrets of the ancient Jewish prayer modes, the *Nusach*, passed on from generation to generation from as far back as the Holy Temple in Jersusalem. Glantz was Professor of Cantorial and Jewish Music at the University for Jewish Studies in Los Angeles, California.

When David Ben Gurion declared the independence of the State of Israel, in May 1948, Glantz was ecstatic. After years of political activism in the Labor Zionist movement, witnessing pogroms in Eastern Europe, anti-Semitism in America, and constant battles between Jews and Arabs in Palestine, Glantz believed he could finally realize his dream to live in Israel.

With his wife, Miriam, and two sons, Kalman and Ezra, the family emigrated to Israel in 1954. His first appearance, the *Midnight Se'li'chot Service*, was a major national event. The *Tiferet Zvi* synagogue in Tel Aviv was packed, with four thousand additional worshippers crowding the surrounding streets, listening to his voice through loudspeakers.

Glantz lived in Israel for ten years. In Israel he enjoyed intimate interaction with a congregation that understood the Hebrew language of the prayers and was accustomed to the Eastern European cantororial style. These worshippers were capable of appreciating Glantz's unique and inspiring musical interpretations of the prayer texts, his religious adherence to the ancient Jewish prayer modes, and his authentic musical innovations. He became widely popular in Israel and throughout the world.

In 1963, two LP records were produced featuring Leib Glantz's *"Midnight Selichot Service,"* which were compiled from the live recordings by *Kol Yisrael* radio from the *Tiferet Zvi* synagogue in Tel Aviv. The complete service was composed by Leib Glantz and is considered his most inspiring work. Many cantors and Jewish music scholars consider Glantz's *Selichot* service the most important cantorial work *ever* published.

In addition to his cantorial career, Glantz appeared in leading tenor roles in several operas, including Alan Hovhaness' "*Shepherd of Israel*," Jacques Halevy's "*La Juive*," and Joseph Tal's "*Saul at Ein Dor*."

Glantz served as a director of ACUM (The Composers, Authors and Publishers Society of Israel), and as judge on the prestigious "Yoel Engel Prize" for original Israeli musical achievements. He was director of the Israeli Composers Association and served as editor of the music periodical *"Bat Kol."*

In 1959, in collaboration with two of his avid admirers and friends, Professor Yehuda Even-Shmuel Kaufman and the famous Israeli writer Eliezer Steinman, Glantz founded the *Tel Aviv Institute for Jewish Liturgical Music*, and under its auspices, an academic level conservatory for training cantors – the *Cantors Academy*. With Glantz at its helm, important scholars and musicians considered it an honor to join the academic faculty, offering a variety of subjects, such as voice training, music, prayer modes, Hebrew language, Jewish and world history, and sacred scriptures.This Institute functioned until Glantz's untimely death in 1964.

Following his sudden passing, while singing on stage at a concert hall in Tel Aviv, the *Institute for Jewish Liturgical Music* was transformed into the publishing organ of Leib Glantz's musical compositions, his research and his literary work. They published seven books of Glantz's 216 musical compositions, the 1965 Hebrew book *"Zeharim – In Memory of Leib Glantz,"* and the 2008 book (in English) *"The Man Who Spoke To God."*

Leib Glantz's funeral was attended by thousands of admirers. Among them his close friend, President of Israel, Zalman Shazar, Ministers of the Israeli Cabinet, Members of Parliament, judges, rabbis, cantors, musicians, and many members of Israel's intelligentsia. He was buried at the *Kiryat Shaul* cemetery in North Tel Aviv.

Excerpts from Essays about Leib Glantz

FROM THE BOOK "THE MAN WHO SPOKE TO GOD"

An excerpt from: *Harmonizing Theory with Creativity: Cantor Leib Glantz's Musical Agenda,* by Dr. Amit Klein, Prof. Eliyahu Schleifer and Prof. Edwin Seroussi, The Jewish Music Research Centre of the Hebrew University, Jerusalem.

Among the giants of modern *Cha'za'nut,* Leib Glantz still stands out as a unique phenomenon; a synthesis of scholar, theoretician, composer and performer. This incredible coexistence of so many virtues in one individual is even more amazing if we understand that some of these virtues actually stood in opposition to each other. The image of the composer and performer is the image of the artist: creative, imaginative, burning with desire to spread out his virtuosity. The image of the scholar is that of the sage: venerable, moderate, wary of foreign influences and innovation. Holding fast to established traditions, while at the same time looking forward for growth and progress of *Cha'za'nut* as an artistic and religious endeavor, typified Glantz's career. He was the brilliant innovator and the formidable conservative.

An excerpt from: *The Glantz/Pinchik Conundrum,* by Dr. Joseph A. Levine, Professor, the Jewish Theological Seminary and editor of the Journal of Synagogue Music.

The underlying theme of Leib Glantz's *Bir'kat Ko'ha'nim* (Priestly Benediction) simulates the lengthy wordless refrain that worshipers sing along with the cantor in traditional synagogues, after the *Ko'ha'nim* conclude each section of their tripartite blessing. The sources from which Glantz may have derived inspiration for his own noble four-part creation are documented. None of these sources approach the grandeur, solemnity and "rightness" for the occasion that Glantz has achieved in adapting them for his elaborate leitmotif. He plucked fragments of *Nu'sach* from the liturgy, biblical cantillation motifs from *Ta'a'mei Mik'ra,* idiomatic turns of phrase from Yiddish folk songs and Chasidic *Ni'gu'nim.* All of these elements he combined, whether consciously or intuitively, with "Mediterranean"-style Zionist paeans to the Land of Israel that were then being written by pioneer settlers in Palestine under the British Mandate. Glantz, always an ardent and supportive member of *Tze'i'rei Tzi'yon,* a Labor Zionist youth organization that promoted *A'li'ya,* Jewish immigration to Israel, and their hymns may have provided the seed that begat his old/new chant for *Bir'kat Ko'ha'nim.*

An excerpt from: *How Shall We Open Our Mouth Before Thee,* by Cantor Abraham Lubin, composer, educator, lecturer and researcher. Former editor of the Journal of Synagogue Music.

Although Glantz stemmed from a similar tradition of learning and exposure to the cantorial chants of the East European synagogue as his other talented colleagues and peers, nevertheless, he grew and developed his artistry in a style all his own, uniquely Glantzian. He elevated his creative efforts to an art form that other musicians and composers, of totally different genres of music, were drawn to appreciate and be inspired by the uniquely original performance of his own liturgical works.

In our attempt to understand Glantz among the traditional school of cantor-composers of Jewish liturgical music, one could compare him, in certain ways, to the great 20th century composer, Arnold Schoenberg (1874-1951). Schoenberg, considered one of the seminal figures of 20th century music was unique among the classic western composers of his century. Just as Schoenberg loosened the grip of traditional tonality and explored new ways of working the 12 notes of the chromatic scales, Leib Glantz explored completely new tracks and paved a new path in rendering the "traditional" modes of East European liturgical song. Like Schoenberg, Glantz conceived and created a most original and revolutionary approach to the interpretation of the liturgical texts of the prayer book in ways never attempted before.

Excerpts from: *The Great Innovator,* by Cantor Max Wohlberg, composer and expert in the field of Jewish music. The article was published in "The Cantor's Voice" journal and in Hebrew in the Israeli daily newspaper *"Ha'A'retz" in 1954.*

From the very beginning of his cantorial career, Leib Glantz displayed an original approach. His voice is a most magnificent lyric tenor, however he does not rely solely on his voice. The text and the interpretation of the words and ideas – these are for Glantz the essence of cantorial. His main focus is on the hidden meanings of the prayers. He tries to penetrate and discover the inner messages, creating music with amazing interpretations.

Glantz's intrinsic contribution to the art of cantorial is intellectual and not only emotional. The daring musical intervals, the surprising modulations and the exciting motifs are based on diligent research and cautious discretion. Only after this stage is resolved in his mind, does Glantz apply his illustrious artistic imagination and his charming compositional talents.

I am convinced that if we succeed in molding for the future a generation of serious and intelligent cantors, that generation will choose Leib Glantz, the cantor, composer, researcher and pedagogue, as the main image to research, to study and to follow. In the history of Jewish music, Leib Glantz is the most daring and most original cantor that ever lived!

An excerpt from: *How Unique Was Leib Glantz?* by Akiva Zimmerman, writer and historian of cantorial and Jewish music.

The pinnacle of Leib Glantz's creativity was undoubtedly the music he composed for the complete Midnight *Se'li'chot* Service. He composed each and every one of the twenty prayers. As a young man in my twenties, I was fortunate to attend his synagogue on *Se'li'chot,* listening in awe. Glantz stood on the *Tif'e'ret Zvi* synagogue pulpit for three solid hours, chanting his unbelievably unique compositions. I will never forget feeling as if Glantz, with his unbelievable tenor voice, was actually *talking* to God in the language of the liturgical poets *(Py'ta'nim).* You could feel his voice penetrating into the hearts of the masses that swarmed to the synagogue to listen to him – an enormous audience of followers and admirers who adored him in Israel from 1954 for the last ten years of his life.

Excerpts from: *The Greatest Innovative and Creative Cantor of the Twentieth Century,* by Cantor Chaim Feifel, Professor of *Cha'za'nut* at the Tel Aviv Cantorial Institute (TACI) and at the Cantorial School of the Hebrew Union College in Jerusalem

I have been asked what was it like to study with Leibele Glantz. He was an exceptional teacher. He always knew how to elevate me to a higher level, to spiritually charge my soul. With each session I absorbed some of his energy. He infused me with *his* truth; he encouraged me to be totally independent, to be brave in expressing my inner soul. Glantz lived his life exactly that way and I felt vibrantly alive every moment of studying with him.

He gave me the capacity to understand the mysteries of cantorial art. Many cantors emotionally express the beauty of our art, but, unfortunately, have little knowledge regarding the essence of their performance. Glantz succeeded in making me attuned to the depth of our traditional language.

Glantz was constantly engaged in serious research in an effort to uncover the historical origins of Jewish music in general, and specifically the prayer modes (*Nu'sach Ha'Tfila).* He stubbornly sought to trace the origins parallel to Jewish history, as far back as the era of the Holy Temples of Jerusalem. It was an almost impossible task.

Leib Glantz possessed great musical skills. His vocal capabilities were limitless, and he was driven by passion with every fiber of his body and soul. As a young man I hadn't realized the mark that he had made on me. Today, after more than four decades as a *Cha'zan,* I have come to the realization that it was Glantz who shaped my identity. He created within me a deep understanding and appreciation of Cantorial Art.

Excerpts from: *A Poet at Heart,* by Professor Yehuda Even-Shmuel Kaufman, philosopher, writer and scholar.

Leib Glantz was a poet at heart – a heart overflowing with song. He sang a psalm of love to Israel's prayers, its music, its festivals, its *To'rah* and its faith.

In a sense, his singing was but a manifestation of the poetry in his heart. He saw the world in terms of poetry, and people that could transcend themselves through song. The "People of Israel" represented for Glantz the "Song of God." The Israel renaissance in Zion was symbolized for him in the words: "O' sing unto the Lord a *new* song!"

Can we comprehend the magnitude of Glantz's love for the Jewish people as they stand before God? Who can describe his admiration of Israel's festivals and of the light radiating from Israel's *To'rah* and customs?

Who among us, who has heard Glantz's prayers, can free himself of the impression that here stood a man whose whole soul was invested in every word he uttered?

Glantz lived in a generation that had devoted its life to the love of the people of Israel, to aspiration for the rebirth of the land of Israel, and faith in the renaissance of the life of the Jewish people in their country. It was a generation of dauntless people that renewed a great deal in the life of the nation, a generation that revived the Hebrew language as its national tongue, an achievement not accomplished by generations of Jewish scholars such as the Tannaites, the Ammoraites, the *Pay'ta'nim* and the poets.

It was this generation that Glantz addressed, calling its sons to come to the synagogue to pray with him. Young people rediscovered their own music – the music of God – finding that it throbs in their hearts as it throbbed in the hearts of their fathers before them. Even the elders felt that Glantz had become a bridge between themselves and their sons, spanning the gap between generations that came before, and the generations yet to come.

Excerpts from: *Artistic Perfection: The Musical Interpretation of Prayers,* by Maestro Elli Jaffe, classical music conductor, composer, and director of the choir of the Great Synagogue in Jerusalem.

The amazing thing about Glantz is that he truly succeeded in uncovering and comprehending the ancient secrets of the *Nu'sach.* This enabled him to navigate his compositions toward distant musical targets, with the confidence of a man who clearly knew where he was coming from and to where he wanted to go.

The focal point of Glantz's cantorial creativity was his famous composition *She'ma Yis'ra'el* (Hear O' Israel). This composition is considered one of the greatest cantorial works ever written, if not the greatest! When we listen to *She'ma Yis'ra'el,* one tends to feel that it is impossible to sing this in any other way – as if this were the final interpretation, of which there can be none other…

Excerpts from: *The Uniqueness of the Chazanic Art of Leib Glantz,* by Cantor Sholom Kalib, author of *The Musical Tradition of the Eastern European Synagogue,* and Professor Emeritus of Eastern Michigan University.

Leib Glantz, or Leibele Glantz, as he was endearingly referred to by masses whom he enthralled by his fiery, often mystical and extraordinarily imaginative approach to *Cha'za'nut,* was unquestionably among the foremost practitioners of the chazanic art of the zenith period of its history. Leibele Glantz was among the last of the chazanic giants of that era, as well as one who stood out in a manner which differed from even his most illustrious contemporaries, due to his personality as well as his rare vocal and musical gifts, resulting in his unique approach to his sacred calling.

The uniqueness of Leibele Glantz, formed by particular characteristics which distinguished him from all other *Cha'za'nim* known to this writer who preceded or followed him, stems first from his depth of the intensity of passion in his liturgical singing. From this metaphoric tree trunk, ever present in his chanting, branches extended in numerous directions.

Chazanic artistry comes to the fore at every level of dynamic nuance within his deeply impassioned approach in addressing the Almighty. Most typically, it is manifest in dramatic, fiery and ecstatic delivery, as if addressing the Master of the Universe, distantly perceived in the heavens above. At other times his delivery comes off as the Jew's profoundly felt, collective cry for mercy across history. Yet at other times – unique to Glantz's delivery – it comes off as an angry protest of the Jew across history for his suffering and persecution. Sharply contrasting to all these is the quasi-whispered intimate prayer to the Father in Heaven, now perceived as close by, on the earth below, as it were.

Excerpts from: *He Who Strikes Flames of Fire,* by Benjamin Z. Maissner, Cantor and music director of Holy Blossom Temple in Toronto, Canada.

Leib Glantz was the paradigm mentor of *Cha'za'nut* in our time. Lovers of cantorial adore his glorious voice, his tears and his joyful music. Every person who was privileged to hear him praying was affected and moved by his passion and his intimate interpretations of the prayer texts. Moreover, there is not one cantor or *Ba'al Te'fi'la* in our time that has not been directly or indirectly influenced by the legacy left for us by Leib Glantz. Consciously or subconsciously, every improvisational sequence in today's cantorial art contains the ingredients originally created by Leib Glantz.

He possessed the quality to heal the souls of his listeners. He provoked anger and made demands of the Almighty. He succeeded in bringing the aura of heaven to earth, so that we mortals could share a glimpse of what the creatures and angels surrounding God's chariot might experience. Glantz evoked in us the deepest of human emotions. We experienced pain as he reminded us of the destruction of our people, our communities and our Holy Temple. His ascending, chromatic rising and falling wailing, made us tremble with anxiety, fear and awe. His pastoral passages of *Ka'va'na* and *D'vei'kut* made us dwell upon the meaning of life.

Excerpts from: *Leib Glantz's Impact on The Art of Cha'za'nut,* by Cantor Moshe Schulhof, teacher of *Cha'za'nut* and *Nu'sach* at the Academy of Jewish Religion in New York.

With an audience in Tel Aviv, capable of understanding the words, Glantz was able to provide ever-deeper interpretations of the prayers, finding hidden meanings and illuminating both the explicit and implicit content. He accomplished this by venturing into new musical areas rarely explored. He used chromatics (12 tone scales), as well as modern musical concepts of tonality. He would use diminished and augmented intervals, and even atonal expressions. He introduced *"Pshat"* (deeper interpretations, literal meanings), as well as expressionism into his music. At times Glantz would "refresh" the *Nu'sach* by veering far away from it, then returning to it, preventing monotony and reinforcing it anew.

His colossal vocal abilities enabled Glantz to venture vocally to wherever his creative mind took him. Though his voice was unique, his style and philosophical approach have deeply influenced all who came after him.

Contemporary composers of liturgical music are currently writing music with modern harmonies, mainly because Glantz proved that one could still be rooted in tradition and at the same time be thoroughly modern. The music performed at Jerusalem's Great Synagogue is a study of how tradition and modernism can be successfully combined – an example set by Leib Glantz.

My cantorial compositions are extremely influenced by Glantz's teachings. I write music to enhance the text, while endeavoring to be emotionally stirring, musically interesting, yet true to the *Nu'sach.* Glantz opened up my imagination and showed me the limitless horizons of creativity, while at the same time remaining true to tradition. I may even write atonally, while at the same time being tonal. I can venture from one mode into another key using any note on the original scale as the new tonic of a new scale. I can use chromatics, dissonant intervals, large interval jumps; in short, I can go fearlessly wherever my imagination takes me, thanks to the path shown by the immortal genius of Leib Glantz. He will forever be an integral part of the continuous development and metamorphosis of cantorial and Jewish Music.

Excerpts from: *The Music of Leib Glantz — Post-Romantic and Extended Instrumental Techniques,* by Cantor Sidney S. Dworkin, Cantor Emeritus of Congregation *Sha'ar Ha'Sho'ma'yim* in Montreal, Canada and past President of the Council of Chazanim of Greater Montreal.

A number of techniques that Glantz employed in composing and/or singing a cantorial recitative point to his grounding in, and familiarity with classical form, nuance, performance practice, and period-related trends.

Some of these techniques are not normally associated with vocal music but rather suggest a musical line that could easily have been written for an instrument. Others are indicative of Glantz's determination, be it deliberate or subconscious, to develop his own unique characteristic style. In essence, this moved his composition into a realm that might aptly be classified as "post-Romantic." The "quasi-classical" compositions that were more or less the order of cantorial composition of the "Golden Era of *Cha'za'nut*" (roughly the first half of the 20th century) contained trace elements of the Baroque, Classical and Romantic periods. It was Glantz alone whose music reverberated with the sound of a new era.

Historically, Leib Glantz was the luminary figure of his time, his cantorial compositions representing the final metamorphosis of the "Golden Era." In addition to his vocal brilliance and personal creativity, the fusion of the traditional cantorial art form with the evolving sounds and trends of period-related classicism, as well as the influence of instrumental music, made Leib Glantz's enigmatic and innovative style unique amongst his peers. It represented a virtual beacon highlighting a pathway toward the future. He was the sole exponent of what can respectfully be called "Progressive 20th Century *Cha'za'nut.*" As Glantz himself once remarked, it would take several generations before his music was truly understood.

Excerpts From Leib Glantz's Writings

From the book "The Man Who Spoke To God"

Excerpt from: *Nu'sach Ha'llel and Tal,* by Leib Glantz, 1961.

When we enter an orthodox synagogue, either in Israel or in the Diaspora, the first thing we notice is the sad, almost tearful, tones. One might get the impression that all Jewish liturgy sounds sad, even when the text expresses joy and thanksgiving.

It might be expected that this exalted verbal content would appropriately call for jubilant music. Unfortunately that is not the case. Almost all cantors sing the passages of *Ha'llel* in the Harmonic Minor. The "peak" of melancholy is reached in conjunction with phrases like "The heavens are the heavens of the Lord, but the earth He has given to mankind", or "To Thee I will offer a thanksgiving sacrifice." What is there to bewail?

I have intensively studied this perplexing question and have found two explanations:

The first explanation is extremely simple: for many generations the situation of the Jews of the Diaspora has been tragic and catastrophic; Jewish blood had flowed like water. Attention to the verbal content of the prayers was neglected. The synagogue services became a suitable opportunity for the Jews to pour out their hearts in lamentation, to cry out and complain to the Almighty about their bitter plight.

The second explanation is not quite as simple. Its source lies precisely in the music formula of the *Ha'llel.* The origin of this *Nu'sach* is rooted in the very first blessing: "He who has sanctified us with His commandments and ordained on us the reading of the *Ha'llel.* "The cantor opens the *Ha'llel* blessing in what seems to be a pure Minor key, but actually it is only an illusory Minor, and as a result both the cantor and the congregation continue with this deceptive minor throughout most of the passages of the *Ha'llel.* There is no thanksgiving and no praise, no song and no exultation. Instead, there are broken sounds and plaints, weak suffering voices. The more tearful the cantor, the greater his reputation...

The great European "Choral Cantors", such as Solomon Sulzer and his followers, reacting against this characteristic lachrymosity, changed the key from the Harmonic Minor to the classic West European Major. It was as though they were saying: What is the matter with you, wailing "Ost Juden," that you weep with tears while singing *Ha'lle'lu'ya*? Go sing *Ha'lle'lu'ya* in a Major key, a la Mozart or Schubert?

The truth of the matter is that neither of these approaches found the proper path to the original Jewish *Nu'sach* of the *Ha'llel.* I am convinced that both the Jewish Major and the Jewish Minor contain something characteristic and specific, that survived from the ancient modes of the oriental peoples, that is not to be found at all in the modern West European scales.

After years of searching, examining and striving to find the musical truth about the *Ha'llel,* I have come to the recognition that the first blessing of the *Ha'llel* is not to be sung in the Minor key, but is actually a direct continuation from the end of *Te'fi'lat Ha'She'va,* from the *Nu'sach* of the *Sha'losh Re'ga'lim* service (the three festivals of *Pe'sach, Sha'vu'ot* and *Su'ccot*) till the beginning of the blessing of *Ha'llel.*

Excerpts from: *Nu'sach A'ha'va Ra'bah,* by Leib Glantz, 1961.

To my great joy, I discovered that the famous 19th century Cantor Pinchas Minkowsky, from the Brody synagogue in Odessa, who was a very modern, choral, almost Reform cantor, knew how to guide his choir and his congregation when chanting the prayer *Tal* — in the "general *Nu'sach.*"

I use the words "to my great joy" because when I composed my composition "*Tal*", (the two portions of *Tal* that are in my recordings,) I did not realize that Minkowsky had done so as well. At that time, I could not bear this neglect, and at the very beginning I sang the words *E'lo'kei'nu Ve'E'lo'kei A'vo'tei'nu* in the *"Nu'sach* from Sinai":

21.

Incidentally, the Chasidim selected this text and clothed it in various and sundry melodies. Indeed there are melodic kernels of *Nu'sach* in many Chasidic tunes. These are tunes that are sung at the Rabbi's table, and songs that are sung before and after the study of the *To'rah.* Some of these tunes are even sung at festive meals, often accompanied by Chasidim dancing with devotion and transcendent ecstasy. But as much as these songs may beautify our family life in the home, they should not be brought into the synagogue to supplant the appropriate traditional *Nu'sach.*

The original Jewish *Tal* must be garbed in "oriental" dress — in oriental scales. The cantor must do everything he can to divest himself of those ordinary Major and Minor keys. The agricultural village life of our country must be given the proper and true musical expression in our prayers. It is very important that the *"Nu'sach* from Sinai" be revived, perhaps in a modernistic manner, but in a clear and concrete fashion.

Excerpts from: *Nu'sach A'ha'va Ra'bah,* by Leib Glantz, 1961.

If it were true that the *A'ha'va Ra'bah Nu'sach* is just an "adopted son" of the Jewish people, then the people of Israel were very good at the "art" of adoption. The Jews fell in love with this adopted "child," nourished it, and turned it into their dearest son *(Ben Ya'kir Ve'Ye'led Sha'a'shu'im.)* Some secular musicologists have claimed that the mode on which the *A'ha'va Ra'bah Nu'sach* is built on is not Jewish but foreign — Gypsy, Armenian, or other. My answer to them is very simple: **They are wrong!**

Let us analyze the *A'ha'va Ra'bah Nu'sach.* We may just discover that it is Jewish in its origin.

The Jews introduced a fundamental and original modification that was purely Jewish: they added an additional Tetrachord that begins from the fifth tone below the E, which is A. In other words, the "Phrygian" and the "Phrygish" combined together. This new Tetrachord is totally different: it does not employ an augmented second. This Tetrachord, which begins on A and continues B – C# – D – E is very surprising because it is a Major Tetrachord, as opposed to the first two Tetrachords that are clearly "Phrygish."

Cantors traditionally begin the *A'ha'va Ra'bah Nu'sach* not from the tone E, but from the tone A (the fifth tone below the E):

9. 

This is a very peculiar and typically Jewish line! The music of no other culture's has anything similar to this.

Excerpts from: *Nu'sach A'do'nai Ma'lach and the Jewish Major,* by Leib Glantz, 1961.

Even regular synagogue worshipers that are not accustomed to be leaders of the prayer services, find themselves chanting this *Ye'kum Pur'kan* or *A'do'nai Ma'lach Nu'sach* to themselves even before the cantor finishes singing each prayer. The Jewish Major has grasped their hearts and they are connected to it with blind love, whether they are aware of it or not!

It is therefore clear why the Yiddish song *"A Cha'zan'dl of Sha'bbes"* has become so popular, even though its lyrics are a bit vulgar. The melody itself is totally *Nu'sach A'do'nai Ma'lach* (or *Ye'kum Pur'kan).* It is exactly the *Nu'sach* of the prayer *Zar'a'cha Cha'ya Ve'Ka'ya'ma:*

14. 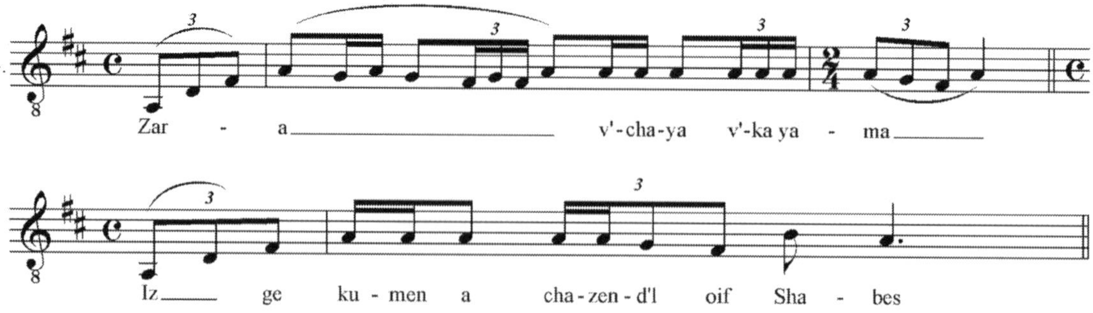

Even more characteristic is the fact that this *Nu'sach* is etched into a very important prayer — the *A'vot* of the *Shach'rit* and *Mu'saf* services of the High Holidays. There we find all four Tetrachords in the most obvious of forms. This is actually the *Nu'sach Mi'Sinai,* which is totally and independently Jewish.

Many *Ba'a'lei Te'fi'la* and even some cantors that are not musically trained, fail in their execution of the High Holiday *A'vot* chant, only because they are not quite aware of how complex and complicated it really is. They need to realize that the chant needs to be opened in a very low tone, because as they rise to the higher stages of this lengthy mode, their voice can actually choke, and they are in danger of temporarily losing their voice! In this case they will find it almost impossible to return to the *Nu'sach.*

Excerpts from: *The Jewish Minor,* by Leib Glantz, 1961.

Nu'sach Ma'gen A'vot wanders musically between Minor and Major. Many composers, both cantorial and secular, have composed beautiful music built on this *Nu'sach.* Anton Rubinstein, a Russian Jewish composer who converted to Christianity, was considered musically *more* Russian than most of his Russian contemporary musicians. However, even having become almost totally assimilated, in the wonderful chorus melody of his famous opera "Demon," he could not "biologically" free himself from the *Ma'gen A'vot Nu'sach...*

Nu'sach Kol Nid'rei is a musical journey from mode to mode, going from *A'ha'va Ra'bah* to Minor, and from Minor to Major, and back. The ending of this enchanting melody is totally in Major. It is therefore understandable why the great German composer Ludwig van Beethoven (1770-1827) fell in love with this sacred melody and immortalized it in one of his most monumental compositions, the String Quartet Number 14 in C Sharp minor. In its sixth movement, *Adagio quasi un poco andante,* the Viola clearly plays the *Nu'sach* of *Kol Nid'rei* over the background of the violins.

Excerpt from: *The Essence of Cha'za'nut,* by Leib Glantz, 1958.

In theory, the cantor improves and beautifies the prayer service, organizes the service, raises it to a level of *Hit'la'ha'vut* (enthusiasm), and to an enlightened musical level. Therefore, an analysis of cantorial must begin with the personal human attributes of the cantor.

Cha'za'nut is not just a musical profession. It is not just a trade. It is wisdom *(Choch'ma).* Wisdom in all its aspects: Wisdom, understanding and knowledge. The integral mission assigned to the cantor consists of demands that are not necessarily musical. A cantor is undoubtedly a singer. However, a singer is definitely not a cantor, even when he performs cantorial in a synagogue. A classical soloist, highly respected by great conductors, can be a wonderful soloist, but he is not a cantor. The greatest Italian opera singer, in order to excel, is not required to be knowledgeable about the Italian people, their history, their customs and their culture. The cantor, on the other hand, must be a complete Jew in spirit and soul. He must be a scholar of Jewish history, ancient Jewish literature, the written and oral *To'rah,* the *Ha'la'cha* (interpretation of the laws of the Scriptures) and the *Mid'ra'shim* (Jewish commentaries on the Hebrew Scriptures). He must be familiar with the literature of the middle ages including its *Pay'ta'nim* (poets) and *Pi'yu'tim* (liturgical poems). He should be familiar with modern Hebrew literature. This Jewish consciousness is the primary basis for the wisdom of *Cha'za'nut,* and serves as the principle attribute of the cantor's mission.

A second attribute, one that is no less important, is the cantor's standard of morality. Many singers and artists conduct their lives in what is often called "bohemian" lifestyle. They frequently indulge in alcohol and unrestrained social behavior. This kind of lifestyle does not disqualify the secular artist. Cantors, as leaders of their communities, are measured according to their morality. Their behavior must be a model for the public. A cantor is not just another member of the community, but an example of which to follow. His singing must originate from holiness and purity.

A third important aspect of the *Cha'zan* is his credo *(A'ni Ma'a'min).* He must be loyal to his people and to their holy values. His religious faith must be unabridged, as he must believe in the words he is uttering, as he is required to be an interpreter of those texts.

Excerpt from: *Rosh Ha'Sha'na – A Festive Day That Provokes Thought,* by Leib Glantz, 1959.

When I analyze the wonderful poem of Rabbi Amnon of Mayence — *U'Ne'ta'neh To'kef Ke'du'shat Ha'Yom* ("We shall observe the mighty holiness of this day"), I become aware that it is free of begging for mercy. There is something more burning, more intense and more penetrating. In *U'Ne'ta'neh To'kef* we hear a poet's artistic description and bold imagination of the Kingdom of the Heavens: "Thou unfoldest the records and the deeds therein inscribed that tell their story" *(Ve'Tif'tach Et Se'fer Ha'Zich'ro'not U'Me'E'lav Yi'ka'reh.)*

This monumental poem stimulates me to call out to all the cantors and Jewish composers of our era and beg of them: Do not cry and do not lament on this glorious day of *Rosh Ha'Sha'na!* We have strayed far away from the penetrating philosophical ideas of the great philosophers of our past. It seems that our generation has chosen to simplify the meaning of our spiritual and cultural wealth to a primitive level that borders with ignorance! There is no need to shout or sob! After all, this is a festive day. The poetry of the prayers of *Rosh Ha'Sha'na* is glorious. The poets who wrote these poems employed thought and passion. Every word was a painting, a song, a philosophy. Sadly, many of us moan, sigh, flatter and plead as if we were beggars knocking on a door.

Excerpt from: *The Music of the Sha'vu'ot Festival Blessing the First Fruit,* by Leib Glantz, 1956.

As we read the *Me'gi'la* of Ruth, the scent of the fields rises not only from the idyllic poetic text, but also from the peaceful, calming melodies — the sounds of nature, soil and harvesting.

These Pentatonic songs seem naïve and simplistic, but those who know the charms of the orient, discover in them a philosophical depth, a creative rural reality, combining sadness and happiness, openness and concealment, innocence and dreaming as well as thought and feeling.

Hundreds of years after the *Nus'cha'ot* appropriate to the reading of the *To'rah* and the *Me'gi'lot* had crystallized, a great poet named Rabbi Meir Ben Yitzchak Nehorai, who was a cantor in Worms, Germany, in the eleventh century generation of Rashi, composed the wonderful poem *Ak'da'mut Mi'lin Ve'Sha'ra'yut Shu'ta* ("I utter these words as a prelude to this discourse"). The poem is about the happiness that will come upon the Israelites and the calamity that will be the destiny of those who persecute them. It is an expression of the eternal optimism of the Jewish people. Interestingly, the melody, which was also composed by the poet himself, is based on the Pentatonic scale.

Excerpt from: *The Music of Yom Ki'ppur,* by Leib Glantz, 1940.

As a child, before I could speak, before I learned how to spell – I instinctively sensed that music, whether instrumental or vocal, was a wonderful form of communication.

As I grew older and began reflecting on the different paths of human language, I began to comprehend the secrets of harmonic musical tones. Music became the special "dialect" that I feel exists between man and God. It is like a ladder reaching up from the earth into the heavens. Whether a gloomy melody or a happy song — both can elevate us from mundane surroundings to spiritual highs.

Yom Ki'ppur, the Day of Atonement, is a day in which the People of Israel devote themselves to purify and sanctify their "contaminated" souls. For one whole day, from the opening *Kol Nid'rei* prayer until the final service of *Ne'i'la* — a crisis takes place, as man comes close to God, and God to man. This is a ceremony that is performed in the most beautiful of languages — the language of music!

Excerpt from a written address to the delegates of the Eighth Annual Conference/Convention of The Cantors Assembly of America (May, 1956).

No words can enable you to grasp the full impact of the dream that is developing into a fascinating reality — a reality that for many years has consisted of difficulties, sorrows, obstacles, and sometimes even pain. I remember when you and I (not long ago) used to exaggerate and be frightened by the difficulties existing in Israel because we were not lucky or privileged enough to enjoy the achievements as well.

I am happy to tell you that now, for the first time, Israel is lifting the weight of her accumulated troubles and is beginning to laugh, rejoice and celebrate. I consider myself a very privileged man and cantor to be able to be part of Israel at this time.

One of the greatest affairs Israel has ever had was the celebration of Independence Day. The sight of thousands of people thronging the streets, glorying in their happiness and freedom, has left on me an unforgettable impression.

Excerpt from: *The Cantor — A Unique Creation of Jewish Life,* by Cantor Leib Glantz, 1947.

Is the cantor a singer, a composer, a musical interpreter, a "deputy of the people" *(Shli'ach Tzi'bur)* a "messenger to God," or is he all of these together? The difficulty of defining the role of the cantor lies in the fact that the institution of "Cantorate" or *"Cha'za'nut"* is a completely Jewish phenomenon, a unique and specifically Jewish creation. It is, therefore, difficult to compare the Cantorate with the existing institutions of other religions.

We find the institution of priests *(Ko'ha'nim)* among the Egyptians, the Phoenicians, the Indians and other nations that were in existence at the time of the creation of the Jewish priesthood. The Cantorate, however, is distinctly originally Jewish, and in order to understand it we must read the Bible again and observe the very roots of Judaism in the days of its birth.

Excerpt from: *The Cantor — A Unique Creation of Jewish Life,* by Cantor Leib Glantz, 1947.

Music in itself is a religious miracle. It cannot be explained in words, neither it's meaning nor its influence. For example, genuine musical audiences are in fact religious audiences, if not consciously, then certainly emotionally and instinctively. There is often religiosity in the heart even when the mind denies it and the most radically minded person is often intensely religious, although he is often unaware of it. The religious feeling that is created and that responds to *Choch'mat Lev* exists in many places and in many hearts and souls, for the "Wisdom of the Heart" may not be clearly defined but it is always rich and deep and reaches more people than the "Wisdom of the Mind."

The Jewish prayer book brilliantly acknowledges the kinship between music and religiosity. It contains a remarkable daily prayer in which God is proclaimed as "the one who chooses music" *(Ha'Bo'cher Be'Shi'rei Zim'ra).* This description of God as a lover of music is based on many manifestations of Jewish religious expression that we find throughout Jewish history, from the days of the Bible through the ceremonial services in both Holy Temples in Jerusalem *(A'vo'da),* up to the early days of the synagogues of the Diaspora.

Excerpt from: *We Must Not Let Cha'za'nut Perish!* by Leib Glantz, 1957.

There is a new generation in Israel — a generation that is not only neglecting, but rejecting one of our most sacred cultural heritages — our original religious music – *Cha'za'nut.*

People of mediocre taste are actively depleting the stature of our traditional music. They are cultivating a fashion of cantorial recordings for the sole purpose of cheap entertainment. At the same time, our writers, poets, artists, intelligentsia as well as our religious scholars are becoming indifferent towards this great cultural asset.

Some define themselves as *"secular"* — careful not to be stigmatized, God forbid, with a trace of Judaism from the past. Religious scholars are engulfed in a peculiar snobbism, totally ignoring our popular original art.

Should not this worry us? Can we afford to let this cultural treasure disintegrate before our eyes? Is it not our holy duty to wake up and struggle for our nation's musical soul, especially in this historical period "When the Lord restores the fortunes of Zion"?

The Man Who Spoke to God

A 565-page Book about Cantor Leib Glantz

by Dr. Jerry Glantz

"The Man Who Spoke to God" is a scholarly and personal tribute to a world famous artist. Edited by his son with contributions by the most important thinkers and practitioners of cantorial and Jewish music, as well as music in general, it provides a comprehensive overview and analysis of Glantz's contributions, including his ground-breaking research into Jewish *Nu'sach*, his pioneering approach to the performance of Jewish music, and his extraordinary ability to speak to the hearts of his listeners. It is an endeavor to define Leib Glantz's historical importance within the culture of the Jewish people.

Just as Glantz's influence spread far beyond his audiences, the book's significance extends beyond Glantz. His legacy is, in large part, an argument for the primacy of orality in the Jewish tradition. Prayers, after all, can be maintained in text. However, music, vocal volume and tonality, must be actually heard to be effective.

Leib Glantz (1898-1964) is considered by many one of the greatest cantors that ever lived. For 100 years, cantors throughout the world have recognized his brilliance as a composer, interpreter, performer, as well as scholar and teacher of Jewish music. Glantz was the people's cantor. Crowds filled the streets when he rehearsed or performed. His many admirers thrilled and wept with emotion at the sound of his voice. His music penetrated souls and inspired young people, many who would later become famous cantors themselves.

The subordination of cantorial art to rabbinic learning was not always the case. During the *Golden Age of Cha'za'nut* (Cantorial), in the first half of the twentieth century, cantors were considered superstars among the Jewish people. Today, many cantors eschew traditional Jewish music in favor of popular, modern tunes, combining foreign elements that originally had no place in this traditional cultural art form. This book makes the case for how much is lost with this popularization of ritual.
The book consists of three parts:

- Reflections on Leib Glantz.
- Analyses of Leib Glantz's Historical Significance as a Cantor, a Composer, a Researcher, a Pedagogue and a Zionist Leader.
- Writings and Lectures of Leib Glantz.

The Appendixes include a comprehensive list of Glantz's 216 compositions, a list of his audio recordings, a list of his published music books and important historical documents.

The book is accompanied by two new compact disks with 30 of Glantz's recorded compositions, some which have never yet been published.

A Dialogue with the Almighty

Cantor Näftali Herstik[1]

There is a story in the Talmud about a great rabbi, Yonatan Ben Uziel, whose intensity of learning and concentration was so great that if a bird flew over his head while studying, it would go up in flames. That was similar to my impression of Leib Glantz when I heard him for the first time in my life — a vision of burning flames shooting in all directions.

I was merely eight years old when my late father, Cantor Moshe M. Herstik, took me to a service led by Leib Glantz at the *Tif'e'ret Zvi* synagogue in Tel Aviv. It was *Sha'bbat Rosh Cho'desh* (Sabbath of the new month) and in the midst of the *Ha'llel* prayer, Glantz suddenly exclaimed: *Lo A'mut Ki Ech'yeh, Va'A'sa'per Ma'a'sei Yah* ("I shall not die, but live, and recount the works of the Lord"). It was as though he was engaged in a "dialogue" with the Almighty. It was so daring that one felt that Glantz was ready to sacrifice his life on behalf of his congregation. It was total dedication: *Me'si'rut Ne'fesh.*

It was as if he was engaged in a "dialogue" with the Almighty. It was so daring that one felt that Glantz was ready to sacrifice his life on behalf of his congregation. It was total dedication!

1 Cantor Naftali Herstik — Chief Cantor of the Jerusalem Great Synagogue from 1979 till 2008. He studied at the Ponivesz Yeshiva, Kfar Chasidim, Israel, and graduated from the Royal College of Music in London. He is the Director of the Tel Aviv Cantorial Institute.

Rabbi Joseph B. Soloveitchik, in his book "The Lonely Man of Faith," described the ultimate form of prayer as standing before the Almighty and speaking directly to Him. Hence the direct form *"Ba'ruch A'ta"* ("Blessed are You").

Listening as a teenager to Leib Glantz's live radio broadcasts of the *Se'li'chot* service,[2] or as an adult to the reissued recordings, I cannot escape feeling that Glantz was talking directly *to* God, or even talking *with* God. It is no wonder that so many households in Israel were glued to their radios for the annual Saturday midnight live broadcast of the *Se'li'chot* service, in order to listen to Leib Glantz.

Listening as a teenager to Leib Glantz's live radio broadcasts of the* Se'li'chot *service, or as an adult on the reissued recordings, I cannot escape feeling that Glantz was talking directly* to *God, or even talking* with *God.

I have always felt that it would be hard to imagine the musical form of the first night of *Se'li'chot* prior to the Leib Glantz era. He created in that prayer service a new dimension, radically different from whatever preceded. It is similar to what was said of Maria Callas and Enrico Caruso — that the world of opera that preceded them was not the same as it was following them.

How does Glantz differ from his predecessors? What are the special tools with which Glantz created such a revolution?

We must establish from the very beginning that Glantz was a great exponent of *Nu'sach Ha'Te'fi'la.* He was an ardent warrior in the battle to maintain these traditional prayer modes as the basis of all liturgical music. It is therefore even more significant, even astonishing, to realize that Glantz's "revolution" took place *within* the boundaries of traditional *Nu'sach.*

In an article written by Leib Glantz himself on the occasion of the Fiftieth Anniversary of the Jewish Ministers Cantors' Association of America (New York, December 1947), Glantz defines the cantor as "a unique creation of Jewish life." That very article highlights Leib Glantz's perception of the ideal cantor — a true *Shli'ach Tzi'bur.* In this article, Glantz refers to the biblical term of *"A'man"* — the artist:

> The definition of the word "artist" in the bible is remarkable. Each time I read the portion of the bible which deals with the artist, I am thrilled by the term which is used to describe him: *"Cha'cham Lev":* He who has wisdom of the heart — that is

2 *Se'li'chot* service — Jewish penitential poems and prayers, especially those said in the period leading up to the High Holy Days. *Se'li'chot* refers to both the service itself and to each of the liturgical poems — *Pi'yu'tim* — that compose the service.

> how the bible describes the artist! The term *"Choch'ma"* in Hebrew means many things: scholarship, wisdom, knowledge and even plain good sense. The biblical distinction between intellectual wisdom and emotional wisdom constitutes a striking definition of art, for it recognizes that art penetrates directly into the heart and often speaks more deeply than words and scholarly definitions. In Jewish prayer services, *"To'rah"* and *"A'vo'da,"* intellectual and emotional wisdom — the wisdom of the mind and the wisdom of the heart — go hand in hand.

Glantz, a true artist and a great scholar, successfully employed all the God-given gifts with which he had so richly been endowed: musical creativity, outstanding vocal ability, an inquisitive mind, and insurmountable energy and feeling.

From *Ash'rei,*[3] the very first word of the *Se'li'chot* service, one is impressed by Glantz's penetrating thought and profound original interpretation of the text. Above all, he creates a unique atmosphere that elevates his listeners towards readiness to pray before the Creator during the period of *Ha'Ya'mim Ha'No'ra'im* — the "Days of Awe." Such is his choral introduction to *Se'li'chot,* which is interwoven with the modes and moods of the High Holiday spirit, encompassing the entirety of prayer from *P'su'kei D'Zim'ra*[4] to *Ne'i'la.*[5] One immediately senses Glantz's clever way of using the Relative Major in order to brighten up the somber mode of the minor chords, hinting at the regal *Mal'chu'yot* element of *Rosh Ha'Sha'na,* the Jewish New Year holiday.

Part of his innovation in the *Nu'sach* of *Se'li'chot* is the use of the aforementioned Relative Major as early as the word *"Od"* in his opening of the *Ash'rei* prayer and in his well-known composition *"Le'chu Ne'ra'ne'na."* It would be impossible to analyze here all of Glantz's uses of modes and scales in his *Se'li'chot* service, but I would mention that unlike the limited modes of the "conventional" *Nu'sach* of the *Se'li'chot,* Glantz skillfully maneuvers among a whole range of traditional modes, from what he calls Major and Minor Pentatonic, to *Yish'ta'bach* and *A'do'nai Ma'lach,* to *A'ha'va Ra'bbah* and *Av Ha'Ra'cha'mim,* to Natural Minor and Harmonic Minor.

It is very interesting to follow Glantz's unique use of the choir as an integral part of his service. I firmly believe that on the one hand Glantz wanted to create an effect of *Shi'rat Ha'Le'vi'im* (the Levites singing in the ancient Holy Temple in Jerusalem) — hence the use of minimalist harmony and open fifths, his unusual emphasis of basses over the tenors, and the descending upper line against the ascending lower line. On the other hand Glantz wanted to create *Shi'rat Ka'hal* (congregational singing) in all its forms — *Te'hi'lim Zo'gn, Ta'cha'nun, Ze'mi'rot, Shi'rat Ha'llel* and so forth. This might be the explanation for the choir singing a great

3 *Ash'rei* — happy are those who dwell in His house.

4 *P'su'kei D'Zim'ra* — ("Verses of Song"), designed in many ways as a warm-up to the central prayers of the service.

5 *Ne'i'la* — the final prayer service of *Yom Ki'ppur* — the Jewish Holy Day of Atonement.

deal in unison, octaves, two-part harmony, and repetition of certain motifs in "strategic" places in the service.

However, the most outstanding feature of Glantz's *Se'li'chot* is his ability to carry the worshipping congregation through every kind of mood and emotion in the liturgy. He could "paint" a vivid and picturesque view of the creation in *"Le'cha Sha'ma'yim,"* a gloomy mood in *"Ki'Chlot Ko'che'inu,"* the trumpets' call to assemble in *"Le'chu Ne'ra'ne'na"* and *"Ki Vei'ti Beit Te'fi'la Yi'ka're Le'Chol Ha'A'mim,"* and supplication in *"HaN'sha'ma Lach"* or *"Re'tze A'ti'ra'tam."*

The most outstanding feature of Glantz's* Se'li'chot *is his ability to carry the worshipping congregation through every kind of mood and emotion in the liturgy.

Leib Glantz described his beloved colleague, Cantor David Roitman, as *"Me'sho'rer Ha'A'mud"* (the poet of the synagogue pulpit), thus distinguishing Roitman from other *Cha'za'nim.* Without doubt, the same can be said of Leib Glantz himself. His portrayal of the text and his interpretive powers were reminiscent of the great poets of years past, who had a magical effect on their listeners and whose words often carried the moral strength of prophets (*"El E'rech A'pa'yim A'ta"* and *"Mach'ni'sei Ra'cha'mim"*). Glantz the poet was a master of timing and rhythm. His deliberate use of repeated words and split phrases, his sense of rhythmic form, and his measured approach to each musical detail are the tools of a master poet.

One cannot distinguish Leib Glantz — the staunch Zionist activist, the fiery speaker and the great orator — from Leib Glantz the cantor. He was truly a great orator at the *"A'mud"* (cantor's pulpit) as well. His deep insight into the texts and his powerful oratory are astonishing in the dramatic outbursts of his composition "*Eich Nif'tach Peh Le'fa'ne'cha.*" Glantz often used his wonderful oratory powers as another means of interpretation in the musical tradition of *Sprechgesang* (spoken song). It is a tool with which Glantz creates tension and expectation of his "coming back" to the more traditional, more familiar modes and tunes. I actually witnessed that "sigh" of joy and relief by the worshippers when Glantz *Kummt Zu'rik A'heim* (arrived back home).

What inspired Leib Glantz to become so unique were his dedicated Chasidic upbringing and his deep faith in *Ne'tzach Yis'ra'el.*[6]

He was very individualistic in his creative approach to *Te'fi'la*, and at the same time he was totally loyal to the "traditional *Nu'sach.*" Most of the time, he successfully melded the two

6 *Ne'tzach Yis'ra'el* can be understood in two ways. It can mean the "Eternal One of Israel" — God. It can also mean "the eternity of Israel" — the survival of the Jewish people, in spite of persecution and assimilation.

> *Like many other geniuses before him, Glantz was frequently misunderstood. In his lifetime, many considered his approach too radical. However, as time went by, his enormous contribution to the world of* Cha'za'nut *is today recognized by all.*

elements into a cohesive expression. Yet like many other geniuses before him (and he was definitely an *I'lui* — a genius), Glantz was frequently misunderstood. In his lifetime, many considered his approach too radical. However, as time went by, his enormous contribution to the world of *Cha'za'nut* is today recognized by all.

During the course of every academic year at the Tel Aviv Cantorial Institute, some young student will come to me, his head still spinning, and he will tell me excitedly that he had just listened to Glantz's *Se'li'chot* for the first time and that it was a life changing event.

I am thankful to the Almighty for the privilege of having known Leib Glantz personally, having heard him in *Te'fi'la*, and having shared conversations with him when I was merely fifteen years old. I hope that thanks to my years of experience at the *A'mud*, I have grown to better understand those conversations, and that I now have greater insight into the Glantz phenomenon, so that I can help the next generation appreciate the greatness of Leib Glantz the *Cha'zan*, the musician, the composer, the poet, the orator, the man whose *Te'fi'lot* (prayers) could at once soar with fiery intensity, and just as quickly could float on heavenly softness. Most importantly, I want the next generation of *Shli'chei Tzi'bur* (leaders of congregations) to see Leib Glantz as I see him — a prime example of *Sa'ne'go'ram Shel Yis'ra'el*[7] — a true advocate, pleading before God on behalf of the people of Israel.

7 *Sa'ne'go'ram Shel Yis'ra'el* — Moses was considered the "advocate" of the Israelites when, according to the bible, he spoke to God in Egypt. Rabbi Levi Yitzchak from Berdichev, one of the legendary figures of Chasidism (1740-1810), was also called *Sa'ne'go'ram Shel Yis'ra'el*, because of his consuming love of God and his people. He became known as the "defender of the people of Israel" as he would argue with God, charging Him with being too stern a father to His children, pleading for an end to the prolonged exile from Zion.

Taking a *Glantz* at Ourselves

How would the great Cantor Leïb Glantz view current-day Chazzanut?

Cantor Ralph Schlossberg[1]

Leib Glantz is important today because in every way he was an example for the cantors of our current generation to follow. His music is important today because it reminds us of how great the sacred art of the cantor can be. **The Leib Glantz Project** is important because this publication of his music now allows the present generation of Jews to experience the true inspirational power of cantorial music at its finest, at a time when the contrast between today's synagogue music and Glantz's concept of what sacred music artistry should be, could not be greater.

Leib Glantz, who passed away in 1964, did not live to witness the major changes in music and prayer that have taken place in much of the synagogue landscape in the last two generations. As a cantor to whom Leib Glantz's music, and his thinking, were a great influence and inspiration, I think it would be useful to imagine what Glantz's response would be to some of these changes – if he were to appear here today and take a look at the scene.

Glantz's thinking concerning his music and the cantorial world of his time was frequently unconventional, always fearless, always faithful to his values and principles, often dazzling, and always relentlessly on target. He articulated concepts of what a cantor should be, as a creative artist, and as clergy, that ought to be recognized as the ideal, the model for the cantorate, and he lived his life accordingly. He also strived to enlighten the general Jewish public, as well as the cantorate, about the nature and historical development of Jewish music.

We will tour today's cantorial landscape with Glantz just as we would show our city to someone visiting again after a long absence. We will try to imagine how he would react. Let us try to derive some lessons and inspiration from Glantz's life and work, and apply them to generate some specific ideas about what we can do to bring the tradition of creative artistry back to its vibrant central role in synagogue song, and thus in Jewish religious life.

Those who have a strong love for the synagogue and who appreciate the importance of its music heritage are aware of the fact that there have been drastic changes in thinking and practice in many congregations in the last two gen-

1. Cantor Ralph Schlossberg served two large and distinguished congregations in the New York Metropolitan Area. He presented *chazzanut* accompanied by his professional choir which included members of the New York City Opera, and by his 100-voice children's choirs and his 50-voice adult choirs. Sixteen members of his choirs went on to become cantors of significant congregations. He has been commissioned by many of the leading cantors, choirs and congregations in the United States and Canada to compose new works of synagogue music.

erations. In an increasing number of congregations a music experience of a limited and simplistic nature is narrowing the very concept of prayer. It is depriving Jews of having a deeper understanding of the liturgy and a more varied and intense spiritual and emotional experience that only sacred music artistry, and more specifically, *chazzanut,* can provide. During his lifetime Glantz witnessed some of these changes. He was among the first to do so. Some of these trends present an increased challenge to the values Glantz promulgated.

In the last decade a small crop of fine cantors came on to the scene. These are highly proficient in the traditional styles of *chazzanut.* They are well trained, serious, and disciplined musicians. They have fine voices, and excellent technical skills. Some have prodigious voices, with phenomenal technical virtuosity. They deliver traditional liturgical music in expressive, idiomatic, authentic *chazzanic* styles. Generally they exhibit good musical taste, excellent artistic instincts and confident performance skills. They appear to have the benefit of a good education, both Jewish and secular, and they live by Jewish values. Most come originally from traditional backgrounds, including a number of *chassidim.* Several have received their training in the Tel Aviv Cantorial Institute, which is a spiritual descendent of the cantorial school founded by Leib Glantz in 1959, and is directed by the excellent Cantor Naftali Herstik.

Most of this new crop are now serving traditionally observant congregations whose rabbis, lay leaders and congregants understand the unique nature and importance of the cantorial art form to the Jewish religion and people. These young cantors, mostly in their 20's, 30's and some 40's as of this writing, already show a level of mature talent in traditional *chazzanut,* rarely seen in the last two generations. Within that small circle of light and joy that they shine on their congregations and communities, the wonderful, expressive, spiritually fulfilling, sacred music art form known as *chazzanut* is alive and well. If Leib Glantz were here today he would be pleased by this. However, he most probably would be dissatisfied that these cantors still mostly repeat the cantorial repertoire and styles of the great classic cantors of the past, and there seems to be little refreshing innovation in *chazzanut* such as Glantz himself accomplished.

Unfortunately, those new talents in traditional *chazzanut* are conspicuous in their rarity. The overall trend seems to be going in the opposite direction, and has been so for quite a while. This trend has been occuring in Orthodox, Conservative and Reform congregations.

In many congregations the role of the *chazzan* has changed from that of the spiritual-musical-artistic sacred spokesperson of the community, to primarily that of a sing-along leader.

More cantors are increasingly presenting *nusach ha'tfila,* our ancient Jewish prayer modes, in an excessively plain manner, devoid of variation and creativity, and repeated note for note every *Shabbat.* In addition, they are doing so in a noticeably hurried manner.

Choirs are disappearing from our synagogues, and our glorious treasury of liturgical choral music is rarely heard.

Cantors are disappearing from our synagogues as well. In too many congregations which can certainly afford a cantor, you can walk into *Shabbat* and holiday services conducted entirely by congregants. Most of them have, at best, a rudimentary and faulty knowledge of *nusach ha'tfilah,* and many display a conspicuous unfamiliarity with any known scale of pitch. The words of the prayers, the impassioned outpourings from the hearts and souls of their authors, are swiftly delivered without emotion or inflection. When someone *davens* that fast, how can there be any emotional appreciation of the meaning of the text?

Wouldn't Glantz ask: Where is the cantor? The purpose of a congregation offering a public religious service is necessarily different from that of an individual praying alone. At a public reading of Shakespeare, wouldn't one prefer it to be presented by an actor who has made it his life's work?

The days of the tear-stained prayer book, when Jews came to *shul* to pour their hearts out in their prayers are gone. Since the congregation does not derive much inspiration from any expressive quality of the chanting of the service by the laity, it puts its energy and focus into congregational singing, with which it only manages to generate a feeling of community and group empowerment. Those feelings are good, but they are more social than religious.

The prayers services seem to be crying out to be clothed in beautiful music, but in too many synagogues, without musical artistry, the experience seems to be missing its most vital dimension. I think that Glantz would be seriously disturbed by this reality.

Increasing the participation of the laity in the synagogue services has become the highest priority in the thinking of many Jewish religious and lay leaders in America for the last two generations. One major contributing factor is the desire to increase attendance, by altering the character of the synagogue services.

These changes were accelerated in the non-Orthodox branches of our tribe, following major studies and conferences where clergy and lay leaders formally codified "Participation" as the new priority, to be pursued with almost no regard for collateral damage to the quality of many people's religious experience.

I am sure that Leib Glantz might concur that increased participation of the laity in religious services is a good thing, especially if it results in an increased membership, increased attendance, and increased interest in the educational and cultural activities that congregations can offer. But wouldn't he insist that we have a responsibility to preserve and transmit our musical tradition and heritage. Glantz might suggest that if you are a congregant who is going to lead a public Jewish worship service, do not think that mere mechanical recitation of the words *only* to fulfill a halachic obligation is sufficient. Glantz was all about expressing and communicating the emotional as well as the intellectual truth of the text.

In many Orthodox synagogues, in conversations with congregants, lay leaders, and rabbis, I've heard "We don't want *chazzanut* – we prefer singing Carlebach."

Leib Glantz loved *chassidic* music. But I am certain he would not approve of the extent to which chassidic-style sing-along has become the central concept of musical expression of the liturgy in many non-*chassidic* synagogues. Wouldn't he be disturbed to see the extent to which it has replaced the vocal artistry of the cantor, and has diminished the very idea of inspired listening, as the primary mode of musical religious expression. Wouldn't he point out that many congregations with an excessive emphasis on congregational singing are mistaking the sense of community and empowerment that is generated by group singing for the entirety of the religious experience. Obviously, a sense of community and empowerment are positive values, but they are definitely not everything, and they are not even the most important thing.

What Leib Glantz would find most disturbing would be the disappearance of *nusach* in today's synagogues.

Nusach ha'tfilah, the Jewish prayer modes, is the spiritual clothing that decorates the Jewish prayers. Through the centuries the Jewish people have evolved a body of traditional prayer chant with distinctive patterns, characteristics and emotional flavors for each occasion in the Jewish calendar. Together with the *Misinai* melodies we have a glorious, diverse treasure of inspirational vocal musical art in many forms and styles. It has added an indispensable dimension of depth, intensity, beauty, nuance and understanding to both the cultural and the religious life of our people. Upon walking into the synagogue and hearing but a few seconds of the prayers of Passover or *Yom Kippur,* chanted by a true master of *nusach,* the correctly educated and well-cultured Jew is instantly transported out of the mundane and into the distinctive emotional framework, historical awareness and heightened spirituality conducive to the religious experience of the occasion. I believe that without this vocal art the Jews would not have developed into the people we are.

Leib Glantz had recognized the importance of the cantorial school of the Jewish Theological Seminary. He once wrote a letter to the students, on the occasion of their graduation ceremony, to offer points of guidance and express encouragement. Today that cantorial school still offers instruction in many of the subjects Glantz thought a cantor should study, and its graduates have a Master's degree in Sacred Music. However, the overall emphasis these days is on accommodating the need of the Conservative congregations to combine many different functions in one person. Today there seems to be an unspoken acquiescence to the notion that inspirational vocal artistry is no longer the first priority, the most important responsibility, of the cantor, but rather just one of many functions of equal or greater importance, that only combined, enable a cantor to be hired by a congregation.

Glantz would certainly agree that the cantor, like the rabbi, must be fully prepared to perform several educational, ritual and clergy functions for his congregation, and he would recognize present day congregation's economic and financial realities. But I doubt he would agree to compromise the primacy of the cantor's art.

Reform cantors are educated in a fine school. The School of Sacred Music actually includes *chazzanut* in the curriculum, however, in the Reform congregational world the situation is very different.

Glantz would consider today's Reform service to be quite alien to his concept of Judaism. The Reform movement differs from Conservative and Orthodox in that it has officially chosen to regard tradition, especially *halachah*, as non-binding. *Halachah* is the collective body of Jewish religious laws, including the biblical law and later the Talmudic and rabbinic law, as well as customs and traditions. Rather than in terms of adherence to tradition, the music and practices here have to be judged on effectiveness

It should be noted that there are a few classic Reform synagogues where most of the service is presented by cantor and choir, and the congregation is inspired by listening. The repertoire includes western European composers heard in Orthodox and Conservative congregations, as well as classic Reform composers, and modern American synagogue composers.

If Glantz were here today he would probably gather his considerable intellectual resources and focus his unmatched creative energy to understand why we Jews, an otherwise highly educated people for whom musical *artistry* has been the primary means of deep emotional religious expression throughout our history, are, in so many of our congregations, in the process of tossing our magnificent music heritage out of the synagogue and creating an artistic desert.

In all three branches of Judaism, advocates of congregational participation and self-expression as a replacement for the inspirational art of the cantor, have dominated the discussion, and it is evident that the majority of congregations are following them. At best, inspiration-by-sacred-music-artistry is allowed to make only brief, token appearances in their synagogue services

Of the many ways Glantz set an example during his lifetime, the most important one for us to follow is active, determined, and sustained advocacy. Glantz made a lifelong effort to educate the public about our music heritage and to raise the level of effectiveness of our cantors. We must do the same, if we want to restore a proper level of culture, and bring synagogue music artistry back into effective use.

I believe Glantz might not wish to eliminate sing-along completely, but would argue for the necessity for both *chazzanut* and some sing-along in our places of worship.

Many congregations have a more diverse membership today, with people of different backgrounds, and different musical, educational, and cultural levels. I believe Glantz might argue that it is the cantor's job to educate the congregation about our music tradition.

Glantz emphasized the importance of excluding "foreign influences" and trying to perform music that has legitimate Jewish ancestry. But we must remember that he emphasized creativity and innovation, and I suspect that he would encourage composers to create music that "sounds Jewish," is in good musical taste, and is appropriate for use in the synagogue, and yet utilizes some compositional elements such as rhythms, harmonization concepts, and even melody, that have some resemblance to musical styles of other cultures.

A truly great cantor, rabbi or religious teacher is a great artist whose performance is effective in evoking spirituality and a truly deep level of understanding and emotion in the hearts of the congregants. Leib Glantz is the perfect example.

Inspirational cantors and rabbis transport their congregations into the content of their presentations. They focus everyone's attention on the message, rather than on themselves or their prowess as the messenger. Yet their presentation is a personal statement; these cantors and rabbis put their hearts and personalities into their communication; They have authenticity without self-aggrandizement, and succeed in communicating their message. Theirs is an effective performance.

The public religious ceremony is not like individual private prayer or meditation. Nor is it purely a collective group activity like sing-along. There is inherent in every public religious service a legitimate and indispensable element of theater, artistic interpretation, dramatization and yes, performance.

I imagine Glantz saying: "What is the Torah Service with its dramatic declamation of the *Sh'ma* and ceremonial parading with the Torah scrolls if not theater and performance? What is the *Yom Kippur* re-enactment of the ceremony of the *Kohen Gadol* (High Priest) entering the Jerusalem Temple's Holy of Holies and bowing all the way to the ground, if not dramatization and performance? Are our prayers not filled with drama, beauty and human emotion? It is totally inappropriate for anyone, cantor or congregant, to present them in a manner that does not show awareness of their drama, meaning and beauty!"

Why does the *Shulchan Aruch* (the Code of Jewish Law) specifically require that our prayer services be led by one with "a pleasant, melodious voice, pleasing to the worshippers"? What volumes that tells us about the central importance of musical beauty and vocal artistry and congregational listening in synagogue services!

If Leib Glantz were here today, would he not urge us to present every persuasive argument we could think of to help improve the music culture in our synagogues?

Concerts of *chazzanut* and other Jewish vocal music do not satisfy our spiritual needs. They are not a valid substitute for vocal artistry when it is exiled from its natural, long-time home – the synagogue service.

A concert is not intended to be a prayer service. It may present sacred music, but the emphasis is on music. The attention is more on the externals – the beauty of the voice and the music, the perfection of the vocal technique, the spectacular coloratura, and necessarily somewhat less on communicating religious truth. The cantorial concert is intended to demonstrate the beauty of holiness, while *chazzanut* in the service is intended to enlist beauty to enhance holiness.

Everything about Glantz's work tells us that in the synagogue service the cantor should be focused on utilizing music to communicate the emotional and intellectual truth of the text and of the particular occasion. Many cantors are focused on other things – perhaps on producing pure beauty, on voice, technique, sound, and listener reaction. They have failed at making the congregants feel and understand the emotional and spiritual truths in the texts. However, the listening public senses this. Some congregants no longer have any expectation of being emotionally or spiritually inspired by a cantor in the synagogue. They have lost trust. But these same people are happy to come to be entertained at a cantorial concert.

Leib Glantz is the perfect example of a cantor who never had this problem. Part of his greatness was that you had absolutely no doubt that every note he uttered came directly from his heart. You were arrested by the intensity of his intention to communicate. He would never allow the listener to be distracted. You were totally drawn in. He made you focus on the text and what it really meant.

Only a small fraction of today's Jewish population had the privilege of hearing Cantor Leib Glantz. The majority of Jews in the last two generations have never experienced a synagogue service conducted by a truly great cantor.

Many of us consider Leib Glantz's high standards to be the benchmark for everything in the field of cantorial music. There is so much to learn from the way he approached every aspect of being a cantor. In a sense, we can all be his students.

Glantz is important to us now because he constantly reminds us that cantorial and choral artistry is an incomparable, irreplaceable living source of inspiration in the synagogue, and that it is vital to Judaism, and to the Jewish people. I think that if he were here today he would find the situation very challenging. Leib Glantz would want *chazzanut* not merely to survive, but to *flourish!*

The Musical Basis of *Nu'sach Ha'Te'fi'la*

LEIB GLANTZ

LECTURE AT THE FIFTH ANNUAL CONVENTION OF THE CANTORS ASSEMBLY, 1952[1]

When cantors ask themselves, "What is the musical basis of *Nu'sach Ha'Te'fi'la*?"[2] — they are seeking first and foremost a viable method, a method which will enable them to understand what they are doing in and with our musical tradition and which will help them to do it with more assurance, more clarity and more confidence.

The day is past when the cantor lived in an environment in which the Jewish musical heritage was an organic part of his being and when the musical tradition permeated every moment of his life, from the chanting of the *Mo'deh A'ni* in the early morning to the *She'ma* he said before retiring. Today, the cantor must learn his art as a separate and often isolated element in his musical education. To do this, he cannot be satisfied merely with knowing the historical basis or the archaeological findings of scholars. These are important, interesting, and significant, but we need something more specifically useful in our actual work.

If we are to retain the purity and beauty of our musical services, where every prayer has its traditional setting and every holiday its specific musical aroma, we must find a way to transmit

1 Lecture by Leib Glantz on May 6th, 1952, at the session devoted to Cantorial Studies, at the Fifth Annual Conference-Convention of The Cantors Assembly and The Department of Music of the United Synagogues of America at The Concord Hotel, Kiamesha Lake, New York.

2 *Nu'sach* – an Aramaic term derived from the Hebrew root *Sach. Nu'sach* is a melodic pattern or prayer mode governing the traditional chanting of the prayer texts. The melodies of the prayers were transmitted informally from generation to generation, and collated into a body called *Nu'sach.* Chanting the prayers according to given melodic patterns and modes was traditional and obligatory. The motifs are subject to repetition and omission and may generally be altered and varied, affording ample opportunity for improvisation. The plural of *Nu'sach* is *Nus'cha'ot.* [Source: *Concise Encyclopedia of Jewish Music,* by Macy Nulman, McGraw-Hill Book Co., NY, 1975].

the knowledge of the subtleties and the differences between the *Nus'cha'ot.* We cannot depend upon memory or mechanical imitation and repetition alone.

Our music has many subtle variations and it is only too easy for the cantor to get lost in a labyrinth. Think for a moment of the similarity between the *Ka'ddish* of the *Ne'i'la* service and the *Ka'ddish* of the prayers of *Tal* or *Ge'shem.*[3] They are both from the group called *"Mi'Sinai" Nus'cha'ot* and some of their intervals are identical.

> ***Our music has many subtle variations and it is only too easy for the cantor to get lost in a labyrinth.***

Nevertheless, the differences are significant. In a culture where every Jew was familiar with the appropriate *Nu'sach,* memory, habit, training and tradition kept the cantor within the proper framework, along with his whole congregation. How few are today the worshippers who know the difference.

We must develop a system by which we may be able to teach the basic musical line for each *Nu'sach* with which the cantors work. I have been thinking along these lines for a long time and I should like to present to you some of my observations. I have found them very useful in providing me with a theoretical basis in terms of which I can understand and differentiate the various *Nus'cha'ot.* I have not yet determined a satisfactory line for all of them, but I believe that this line of inquiry has already brought into the light some of the secrets of how the *Nus'cha'ot* are built. In certain of the *Nus'cha'ot,* where I was able to work out complete and correct lines or scales, the similarities, the differences and the confusions between them were clarified. Elements that formerly had to be described as accidental, or capricious, found their place in a regular pattern.

Before we begin our analysis of the *Nus'cha'ot* in terms of musical intervals, lines, modes and scales, let us first briefly review the concept of *Nu'sach* itself. The Jews used this term in the same way as did other Eastern peoples, such as the Arabs and the Hindus. They used it to describe a short musical line, a musical group, or a musical phrase, which was the basis of their melodies. Once the performer knew these short musical lines, he was left to himself to improvise and elaborate upon that basic line.

The Jewish people developed two types or groups of *Nus'cha'ot.* The first type fits the description as given above more exactly. It is a group of musical phrases built upon the biblical cantillation modes.[4] The cantors use these *Nus'cha'ot* as a basis for their recitatives, improvisations

3 *Ge'shem* and *Tal* — rain and dew.

4 Biblical cantillation modes — the art of chanting the *To'rah* is over two thousand years old and evolved from a solely oral tradition, to a formalized system of musical notation that we now call trope, *Ta'a'mim,* or musical cantillation. This biblical cantillation system is made up of 28 signs and each sign stands for a specific musical pattern or melodic motif.

or compositions. The improviser or composer had full freedom to elaborate, to develop, to introduce modulations, within the framework of the particular musical line. Examples of such *Nus'cha'ot* are the *"A'do'nai Ma'lach" Nu'sach* of Friday night, which is identical with the *"Ye'kum Pur'kan" Nu'sach* of Saturday morning, the *"Ma'gen A'vot" Nu'sach,* the *"Yish'ta'bach" Nu'sach* of Saturday morning, and the *"A'ha'va Ra'bbah" Nu'sach.*

There is a second type, also called *Nus'cha'ot,* which differs from the first group, because it consists of a group of *fixed prayer melodies* that have been associated with certain texts from time immemorial. These fixed melodies are not subject to improvisation, elaboration or any kind of change. They are always sung in the definite crystallized form. These are called *"Mi'Sinai"* melodies, or "melodies from Sinai" and they include some of the most beloved and important prayers of the liturgy. Of course, even the fixed melodies vary in different parts of the world. The Oriental [Middle Eastern], the Sephardic, and the Ashkenazic communities have crystallized different melodies for the same texts.

Poetic legend has it that God himself sang these melodies to Moses on Mt. Sinai, when He gave him the *To'rah.* To our forefathers it was unthinkable that God should not reveal Himself in music. How lofty an origin does our tradition ascribe to the music of our prayers!

Although legend and folklore place the origin of the *Mi'Sinai* prayer melodies even further back in the mists of history than the biblical cantillations, musicological research has demonstrated that these *Mi'Sinai* melodies developed later — in the Diaspora. The first group, the musical lines based upon the biblical cantillation modes, has history that goes back at least 2400 years. Both the biblical modes and the *Mi'Sinai* melodies were exposed to many different influences and to many different cultures in their long history, but their main features have remained the basis of synagogue music to this day.

Although legend and folklore place the origin of the* Mi'Sinai *prayer melodies even further back in the mists of history than the biblical cantillations, musicological research has demonstrated that these* Mi'Sinai *melodies developed later — in the Diaspora.

In any discussion of the origin of Jewish music, full recognition must be given to the great musicologist, Avraham Zvi Idelsohn (1882-1938), who in the short span of his life succeeded in proving that the biblical cantillation modes were well preserved in their raw state by the Oriental [Middle Eastern] Jewish communities. He also proved that the Byzantine and the Western Christian world inherited and utilized the same modes in their Gregorian chants. There is also a contemporary musicologist, Shlomo Rosowsky (b. 1878), who is making tremendous contributions in the study of biblical cantillation. A few others are engaged in this field and we are beginning to see light on all of these mysteries of the Jewish contribution to the art of music.

I do not belong to that school of thought that believes that the roots of a culture are necessarily the same as the flowers and the fruits of a culture. It is very important to know the roots and the sources. It is just as important to cherish and to value the manifold developments of a culture throughout its entire history.

There is a danger, it is true, that strange and illegitimate elements often find their way into a culture. These must be discriminated against and eliminated wherever possible. But in the dynamic life of a people, much is absorbed from the outside, assimilated and transformed into the true image of that people and that culture.

In our enthusiasm for the tremendously important scientific researches into the musical origins of our *Nus'cha'ot,* we may tend today to overestimate the importance of that part of our musical heritage that was frozen at a very primitive level by the Eastern Jewish communities. There is a tendency among certain circles to minimize much of the dynamic musical development of the Ashkenazic and Eastern European musical culture, while overestimating the value of that portion of our musical heritage that was kept in the "deep-freeze" by the Eastern Jewish communities. If we had relied upon the Eastern Jewish communities alone for our music, we would find ourselves today with only a few bare roots. If I may be allowed to draw a parallel, although no analogy is perfect, the Eastern Jewry played almost the same role in Jewish music as the *Karaite*[5] sect played in the freezing of Jewish *Ha'la'cha*[6] on the basis of the Five Books of Moses alone.

If the biblical cantillation modes may be considered the *"To'rah She'Bich'tav"* (written law) of Jewish music, then the later development of the *Nus'cha'ot* by the different communities, especially by Ashkenazic and Eastern European Jewries, may be likened to the *"To'rah She'Ba'al Peh,"* the oral commentary and interpretation of the raw material of the biblical cantillation.

The dynamic vitality of the Ashkenazic Jewry and later the Jewry of the Eastern European countries, which created the Rabbinic literature, the *Ka'bba'la,*[7] the Chasidic movement, the great modern Hebrew and Yiddish literatures, that same vitality also flourished in the field of music. It continued to create and to re-create, change and interchange, and also to weave-in new threads, new intervals, new musical lines, and even one great new *Nu'sach,* the *A'ha'va Ra'bbah Nu'sach,* into the Jewish liturgy.

We must recognize that just as the time came for the Talmud to be recorded and published, so the time has come when Jewish music can no longer withstand the great onslaughts of accidental singing. The time of *Ge'ni'za* (archiving) of Jewish music has arrived. The cantor and the composer must have the true musical line for each and every prayer. We must stop the guesswork and replace it with true understanding of the elements of cantorial creativity.

The time has come when Jewish music can no longer withstand the great onslaughts of accidental singing . . . We must stop the guesswork and replace it with true understanding of the elements of cantorial creativity.

Let us now begin to look into the nature of our *Nus'cha'ot.* On the one hand, it is clear that they cannot be understood in terms of the crystallized Major and Minor scales of Western music. On the other hand, an analysis of the *Nus'cha'ot,* in terms of the biblical cantillation modes alone leads us into a labyrinth of such complexity that only the most articulate and skillful of musical scholars can find his way around.

5 *Karaites* — a Jewish sect founded in the eighth century and located chiefly in the Crimea and nearby areas, and in Israel, which rejects rabbinical interpretation in favor of a literal interpretation of the scriptures.

6 *Ha'la'cha* — Jewish law and jurisprudence, based on the Talmud.

7 *Ka'bba'la* — the ancient Jewish tradition of mystical interpretation of the Bible, first transmitted orally and using esoteric methods (including ciphers). It reached the height of its influence in the later Middle Ages and remains significant in Chasidism.

If I may be permitted to paraphrase a popular expression, "The Greeks had a line for it." Although it may be historically true that the Greek modes themselves were shaped upon the biblical modes, there is no doubt in my mind that the Greek modes offer the most useful lines for the understanding of our own musical formations.

The basic element of the Greek mode is the Tetrachord, a line of four steps. Various modes are different combinations of different Tetrachords.

Certain Jewish prayers can be analyzed in terms of known and recognized Greek modes. They can be understood by simply following the five-step (Pentachord), seven-step (Heptachord), or eight-step (Octachord) lines of the Greek modes.

There are others, however, which remain incapable of being so easily described. These, of course, are the ones that present the real problem to us. My observation is that the Ashkenazic Jews created new scales based upon new combinations of the elements of the Greek modes. We can find *Nus'cha'ot* based on a ten-step line, a twelve-step line, and a thirteen-step line, all of them new combinations of three or four Tetrachords in varying sequence.

The Ashkenazic Jews created new scales based upon new combinations of the elements of the Greek modes.

It would not be possible in a single lecture to analyze every important prayer in the liturgy. This would require a series of lectures. In this presentation, we will have to limit ourselves to only a few examples.

On Sabbath morning the *Ba'al Shach'rit*, who usually precedes the cantor, sings the *Psu'kei De'Zim'ra* in a pure Pentatonic, or five-step line. This *Nu'sach* can definitely be traced to the biblical cantillation, but for all practical musical purposes, the modern musician can understand it as a *Nu'sach* built on the pure and simple Pentatonic line. This portion of the Sabbath service was most often chanted by a layman rather than by a professional cantor. Therefore it retained the simplicity of the original, and was not subjected to the musical development that other *Nus'cha'ot* experienced.

ILLUSTRATION 1

1a) *P'su'kei De'Zim'ra* phrase:

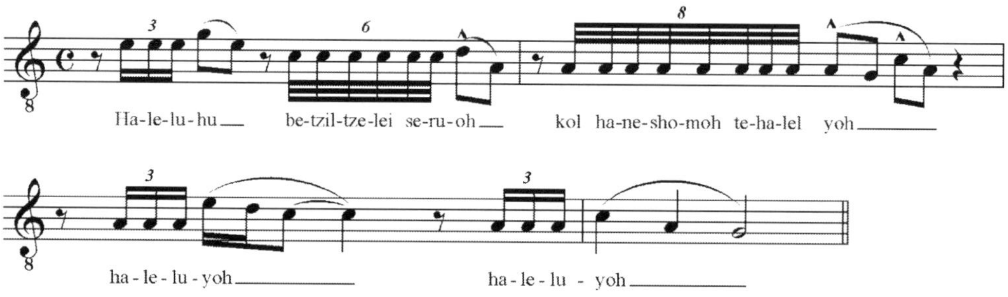

1b) The Pentatonic line:

The *Ak'da'mut* prayer of the *Sha'vu'ot* festival service can also be clearly understood through the application of the plain and simple Pentatonic line. It, too, has remained in an elementary form, because it is considered to be a *Mi'Sinai Nu'sach,* and as such was not subject to development. Of course, certain *Ba'a'lei Kri'ah* (masters of musical reading of the *To'rah*) may add some western intervals to the *Ak'da'mut,* but the Pentachord is so prominently dominating in it, that we can easily discard those additions as accidental and definitely ascertain the right line upon which it is built. To mention at least one more type of prominent prayer built on the Pentatonic, let us not forget the *A'vot* of the weekday *A'mi'da,* which is definitely sung in the Pentatonic all over the world, although different communities sing the entire weekday *A'mi'da* (which follows after the *A'vot)* in a different musical line. The *A'vot* remains the same Pentatonic in almost every place where Jews conduct prayer services.

ILLUSTRATION 2

2a) The *"Ak'da'mut"* phrase:

2b) The Pentatonic line:

2c) The *"A'vot"* of the weekday *A'mi'da:*

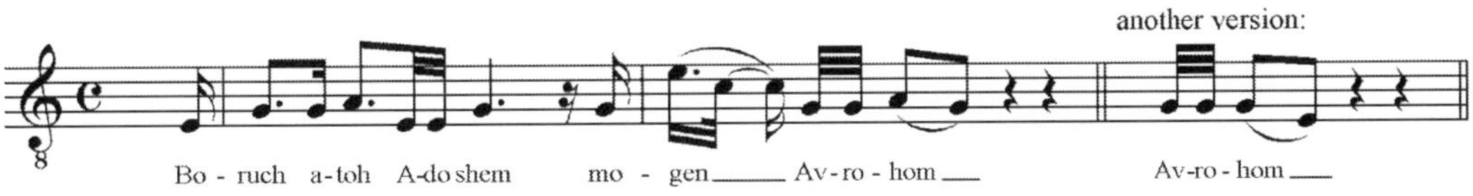

Let us now look at the *Nu'sach* of the *A'do'nai Ma'lach* of the Friday night service, which is identical with the *Ye'kum Pur'kan Nu'sach* of the Saturday morning service. The name *Ye'kum Pur'kan* was used mostly by Eastern European cantors. It is the most typical Major *Nu'sach* of the Jewish liturgy. This *Nu'sach* is used in almost every prayer that is sung in the Jewish Major scale. The most important of these are the *A'vot* of the Sabbath and festival morning services, and the *Na'a'ritz'cha* of the *Mu'saf* service.

When we apply the Greek Mixolydian mode, which consists of two conjunctive Tetrachords, the last note of the first Tetrachord, forming the first note of the second Tetrachord of this mode, forms a line of the following intervals:

one-tone, one-tone, one-half-tone.

ILLUSTRATION 3

3a) *Ye'kum Pur'kan* elementary short phrase:

3b) The Mixolydian mode:

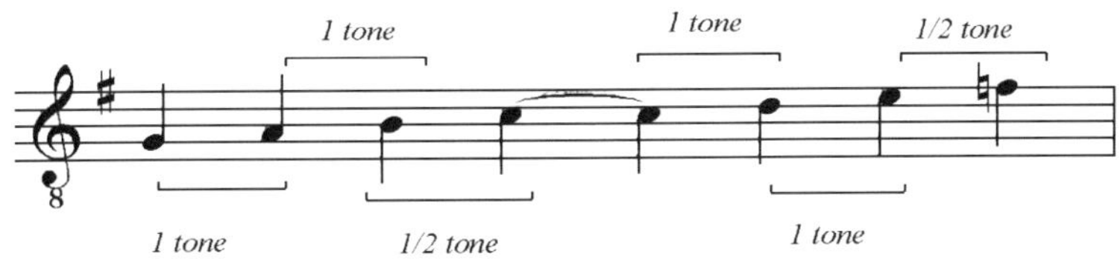

But when we look deeper into the *Ye'kum Pur'kan Nu'sach*, we find two prominent peculiarities:

1. When we proceed above the second Tetrachord, we must use Bb instead of B natural.
2. We use F# instead of F natural when we proceed below the first Tetrachord.

These two peculiarities have "tormented"' my thoughts for a long time. I am happy to present a solution to this problem:

The Jews added an identical Tetrachord on top of the second Tetrachord, and then added another identical Tetrachord below the first. The first addition creates a ten-step line, or a three-Tetrachord line, upon which some of our *Mi'Sinai Nus'cha'ot* are built. The second addition creates a thirteen-step line or four-Tetrachord line, upon which other *Mi'Sinai Nus'cha'ot* are built. We may compare it to a two-car train to which a car was added in front and another similar one added in the back.

ILLUSTRATION 4

4a) The 10-step *Ye'kum Pur'kan* line:

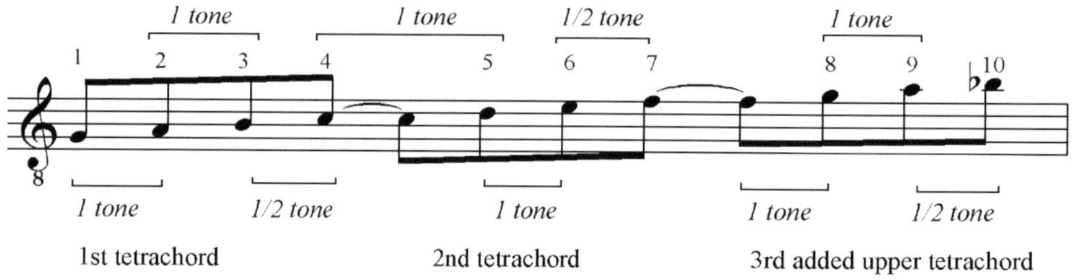

4b) The 13-step *Ye'kum Pur'kan* line:

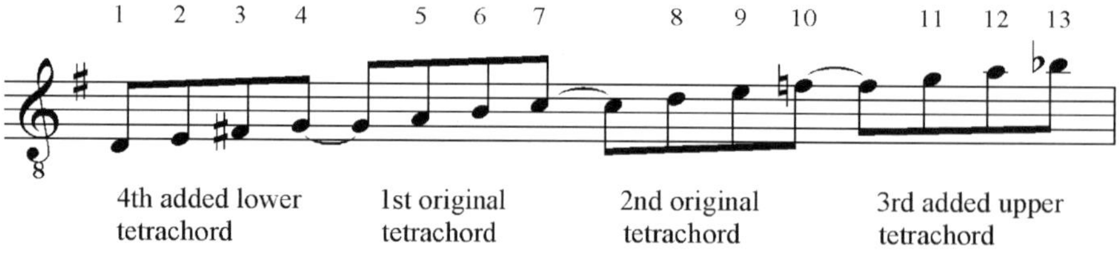

The original *Ye'kum Pur'kan* prayer of the Sabbath *Mu'saf* service, as well as the other basic Sabbath prayers, which are shaped in the *Ye'kum Pur'kan Nu'sach,* contain in themselves all of the features mentioned above. It is fascinating to observe that some of the *Mi'Sinai Nus'cha'ot*

of fixed prayer melodies, contain only one feature or one variation of this *Ye'kum Pur'kan Nu'sach* — either the seven-step, ten-step, or thirteen-step line. As a striking example of the most elementary type of Major scale, namely — the original Mixolydian seven-step, two Tetrachord line, we can mention the *Ka'ddish* prayer of the *Ne'i'la* service of *Yom Ki'ppur.*

Please keep this in mind. This analysis refers only to the *Ka'ddish* prayer of the *Ne'i'la* service. Although the *Ka'ddish* prayer for *Ge'shem* (rain) and *Tal* (dew) contain many elements of the same melody, it is definitely built on another line that we shall discuss later.

If we start the *Ne'i'la Ka'ddish* prayer from the G, while bearing in mind the seven-step line, and we work only within these seven steps, we can never lose the pattern of the *Nu'sach* of the *Ne'i'la* service.

ILLUSTRATION 5

5a) The *"Ne'i'la Ka'ddish"* phrase:

5b) The Mixolydian 7-step line:

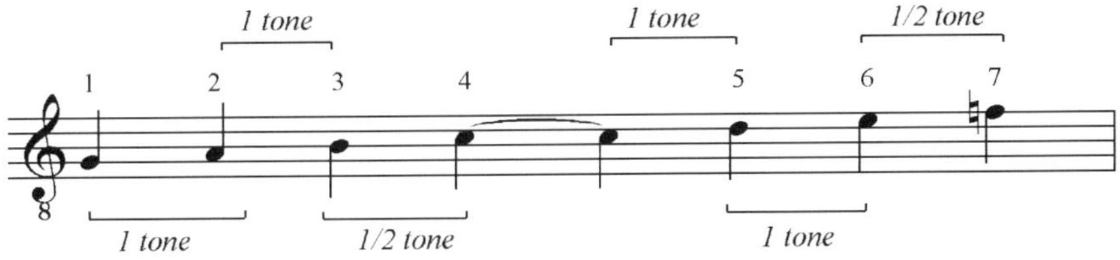

Another striking example of the seven-step major line is the *Nu'sach* of the *Ha'gga'da* (the story of the Exodus of the Israelites from Egypt) for *Pe'ssach* (Passover holiday*)*. With the exception of the melody for the "Four Questions," *Ma Nish'ta'na* ("Wherefore is this night distinguished from all other nights?"), which I venture to call a *Mi'Sinai* prayer melody, as it is almost an exact imitation of the biblical cantillation, the rest of the *Ha'gga'da* can be analyzed and understood much more easily in terms of the two Tetrachord, seven-step Major line.

ILLUSTRATION 6

6a) ***"A'va'dim Ha'yi'nu"*** **(from the Passover** ***Ha'gga'da*** **):**

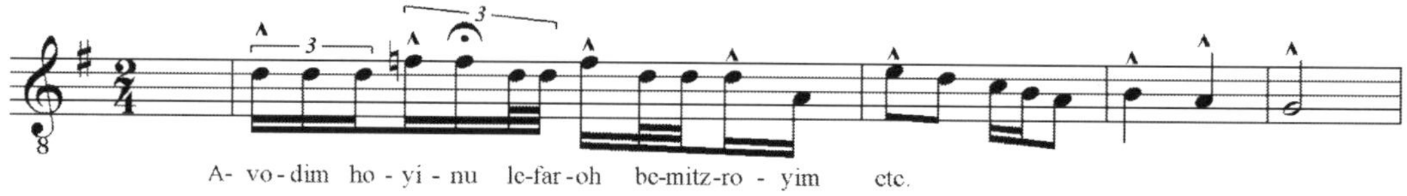

6b) The Mixolydian 7-step line:

6c) ***"A'dir Hu"*** **(from the Passover** ***Ha'gga'da*** **):**

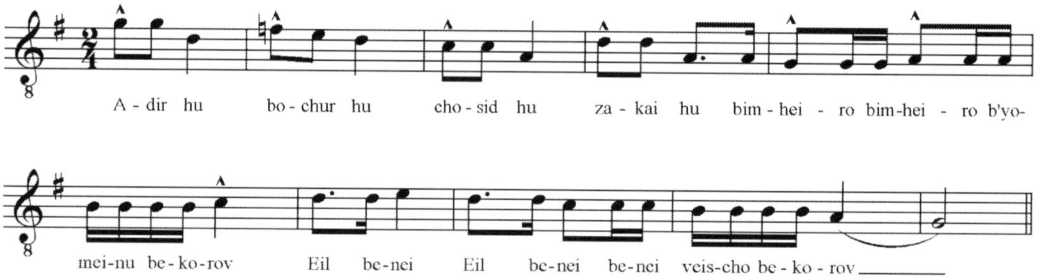

A unique demonstration of the ten-step line is the *Ba're'chu* prayer of the evening Festival service. It is unique because the entire evening *Ma'a'riv* service of the festival is performed by the Ashkenazic and Eastern European communities in a Minor key. The *Ba're'chu,* curiously enough, starts with a Major, and climbs up to the Bb at the end of the third Tetrachord. This same three-Tetrachord line runs through the Festival morning *A'mi'da Nu'sach.*

ILLUSTRATION 7

7a) ***"Ba're'chu"*** **for Festival evening services:**

7b) The Festival *"A'mi'da"* morning service phrases:

7c) The three Tetrachord, 10-step line, *Ye'kum Pur'kan Nu'sach:*

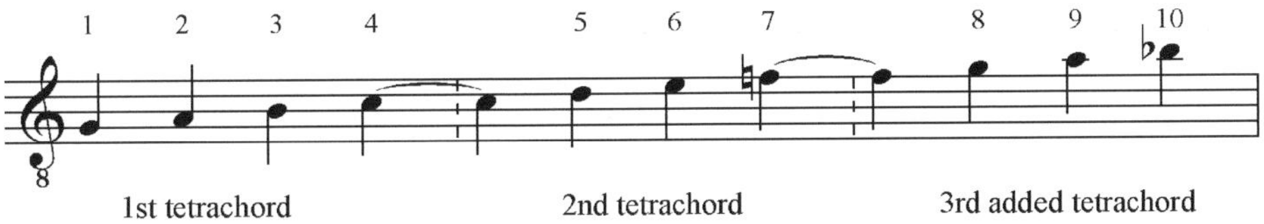

An even more striking example of the three-Tetrachord line, is the first part of the *Ve'Ha'Ko'ha'nim* prayer from the *A'vo'da* ceremony of *Rosh Ha'Sha'na* and *Yom Ki'ppur.* This is a fixed prayer melody, a *Mi'Sinai Nu'sach,* and is one of the most difficult for any cantor to understand or to analyze. I am glad to say that since I discovered the two-fold *Nu'sach* of the *Ve'Ha'Ko'ha'nim* prayer, I find it easier and more interesting to chant.

The secret of the *Ve'Ha'Ko'ha'nim* lies in the fact that it is built on two different *Nus'cha'ot.* The first part is based on the ten-step *Ye'kum Pur'kan Nu'sach.* However, it has its own particular combination of Tetrachords, in which the third Tetrachord is added below the first instead of above the second line. This gives us a line from D to F (above the octave).

If we start the *Ve'Ha'Ko'ha'nim* from G in the Jewish Major scale, one might be misled into thinking that this is the basic tonic of this musical scale. But we are amazed to learn in the course of chanting the *Nu'sach* that the tonic stems from the D below. Suddenly, in the middle of the *Ve'Ha'Ko'ha'nim,* we find a modulation from the Major of the *Ye'kum Pur'kan Nu'sach* to the *Nu'sach* of the *A'ha'va Ra'bbah,* which I shall discuss later.

ILLUSTRATION 8

8a) *"Ve'Ha'Ko'ha'nim"* (first part) built on the three Tetrachord, 10 step-line of the *Ye'kum Pur'kan Nu'sach*:

8b) *"Ve'Ha'Ko'ha'nim"* (second part) — modulates to *A'ha'va Ra'bbah Nu'sach*:

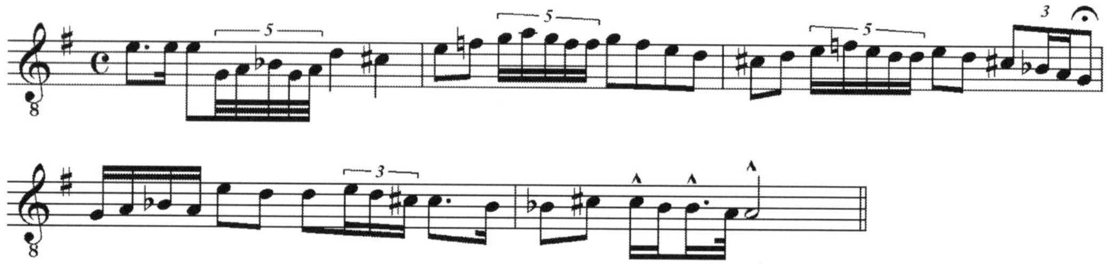

Please note that this *A'ha'va Ra'bbah* part has no augmented second interval in the second Tetrachord, which we will discuss later when we take up the special members of the *A'ha'va Ra'bbah* family.

Another type of *"Ve'Ha'Ko'ha'nim"* also modulates into *A'ha'va Ra'bbah* but in the first lower Tetrachord and not in the second as we have seen above.

8c) A second type of *"Ve'Ha'Ko'ha'nim"*:

The last and most important illustration of the *Ye'kum Pur'kan Nu'sach* in its entirety, namely the thirteen-step line, embracing all the four Tetrachords, I found in one of the greatest fixed prayer melodies, the *A'vot* of the High Holidays. I sometimes allude to this *Nu'sach* as an 'escalator' melody, for the rising thirteen-step line makes it the most difficult of all prayers.

As a child, I used to pity my grandfather and my father, who were both cantors, when they entangled themselves in that melody and had difficulty finding the way back to the tonic. When I grew older, I begged every cantor and every *Ba'al Te'fi'la* (prayer master) to demonstrate the *A'vot* for me in an effort to get at the mystery of its structure.

One of the oldest *Ba'a'lei Te'fi'la,* whom I met in a small town near Odessa, sang the *A'vot* for me in a most peculiar fashion. He assured me that he had heard it from Bezalel Odesser (1790-1860), the famous cantor and *Ba'al Te'fi'la,* who was considered the father of *Nu'sach Ha'Te'fi'la* for the Eastern European *Cha'za'nut* of the nineteenth century.

When I was sent by my father to Kishinev in order to hear the famous cantor, Avraham Berkovitch-Kalechnik, that cantor again sang the *A'vot* in the same manner as the old man mentioned above. On asking Kalechnik about the origin of the *A'vot* that he sang, he told me that it was given to him as an authentic *Nu'sach* from the mouth of Bezalel Odesser. Lately, while looking for an example of a *Mi'Sinai Nu'sach* in the thirteen-step line, I found in the *A'vot* version of those two people, the complete thirteen-step *Ye'kum Pur'kan* line. In the *A'vot,* as well as in the *Ve'Ha'Ko'ha'nim,* we discover that the Major melody is suddenly cut off and modulates into the same *A'ha'va Ra'bbah Nu'sach.* If one knows the full thirteen-step line of the *Ye'kum Pur'kan Nu'sach* and the *A'ha'va Ra'bbah* line as well, he is always on solid ground when he executes this complicated prayer.

The *A'vot* always presents an additional vocal difficulty to cantors, for its proper presentation requires a voice of considerable range.

This is clear as soon as you realize that it is based on a line of thirteen steps, each one playing an important role in the *Nu'sach.* The cantor should know which is the lowest of the thirteen steps in order to make it possible for him to climb up to those in the highest Tetrachord.

ILLUSTRATION 9

9a) *"A'vot"* of the High Holidays (first part) built on a four Tetrachord, 13-step *Ye'kum Pur'kan* line:

9b) Modulation of the *"A'vot"* into *A'ha'va Ra'bbah*:

9c) The 13-step line used in this *"A'vot"*:

9d) The *A'ha'va Ra'bbah* line used in the *"A'vot"*:

Please note again that in the second Tetrachord of the *A'ha'va Ra'bbah Nu'sach* there is no augmented second interval.

I mentioned the *A'ha'va Ra'bbah Nu'sach* in passing as being one of the parts of the *Ve'Ha'Ko'ha'nim* and of the *A'vot.* Let us look into its structure for a moment. Musicologists tell us that there is no trace of this *Nu'sach* in the biblical cantillation. Therefore, it is looked upon by some people as being under suspicion of illegitimacy. Some say it is a gypsy mode, others that it is a copy of the Hedjaz or the Tartaric music. Still others think that the Jews took it over from the Ukrainians. Whatever its birth, I think no one can deny that the *A'ha'va Ra'bbah Nu'sach* has become a love child in the family of Jewish *Nus'cha'ot.* We have molded and transformed it into our own true image.

It is generally considered that the tonic of this *Nu'sach* is E. That is why it is also called the Phrygian, or as the Eastern European cantors called it, Phrygish. The name probably was accepted because the medieval Phrygian mode also begins with E. The most important feature of this *Nu'sach* is the fact that the second interval has an augmented second. However, there is another feature in this *Nu'sach,* which is even stranger than the augmented second. This is the fact that when we go down below the E, we must sing D and C# instead of C natural, which again creates the peculiar situation that within one scale we have C natural and C#, and D natural and D# as well.

My answer to this is the same. The Jews did something of their own to an existing mode. We added a Tetrachord of another type below the tonic. The original two Tetrachords both have the following intervals:

half-tone, tone and-a-half, half-tone.

The connection between the Tetrachords is a disjunctive one. This means that the beginning of the second Tetrachord does not start with the last note of the first. The added Tetrachord, added down below the tonic is a major Tetrachord. Its intervals are:

one-tone, one-tone, half-tone.

This then gives us the following line of 12 tones:

(A, B natural, C#, D) (E, F, G#, A) (B, C natural, D#, E).

Anyone who is acquainted with the way that cantors treat the peculiar patterns of the *A'ha'va Ra'bbah Nu'sach* will admit that the most interesting feature, besides the augmented second, is the additional strange Tetrachord, which was hooked on to the other two. It is this that gives it the specific Jewish flavor, which you cannot find in any other formation.

These features are easily recognizable in the prayer *Be'Mo'tza'ei* of the *Se'li'chot* service and in many other prayer-melodies of the weekday, Sabbath, High Holidays and Festival services.

The entire *A'mi'da* of both *Shach'rit* and *Mu'saf* services on Sabbath is sung in the *A'ha'va Ra'bbah Nu'sach.*

ILLUSTRATION 10

10a) The basic line of the *A'ha'va Ra'bbah Nu'sach*:

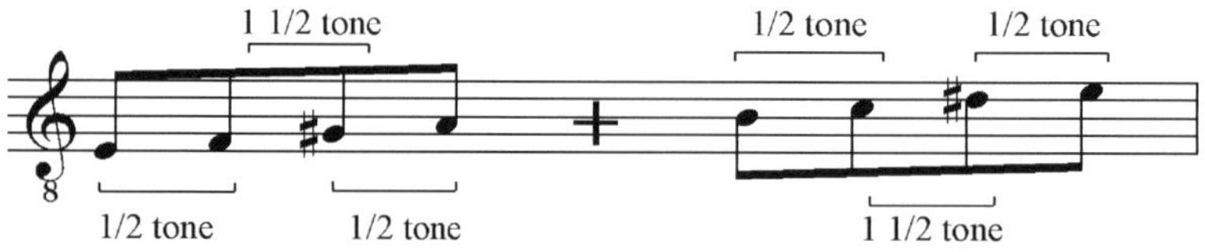

10b) The addition of a Major Tetrachord below the tonic:

10c) A typical *A'ha'va Ra'bbah* cantorial phrase built on a three Tetrachord, 12 step line:

10d) The complete 12-step line in *A'ha'va Ra'bbah*:

Here of course we should remember that some of the members of the *A'ha'va Ra'bbah* family omit the D# in the second Tetrachord and we have the augmented second only in the first lower Tetrachord.

A specific example of the *A'ha'va Ra'bbah Nu'sach* is the *Yit'ga'dal* prayer of the High Holiday *Mu'saf* service. It is another fixed *Mi'Sinai* prayer melody that is made up of a combination of two basic *Nus'cha'ot.* The first one is definitely in the *A'ha'va Ra'bbah Nu'sach.* The second part is in the regular *Ma'gen A'vot Nu'sach,* which I shall analyze later.

ILLUSTRATION 11

11a) The beginning of the High Holiday *"Ka'ddish"* in E mode of the *A'ha'va Ra'bbah Nu'sach*:

11b) The second part of the *"Ka'ddish"* in *Ma'gen A'vot* (Aeolian mode) in A:

It is also interesting to note that the *A'ha'va Ra'bbah Nu'sach* has several expressions and formations. One of the most attractive of these is the kind of *A'ha'va Ra'bbah Nu'sach* which runs through the famous High Holiday prayer, *O'chi'la La'El.* I therefore call this type by the name *O'chi'1a La'El Nu'sach.* This prayer has a *Mi'Sinai* melody, which is both strange and beautiful. Its peculiarity consists of two features:

- It drags the basic tone down below the E, and it lands on the D;
- The second Tetrachord, going upward, omits the interval of the augmented second, which it had in the first Tetrachord. It is obviously a different Tetrachord that is a plain Minor, with the following steps:

  (A B C D)

When we construct the entire mode from these two Tetrachords going upward from D to D, we get the full line of the *O'chi'la La 'El Nu'sach,* which has all the flavor and all the peculiarities of the *A'ha'va Ra'bbah Nu'sach.* However, the augmented second interval appears here not between the second and the third step, but between the third and fourth step, since the basic tone here is not E, but D. And. of course, as I said before, that augmented second interval appears only in the first Tetrachord and disappears in the second one.

A similar *A'ha'va Ra'bbah Nu'sach* is found in the latter part of the *A'vot,* in *A'ta Gi'bor Le'O'lam A'do'nai,* which is also built on the D tonic instead of the E. The same is true of the *O'chi'la La'El Nu'sach* principle.

ILLUSTRATION 12

12a) The *O'chi'la La'El* branch of the *A'ha'va Ra'bbah Nu'sach*:

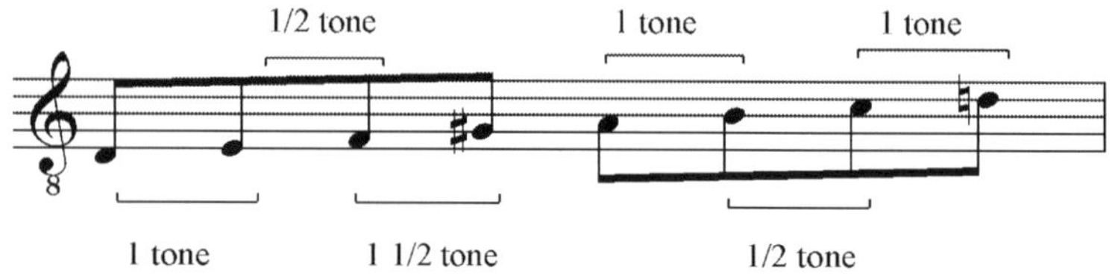

12b) The *O'chi'la La'El* phrase:

12c) *"A'ta Gi'bor"* and other later parts of the *"A'vot"* have the same musical line as the *O'chi'la La'El* (as in illustration 12b).

The *A'ha'va Ra'bbah Nu'sach,* in all of its manifestations, has become so dear to the Jewish people that it is an almost inescapable pattern in many folk songs and in many Chasidic *Ni'gu'nim* (melodies). Among these are "*Ei'li Ei'li*" and "*The Re'bbes Ni'gun.*" It is interesting to see that when Louis Lewandowski (1821-1894) succeeded in freeing himself entirely from German influences, he created one of his best and most authentically Jewish compositions — "*Ki Ke'Shim'cha*" — in the purest *A'ha'va Ra'bbah Nu'sach.*

One of the greatest of the contemporary Jewish and universal composers, Ernest Bloch (1880-1959), also could not escape its charm. His *"Tzur Yis'ra'el"* composition is a real gem in that same *Nu'sach.*

When we approach another basic *Nu'sach,* the *Ma'gen A'vot* of Friday night, we know that this one is definitely linked with the biblical cantillation. It is generally treated as a D mode with Bb in it. But again and again, I must emphasize that we can better understand it by applying the Aeolian mode as its basic musical line. This line does not require any accidentals (as the D line would), requiring the use of the Bb. Of the *Mi'Sinai* melodies built on the *Ma'gen A'vot Nu'sach,* let me mention at least two: *She'ma Yis'ra'el* at the opening of the Ark on the High Holidays, and the *P'tach La'nu Sha'ar* of the *Yom Ki'ppur Ne'i'la* service.

ILLUSTRATION 13

13a) The *Ma'gen A'vot* (Aeolian mode):

13b) *"She'ma Yis'ra'el,"* opening the Ark on the High Holidays:

13c) *"P'tach La'nu Sha'ar"* (*Yom Ki'ppur Ne'i'la* service):

The original *Ma'gen A'vot Nu'sach* branched out into many variations. It created a whole family of the Jewish Minor scale. I shall illustrate briefly just five of the many members of this family:

- *Yish'ta'bach* of the Sabbath *Shach'rit* service;
- *Mi'She'Bei'rach* of the Sabbath *Mu'saf* service;
- *A'ta Zo'cher* of the *Rosh Ha'Sha'na Mu'saf* service;
- the *Shach'rit* service of *Rosh Ha'Sha'na* morning; and
- the *Ge'shem/Tal Nu'sach.*

The *Yish'ta'bach Nu'sach* can be easily understood when it is seen as an eight-step line, from E to E, built upon two Tetrachords of the plain Greek Dorian or the medieval Phrygian mode.

The East Europeans modulated very easily from the *Yish'ta'bach* weekday *Nu'sach* to the *A'ha'va Ra'bbah Nu'sach,* even in the middle of the *Yish'ta'bach* prayer itself.

ILLUSTRATION 14

14a) The *"Yish'ta'bach"* phrase (Sabbath morning):

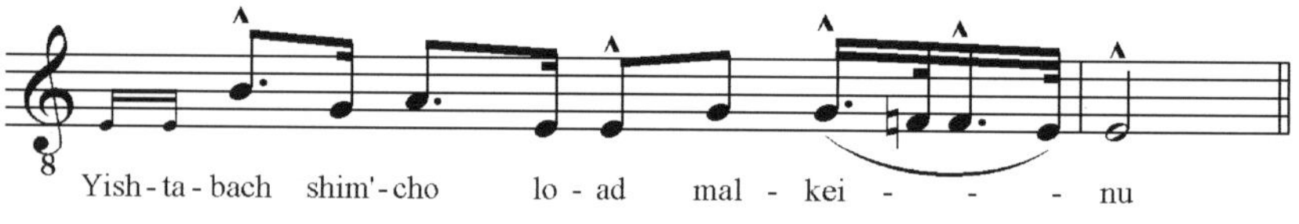

14b) The Greek Dorian or medieval Phrygian mode:

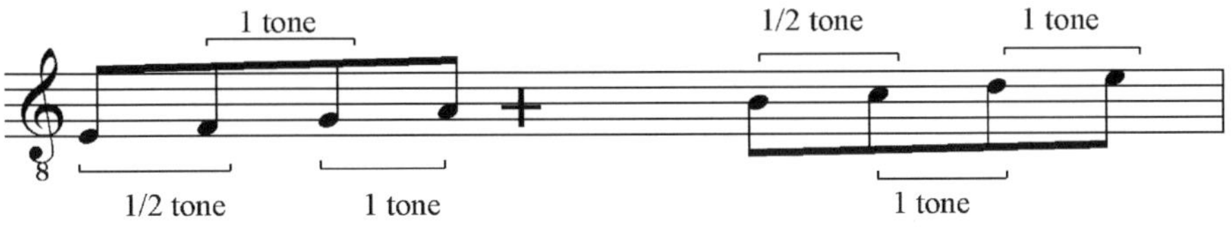

14c) Modulating from *Yish'ta'bach* to *A'ha'va Ra'bbah* in Eastern European synagogues:

The only change they make is from G natural to G#.

A really striking branch of the Minor family is the great *A'mi'da Nu'sach* from the *Rosh Ha'Sha'na Mu'saf* service, the *Mal'chu'yot, Zich'ro'not* and *Shof'rot.* I do not agree with the contention of some, that this *Nu'sach* is identical with the *Mi'She'Bei'rach Nu'sach* of the Sabbath *Mu'saf* service. The differences appear to be very slight but they are the result of two separate and distinct musical lines. Furthermore, they each create a different mood and impression.

Both are built from D to D on the white keys of the piano. They both use the Bb on the sixth step. The difference lies in this: The *Mi'She'Bei'rach* has an augmented second between the F and the G#, and is therefore likened to the Ukrainian-Dorian. It is considered to be the result of Slavic interference.

ILLUSTRATION 15

15a) The *"Mi She'bei'rach"* phrase (Saturday morning *Mu'saf* service) in D mode:

* Editor's note: In the original article, a mistake was made by the printer and the starred note above was printed as a Bb and not a B natural. Glantz, in a later printing, corrected the mistake. The corrected version is above.

15b) The *Mi She'bei'rach Nu'sach* line (Ukrainian/Dorian):

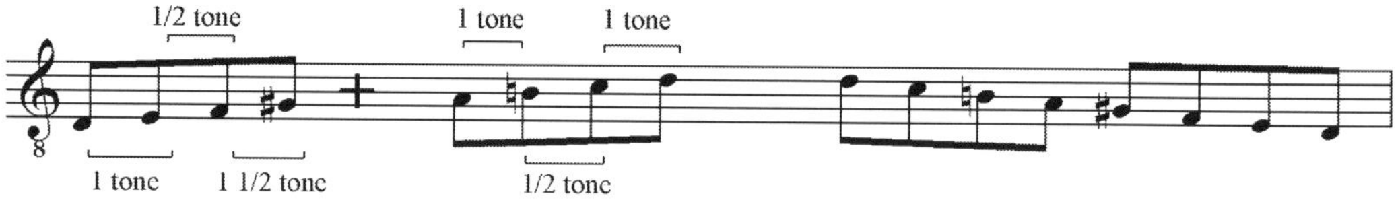

The *A'mi'da Nu'sach* of *Rosh Ha'Sha'na,* which some cantors call the *A'ta Zo'cher Nu'sach,* is distinguished from the *Mi'She'Bei'rach Nu'sach* by avoiding the augmented second and also by frequent modulation into the Major scale built on its third step.

There is another great feature of the *A'ta Zo'cher Nu'sach.* It is closely related to the *Shach'rit Nu'sach* of the *Rosh Ha'Sha'na* service, also a prominent member of the Minor scale family. Each is built on two Tetrachords with the following intervals:

one tone, half-a-tone, one tone.

The difference lies in the fact that in the *Shach'rit Nu'sach* there is an additional Tetrachord placed below the basic D on the conjunctive principle: the beginning of the second Tetrachord is the last tone of the first Tetrachord. This line is:

(A B C D) (D E F G),

whereas in the *A'ta Zo'cher Nu'sach,* the same Tetrachord is placed on top of the basic Tetrachord on the disjunctive principal, which gives the line:

(D E F G) PLUS (A B C D).

All three Tetrachords are Minor and have identical intervals.

ILLUSTRATION 16

16a) The *"A'ta Zo'cher"* phrase — D mode modulating into *Ye'kum Pur'kan Nu'sach* from its third step (F):

16b) The D line of *"A'ta Zo'cher"*:

16c) The F line of the *Ye'kum Pur'kan* — Mixolydian transposed from G:

16d) The *Shach'rit Nu'sach*:

16e) The added Tetrachord:

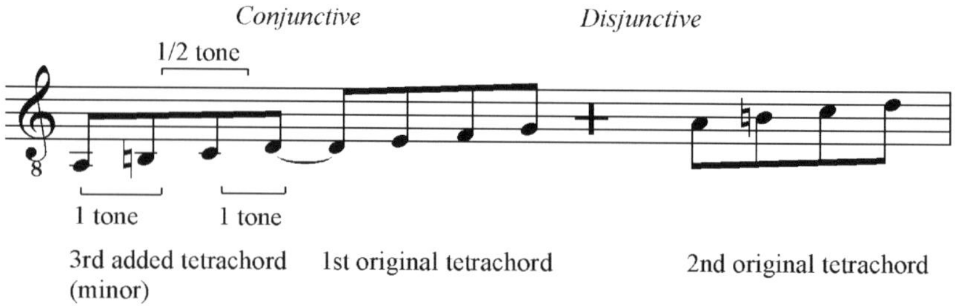

The last illustration for which we shall have time today and which will conclude the description of the Jewish Minor scale family is an analysis of the *Nu'sach* of *Ge'shem and Tal.* The pure Greek Phrygian mode, otherwise known as the medieval Dorian, from D to D gives us the clue to this *Nu'sach.* The difference between the original *Ma'gen A'vot Nu'sach* and the *Ge'shem* or *Tal Nu'sach* lies in one interval. This interval appears between the fifth and the sixth step. If we build the *Ma'gen A'vot Nu'sach* from D to D, there must be a Bb on the sixth step.

When we build the same line for *Ge'shem or Tal,* we notice a struggle between the B natural and the Bb. I think that the B natural is the prevailing feature of the *Ge'shem/Tal Nu'sach.* Years ago, when I recorded my composition *"Tal"* for the RCA Victor recording company, I dared to use the B natural in a revolutionary way, although at that time I could not yet theoretically explain why I did it.

Today I believe that I can give the full reasoning. The following illustration for the *"Af Brie"* — the *Pi'yut* (liturgical poem) that is a real *Mi'Sinai/Ge'shem Nu'sach,* shows clearly how the B natural pushes forward and struggles for its recognition.

ILLUSTRATION 17

17a) *"Af Brie" (Ge'shem Pi'yut) Nu'sach* built on D (both B natural and Bb are features of this *Ge'shem Nu'sach*:

17b) The D line which forms the *Ge'shem-Tal Nu'sach*:

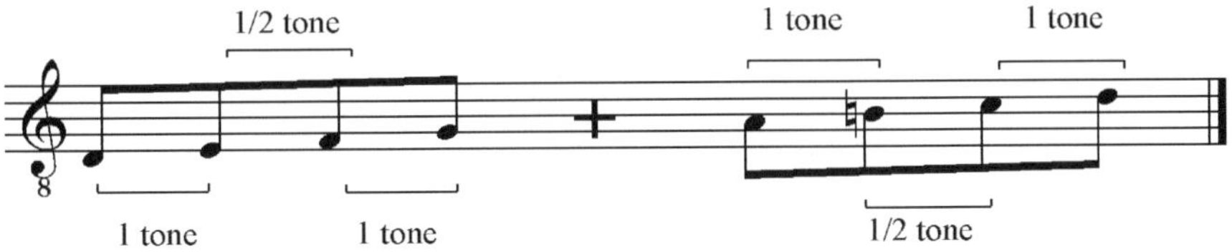

As we could see from the above illustration, both the Bb and the B natural manage to live together in this *Nu'sach.* That is why, if we want to be true to its particular two-fold flavor, we must emphasize that double feature in the concluding phrase of the *Nu'sach:*

Bb, A, B natural, G, A.

From this we can see the tremendous difference between the *Ka'ddish* of *Ne'i'la* and the *Ka'ddish* of *Tal.* One only has to know that the *Ne'i'la Ka'ddish* is based on the elementary *Ye'kum Pur'kan* Jewish Major, which is understood when we have in mind the Mixolydian mode, and that the *Ge'shem/Tal Nu'sach* is based on a Minor scale and is a branching out of the *Ma'gen A'vot Nu'sach.*

In conclusion, I should like to make one general remark. I do not claim to know all the secrets of all the *Nus'cha'ot.* All I can say is that knowing this much, we shall be able to proceed further. The material is fascinating, the theme is so dear, the problem so important, that we should try to study our wonderful *Nus'cha'ot* with patience and love. We are entrusted with the task of guarding our musical heritage; therefore we must also carry forward and develop it.

We are entrusted with the task of guarding our musical heritage; therefore we must also carry forward and develop it. The future of Jewish music depends on us.

The future of Jewish music depends on us. It depends on the degree of our own deepening of our studies, and also our teaching it to the entire Jewish people.

1. *Shomer Yisrael*

THE ARRANGEMENT FOR THIS COMPOSITION WAS COMMISSIONED BY
CANTOR AVSHALOM ZFIRA
IN HONOR OF HIS DEAR WIFE RONI ZFIRA

About *Shomer Yisrael*:

There is an interesting story behind this amazing composition.

In 1930 the young Leib Glantz, who was an ardent and active Zionist leader, visited *E'retz Yis'ra'el* (British Palestine) in order to personally meet with the Jewish pioneers (*Ha'lu'tzim*) and to uplift their spirits following the Arab massacres of 1929.

While visiting the town of *Tzfat* (Safed), he entered one of the picturesque synagogues and joined in for the afternoon *Min'cha* service.

The mode, the tone, and the sensitive supplication in which the members of that *Min'yan* recited *Ta'cha'nun,* left an unforgettable imprint on his soul and kept haunting him until he could find the time to compose and record this masterpiece.

You can actually imagine the people crying for help from the Almighty amidst the joy of the pioneers' achievements and the rejuvenation of Zion.

—*Cantor Naftali Herstik*

Glantz begins *Shomer Yisrael* with a typical *Nu'sach* melody that a simple Jew would pray in the synagogue in every morning service. He slowly builds up intensity upon that motif. The listener becomes caught up in this growing intensity and is deeply moved. At the same time, he becomes almost disturbed. I recall being introduced to this number by a cantor who was an avid fan of Glantz. He heard Glantz sing *Shomer Yisrael* at a concert, and became so emotionally shaken that he had to leave the auditorium! Indeed, every time I hear this composition, I am still in absolute awe. I have yet to hear anyone other than Glantz sing it.

His colossal vocal abilities enabled Glantz to venture vocally to wherever his creative mind took him. Though his voice was unique, his style and philosophical approach have deeply influenced all who came after him. Even some of his contemporaries in their later years began to use his concepts.

Contemporary composers of liturgical music are currently writing music with modern harmonies, mainly because Glantz proved that one could still be rooted in tradition and at the same time be thoroughly modern.

My cantorial compositions are extremely influenced by Glantz's teachings. I write music to enhance the text, while endeavoring to be emotionally stirring, musically interesting, yet true to the *Nu'sach.* Glantz opened up my imagination and showed me the limitless horizons of creativity, while at the same time remaining true to tradition.

—*Cantor Moshe Schulhof*

Score

שומר ישראל

Shomer Yisrael

Leib Glantz
Arr: Raymond Goldstein

- el v'-al yo - vad v'-al yo - vad Yis-ra - el ha - om - rim v'-al
yo - vad Yis-ra - el ha - om - rim Yis - ra - el ha - o - m'-rim ha - o - m'-rim sh'-
ma Yis - ra - el Yis-ra - el

sho - mer goy e-chad sh'-mor sh'-mor sh'-e-rit am e-chad am
e-chad v'-al yo - vad v'-al
yo - vad oi goy e-chad v' - al

12
yo - vad v'-al yo - vad v'-al yo-vad goy e-chad ham-ya-cha-dim shim-cha ham-
13
ya - cha-dim shi - m'-cha
A-do-shem E-lo-kei-nu A-do-
15
shem e - chad
sho -
mp

17
- mer goy ka-dosh sh'-mor sh'-e-rit am ka-dosh v' - al v'-al
18
yo - vad v' - al yo-vad goy ka-dosh v' -
19
- al yo-vad goy ka-dosh v'al yo - vad v'-al yo-vad v'-al yo-vad goy ka-dosh v'-al

20
5
5
al v' -
21
5
3
al v'al yo-vad goy ka-dosh ha - m' -
22
3
shal - shim b' - sha - losh k' - du - shot l' - ka - dosh ha - m' - shal - shim ha-m'sha-l'-

23
shim b' - sha - losh k' - du - shot k' - du - shot l' - ka - dosh l' - ka -
24
dosh mit - ra -
25
tze b'ra - cha - mim u - mit - pa - yes b'- ta - cha - nu - nim hit - ra - tze v' - hit - pa - yes l' -

dor a - ni l'-dor a - ni ki ein o - zer
pp
mf
appassionato
mit - ra -
f
tze b'-ra-cha-mim u-mit-pa-yes u-mit-pa-yes b'-ta-cha-nu-nim hit-ra-tze v'-hit-pa-yes l'-
mf

30
dor a-ni l'-dor-a-ni ki ein o - zer
32
a-vi-nu mal-ke-nu a-
34
vi-nu mal-ke - nu cho-ne-nu va-a-ne - nu cho-ne-nu va-a-ne - nu cho-ne-nu va-a-
mf

ne-nu cho-ne-nu va-a-ne - nu ki ein ba-nu ma-a-sim ki ein ba-nu ma-a-
mp
sim
mf
a tempo
a-vi-nu mal-ke-nu cho-ne-nu va-a-ne-nu a-vi-nu mal-ke-nu cho-ne-nu va-a-ne-nu a-

39
vi-nu mal-ke-nu cho-ne-nu va-a-ne-nu cho-ne-nu va-a-ne-nu cho-
Ped. Ped.
40
ne-nu va-a-ne-nu ki ein ba-nu ma - a-sim a - se i-ma-nu tz'-da-ka va-
f
fz
mp
42
che - sed a - se i-ma-nu tz'-da-ka a -
mp
fz

44
5
se i - ma-nu tz'da - ka va - che - sed
45
oy
oy
fp
46
3
tr
v' - ho - shi - e - nu
f
ff

Leib Glantz at age 7 with his father, Cantor Kalman Glantz, in Kiev, Ukraine, 1905

2. *Kol Ha'shem*

THE ARRANGEMENT FOR THIS COMPOSITION WAS COMMISSIONED BY
CANTOR UDI SPIELMAN AND DR. VARDA SPIELMAN
IN MEMORY OF THEIR FATHERS – ABRAHAM NOGA AND JOSEF SPIELMAN,
AND IN HONOR OF THE GREAT CANTOR NAFTALI HERSTIK
AND THE BOCA RATON B'NAI TORAH CONGREGATION AND ITS RABBI – DAVID STEINHARDT

About *Kol Ha'shem*:

Leib Glantz's recording of this piece is all about *Chazzanic* style.

One can certainly analyze the musical intricacies of the melodic line, but it would be only of academic interest. The true soul of this piece, as conceived by Glantz, does not reside in the notes on paper. To truly appreciate how great this is one has to be very familiar with, even immersed in, the style and the *Nu'sach.*

To anyone considering performing this piece, to really capture the expressiveness the composer intended, be advised to bring a crystal-clear *coloratura* capability and a considerable feel for the style.

In his own recording Glantz shows a great resemblance to both cantors Mordecai Hershman and David Roitman at their very best. If you understand what that means, then you have a good understanding and appreciation of Eastern European *Chazzanic* art.

—Cantor Ralph Schlossberg

While Glantz adheres to the *Nu'sach* in this cantorial piece, he also gives vent to his creativity as he reinterprets the text through artful elaborations of the basic *Nu'sach.*

Already with the very first musical phrase, Glantz must have felt that the basic melody of the *Nu'sach* does not adequately express the magnitude of the scene described in the text. The verses of this Psalm refer to the might of God which is expressed in his dominion over the earth through his voice. Seven times throughout the psalm, God's voice is described in different forms of dominion ("The voice of the Lord is upon the waters ... The voice of the Lord breaks the cedars", etc.). Likewise, verses 7 and 8 are praising the strength of God's voice ("The voice of the Lord flashes forth flames of fire. The voice of the Lord shakes the wilderness; the Lord shakes the wilderness of *Ka'desh*"). Moreover, according to the traditional Jewish interpretation, verses 7 and 8 describe the giving of the *To'rah* on Mount Sinai. The verses of the Pentateuch and the *Mid'rash* that the learned Glantz must have had in mind describe the giving of the *To'rah* on Mount Sinai as an awesome and inspiring theophany. Glantz apparently sensed that this perception is not fully conveyed by the simplicity of the *Nu'sach.* After quoting the opening melodic theme of the *Nu'sach* (thus expressing his commitment to the venerable melody) Glantz departs to a different, more grandiose, direction in the second half of verse 8 in the words *Ya'chil A'do'nai Mid'bar Ka'desh.* After the recitation on the notes B and G# (which belong to the tonic chord) in the first part of the verse, Glantz diverts from the paved path of the *Nu'sach* to an original melodic climax. The recitative departs from the simple melody of the *Nu'sach* into a bursting statement on the might of God, with a climax on the tonic chord in the high register, developed by Glantz in an unconventional melodic movement.

At the end of the composition, on the last verse of the Psalm, Glantz completely abandons the melody of the *Nu'sach* in favor of a classic cantorial finale. An intricate melismatic phrase reaches the subtonic degree and thereupon the final tonic.

—Dr. Amit Klein, Professor Eliyahu Schleifer, and Professor Edwin Seroussi

Score

קול השם

Kol Ha'shem

Leib Glantz

Arr: Raymond Goldstein

5
C
ya-chil A-do-nai mid-bar mid-bar mid-
S
mf mid-bar
A
mf mid-bar
T
mf mid-bar
B
mf mid-bar
7
C
bar ka-
S
p Oo Oo
A
p Oo Oo
T
p Oo Oo
B
p Oo Oo

9
C
S
A
T
B
- - desh kol
11
A - do - nai y'-cho - lel y'-cho-lel a-ya-
p Oo
Oo

13
C
lot vaye-che-sof y'-a-rot y'-a-
S
y'-a-
A
y'-a-
T
pp
Oo y'-a-
B
pp
Oo y'-a-
14
C
rot vaye-che-sof y'-a-
S
rot
A
rot
niente
T
rot
B
rot

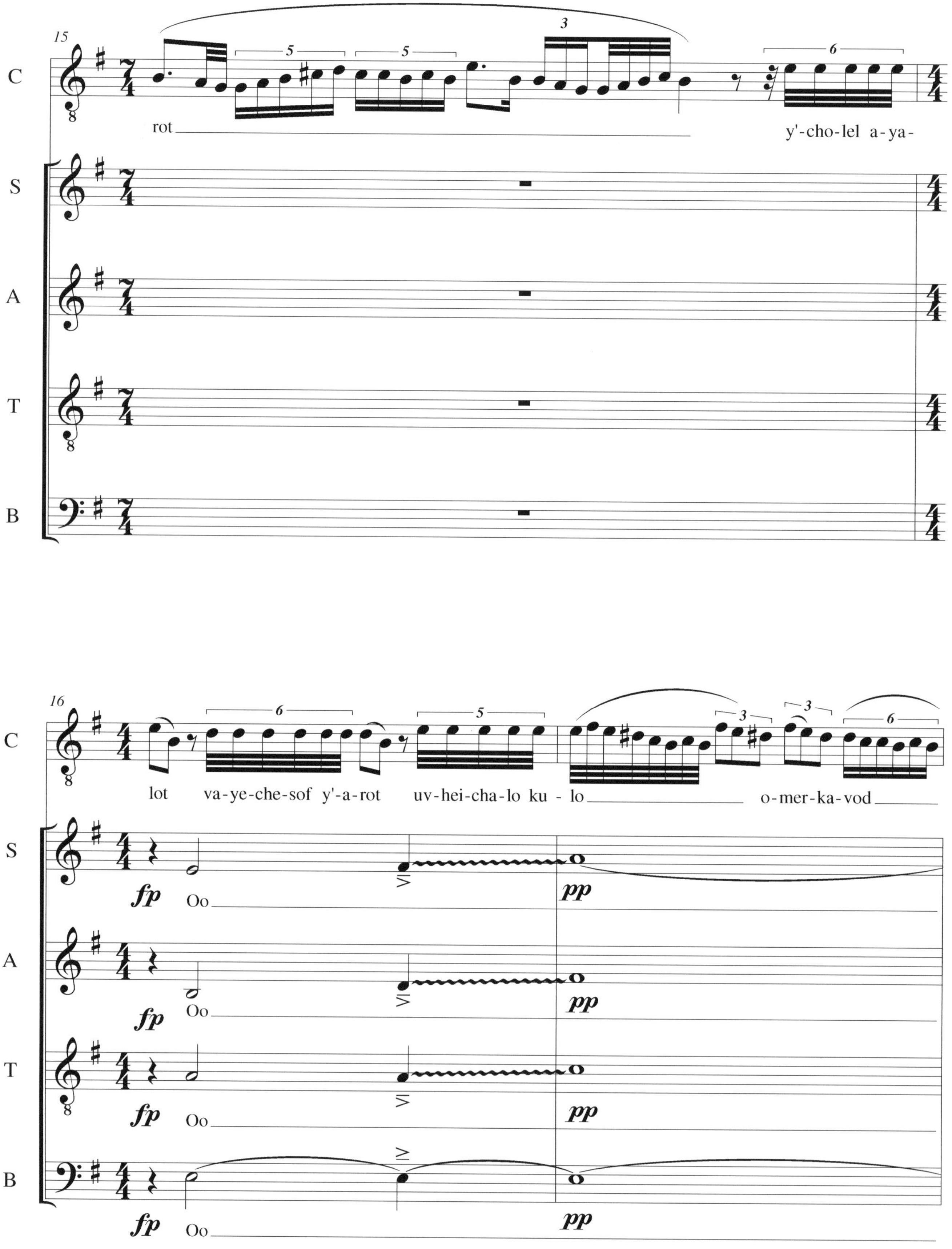
15
C
rot
y'-cho-lel a-ya-
S
A
T
B
16
C
lot va-ye-che-sof y'-a-rot uv-hei-cha-lo ku-lo o-mer-ka-vod
S
fp
Oo
pp
A
fp
Oo
pp
T
fp
Oo
pp
B
fp
Oo
pp

18
C
S
A
T
B
A-do - nai la-ma-bul ya-shav va-ye-shev A-do-nai me-lech me-
fp
Oo
20
lech me-lech l'-o-
p
Oo

22
C
S
A
T
B
lam
me - lech l'- o - lam
In 8
25
mf
mp
A - do - nai oz
oz l'-a-mo l'-a-mo yi-ten
oz l'-a-mo l'-a-mo yi - ten
oz l'-a-mo yi-ten
oz l' - a - mo yi - ten

28
C
A - do - nai y'-va-rech
9
S
pp
Oo
A
pp
Oo
T
pp
Oo
B
pp
Oo
30
tr
C
y' - va - rech et a - mo
a - mo va - sha - lom
S
a - mo a - mo va - sha - lom.
A
a - mo a - mo va - sha - lom.
T
a - mo a - mo va - sha - lom.
B
a - mo a - mo va - sha - lom.

Leib Glantz at age 8, with tuning fork, officiating as cantor on the prayer pulpit in the Tolner Synagogue in Kiev, Ukraine, 1906

3. *Ana Be'choach*

THE ARRANGEMENT FOR THIS COMPOSITION WAS COMMISSIONED BY
UDI AND AVIVA HERMON (CHERSONSKY)
IN MEMORY OF UDI'S FATHER – NAFTALI CHERSONSKY, LEIB GLANTZ'S NEPHEW,
AND HIS MOTHER PAULA COHEN CHERSONSKY, Z"L.

About *Ana Be'choach*:

The text of this ancient prayer is attributed by Talmudic sources to Rabbi *Ne'chun'ya ben Ha'ka'nah,* and yet is considered by many a mystic-Kabalistic text. When Leib Glantz sang *Ana Be'choach* in his synagogue in Tel Aviv, the whole congregation used to meditate with him in a whispering hum. There was a mystical atmosphere present in the packed place of worship. Hence the very haunting harmonization of this prayer in Raymond Goldstein's arrangement, with his strong emphasis on extreme dynamics ranging from a whispering *pianissimo* to a *fortissimo* outcry as was indeed the case in Glantz's live performances.

It is worth noting that in Chassidic/Kabalistic circles the tradition is to say every word of *Ana Be'choach* seven times, as I experienced when my father *a"h* would light the *Chanukah* candles.

The extremity of the range has led us to divide the solo line between the various voices in order to enable the performers to recreate the original effect.

—*Cantor Naftali Herstik*

Leib Glantz's profound understanding of the liturgical texts and contexts is demonstrated in his setting of *A'na Be'Cho'ach,* which reveals an additional layer of Glantz's ability to compose his music in accordance with the special role of the prayer. Glantz was dissatisfied with the common practice of Eastern-European cantors designating a wail or whimper-like tune to every prayer, be it a lamentation or a Gloria. The all-too-common utilization of wailing and melismatic melodies suffered from the three flaws that Glantz so persistently stood up against:

1) It did not (always) align with the *Nu'sach;*
2) It created melodic lines that were dull and monotonous and lacked the much needed compositional renovation; and –
3) It did not (consistently) reflect the meaning of the text and rarely provided an insight into the inner layers of interpretation that underlie the explicit meaning of the text.

Thus, Glantz sought new and innovative ways to express the spirit of the prayers through music. True to his own guidelines, Glantz composed the prayer *A'na Be'Cho'ach* in a very different style than other composers. Glantz provides a glimpse into the mystery of the text by hinting at its concealed meanings.

This piece is neither an operatic recitative nor is it the classical cantorial recitative. The usual speech-like manner of traditional *Cha'za'nut* is grounded in a melodically static line recited in a flowing rhythm. The new style introduced by Glantz, however, reverses this formula: the rhythm is static whereas the melody is unconstrained. Glantz evidently delved into an active search for innovative forms of speech-mannered music, which would serve his purpose in this composition.

The abrupt dramatic shouting of the words *Shav'a'tei'nu Ka'bel U'She'ma* and the multiple repetitions of the verse, seem to generate a demand, perhaps even an impudent one. Note the *Schprächgesang* style in the high notes. The image envisioned as we hear Glantz audaciously confronting God may be that of Rabbi Levi Itzchak of Berdichev. Glantz approaches God in a familiar manner that is reminiscent of the practice of this Chasidic leader, who was known to accost God with protestations and grievances, or even with exasperation.

—*Dr. Amit Klein, Professor Eliyahu Schleifer, and Professor Edwin Seroussi*

Score

אנא בכוח

Ana Be'choach

Leib Glantz
Arr: Raymond Goldstein

Misterioso

7
S
A
T
B
f
ve-nu ta-ha-re - nu no - ra __ no-ra
na __ gi - bor ______ gi - bor gi-bor __
ve-nu ta-ha-re - nu no - ra __ no-ra
na gi - bor ______ gi - bor gi-bor __
ve-nu ta-ha-re - nu no - ra __ no-ra
na __ gi - bor ______ gi - bor gi-bor __
ve-nu ta-ha-re - nu no - ra no-ra
na gi - bor ______ gi - bor gi-bor __
f
11
C
dor - shei yi-chud'-cha k' - va - vat __ shom-rem
mp
Oo ______ k'-va - vat __ shom-rem __ bar'-
Oo ______ k'-va - vat __ shom-rem __ bar'-
Oo ______ k'-va - vat __ shom-rem __ bar'-
Oo ______ k'-va - vat shom-rem __ bar'-

15
C
ra-cha-mem tzid-kat'-cha ta-mid gom-lem
S
chem ta-ha-rem mp Oo cha-
A
chem ta-ha-rem mp Oo cha-
T
chem ta-ha-rem mp Oo cha-
B
chem ta-ha-rem mp Oo cha-
18
C
b' - rov tuv-cha na-hel a-da - te - cha
S
sin ka-dosh ka - dosh ka-dosh Oo mp ya-
A
sin ka-dosh ka - dosh ka-dosh Oo mp ya-
T
sin ka-dosh ka - dosh ka-dosh Oo mp ya-
B
sin ka-dosh ka - dosh ka-dosh Oo mp ya-

22
C
zoch - rei zoch-rei
S
chid ge-e l'-a-m' - cha p'-ne k'-du-sha-
A
chid ge-e l'-a-m' - cha p'-ne k'-du-sha-
T
chid ge-e l'-a-m' - cha p'-ne k'-du-sha-
B
chid ge-e l'-a-m'-cha p'-ne k'-du-sha-
25
C
cha - sin ka-dosh ka - dosh ka-dosh b'-rov tuv'-cha na-
S
te - cha Oo
pp
A
te - cha Oo
pp
T
te - cha Oo
pp
B
te - cha Oo
pp

29
C
hel a-da-te-cha ya-chid ge-e l'-a-m'-cha p'-ne zoch-rei zoch-rei k'du-sha-
S
A
T
B
poco dim.
mf
Oo
33
te - cha shav-a-te-nu ka-bel ush-ma tza-a-ka-te-nu yo - de-a yo-de-a ta-a-lu-
sempre piano
Oo

37
C
mot shav-a - te-nu ka-bel ush-ma tza-a-ka-te - nu yo - de-a yo-de - a ta-a-lu-
S
Oo
A
Oo
T
Oo
B
Oo
41
C
mot
misterioso
S
shav-a - te-nu ka-bel ush-ma tza-a-ka-te - nu yo - de-a yo-de - a ta-a-lu-
pp
A
shav-a - te-nu ka-bel ush-ma tza-a-ka-te - nu yo - de-a yo-de - a ta-a-lu-
pp
T
shav-a - te-nu ka-bel ush-ma tza-a-ka-te - nu yo - de-a yo-de - a ta-a-lu-
pp
B
shav-a - te-nu ka-bel ush-ma tza-a-ka-te - nu yo - de-a yo-de - a ta-a-lu-
pp

45
S
mot shav-a - te-nu ka-bel ush-ma tza-a-ka-te - nu yo - de-a yo-de - a Oo
A
mf
mot shav-a - te-nu ka-bel ush-ma tza-a-ka-te - nu yo - de-a yo-de - a ta-a-lu-
T
mf
mot shav-a - te-nu ka-bel ush-ma tza-a-ka-te - nu yo - de-a yo-de - a Oo
B
mf
mot shav-a - te-nu ka-bel ush-ma tza-a-ka-te - nu yo - de-a yo-de - a ta-a-lu-
mf

49
C
shav-a - te-nu ka-bel ush-ma tza-a-ka-te - nu yo - de-a yo-de - a
S
meno forte
Oo
A
meno forte
mot Oo
T
meno forte
Oo
B
meno forte
mot Oo

53
C
S
A
T
B
f
ta-a-lu-mot shav-a-te-nu ka-bel ush-ma tza-a-ka-te-nu yo-de-a yo-de-a
mf
Oo
57
ta-a-lu-mot
a tempo
rit. e dim
p
yo-de-a yo-de-a ta-a-lu-mot

Leib Glantz in Kiev, 1918

4. *Amar Rabbi Elazar*

THE ARRANGEMENT FOR THIS COMPOSITION WAS COMMISSIONED BY CANTOR NATHAN LAM OF STEPHEN S. WISE TEMPLE, LOS ANGELES, CA, IN HONOR OF HIS GRANDCHILDREN – LYLA PITSON, MAX LAM, AND OLIVIA PITSON.

About *Amar Rabbi Elazar*:

When Raymond Goldstein presented me with the score for *Amar Rabbi Elazar,* it struck me that I recognized the melody from somewhere else. I wondered if Leib Glantz might have borrowed it from someone else?

Then I recalled that the melody was actually Glantz's *Ra'za De'Shabbat* (the secret of the Sabbath). His longtime choir conductor, Yehoshua Zohar, had once showed it to me.

I can imagine the anguish Glantz felt when he realized that most of the great synagogues that could afford to hire regular cantors prayed in *Nu'sach Ash'ke'naz,* where *Ra'za De'Shabbat* was never recited. Instead they would sing the chapter *Ba'meh Mad'li'kin* from the *Mish'na** and then *Amar Rabbi Elazar* (Rabbi Eleazar said).

As was the case with great composers such as Rossini, Verdi, and others, Glantz didn't want his beautiful composition to be consigned to oblivion, so he found the perfect place to attach his music: in exactly the same spot in the Friday evening *Ka'ba'lat Shabbat* prayer service.

In order to appropriate the music from *Ra'za De'Shabbat* to the new text of *Amar Rabbi Elazar,* changes were required. As a result, the mystical interpretation of the "Secrets of the Sabbath" now provided for a different understanding of the scholarly text of *Tal'mi'dei Cha'cha'mim Mar'bim Sha'lom Ba'O'lam* (Torah scholars increase peace in the world).

This interpretational concept guided us when we engaged in the creation of this new arrangement.

—*Cantor Naftali Herstik*

*The *Mishna is* an authoritative collection of exegetical material embodying the oral tradition of Jewish law and forming the first part of the Talmud.

Score

אמר רבי אלעזר

Amar Rabbi Elazar

Leib Glantz
Arr: Raymond Goldstein

9
1.
2.
dei cha-cha-mim mar-bim sha-lom sha-lom ba-o - lam a- -lom ba-o - lam a-
12
5
3
mar a-mar a-mar Ra-bi Ra-bi Ra-bi El-a-zar a-
colla parte
15
mar a-mar a-mar Ra-bi Ra-bi Ra - bi Cha-ni - na tal-mi-

Piu Mosso
18
dei cha-cha-mim mar-bim sha-lom ba-o-lam she-ne-e - mar v'-chol ba-
mf
20
7
6
tr
na - yich li-mu-dei A-do-nai v'-rav sh'-lom ba-na - yich al tik-
22
3
rei ba-na - yich e-la e-la e-la e-la bo - na - yich A -

אמר רבי אלעזר

Un poco piu mosso
rav l'o-ha-vei to-ra-te-cha to-ra - te - cha v' - ein la - mo mich-
mp
shol shalom rav l' - o-ha-vei to-ra-
mf
p
te - - - cha v' - ein la - mo mich -
tr

41
shol y'-hi sha-lom b'-chei-lech shal-va b'-ar-m'-no-
43
ta - yich y'-hi sha-lom b'-chei-lech shal-va b'-ar-m'-no-
45
ta - - - - yich l'-ma-an
6
pp

47
l' - ma-an a-chai v'-re - ai a-da-b'-ra na sha-
mp
49
3
lom bach l'ma-an a-chai l'ma-an a-
51
chai v'-re-ai a-dab'-ra na sha-lom sha - lom bach l'-ma-an
p

53
beit A-do-nai E-lo-hei-nu a-va-k'-sha tov, tov a-va-k'-sha tov lach
mf
f
56
in 8!
tov lach A-do-nai oz l'-a-mo yi-ten l'-a-mo yi-ten A-do-
mp
legato
59
nai y'-va-rech y'-va-rech et a-mo et a-mo va-sha-lom

Leib Glantz in Kishinev, Bessarabia, age 22, 1920

5. *Yigdal*

THE ARRANGEMENT FOR THIS COMPOSITION WAS COMMISSIONED BY CANTOR MO GLAZMAN OF CONGREGATION KOL AMI IN WHITE PLAINS, NY, IN HONOR OF OUR FRIEND AND TEACHER HAZZAN BENY MAISSNER.

About *Yigdal*:

Throughout my years of constant investigation into the manuscripts of Leib Glantz, I was often amazed to find tunes and set works copied out on scraps of paper, sometimes not even on music notation sheets. It showed that sometimes the muses obviously captured this man's very inventive mind at the spur of the moment.

The *Yigdal's* original single sheet of manuscript must have been overlooked when the original lists of his compositions were compiled and it could easily have been misplaced at the time. But lo and behold, there it was, the basic tune, with some traditional harmony, the same for all the verses, a typical ping-pong between the cantor and the corresponding answering verses by the choir. Of course, it can be rather boring, if the same tune is repeated in strophic form without any variant in the harmonies; hence I felt it my duty as an arranger to reshape the question-answer form giving us a new harmonic color – thus capturing the essence of what is a very pleasant jaunty tune for an end of a *Shabbat* service. Intervallically, it is very recognizable as a Glantz work by some tell-tale use of various intervals, like ascending sixths and fourths, as found in many of his compositions.

—*Raymond Goldstein*

Score

יגדל

Yigdal

Leib Glantz

Arr: Raymond Goldstein

9
C
Ein lo d'-mut ha-guf v'-ei-no guf lo
S
lam v'-gam ein sof l'-ach-du-to.
A
lam v'-gam ein sof l'-ach-du-to.
T
lam v'-gam ein sof l'-ach-du-to.
B
lam v'-gam ein sof l'-ach-du-to.
Pno.
legato
13
C
na-a-roch e-lav k'-du-sha-to
S
kad-mon l'-chol da-var a-sher niv-ra ri-
A
kad-mon l'-chol da-var a-sher niv-ra ri-
T
kad-mon l'-chol da-var a-sher niv-ra ri-
B
kad-mon l'-chol da-var a-sher niv-ra ri-
Pno.

17
C
S
A
T
B
Pno.
Hi - no a-don o-lam l' - chol no - tzar yo-
shon v'-ein re-shit l' - re - shi - to
legato
mp legato
23
re g'-du-la-to u - mal - chu - to
she - fa n'-vu - a - to n' - ta - no el an-

27
con calore
C
Lo kam b'-Yis-ra-el k'-Mo-she od na-
S
shei s'-gu-la-to v'-tif-ar-to.
A
shei s'-gu-la-to v'-tif-ar-to.
T
shei s'-gu-la-to v'-tif-ar-to.
B
shei s'-gu-la-to v'-tif-ar-to.
con calore
Pno.
mf
31
C
vi u-ma-bit et t'-mu-na-to
S
A
T
To-rat e-met na-tan l'-a-mo El, al
B
To-rat e-met na-tan l'-a-mo El, al
Pno.
mf

35
C
S
A
T
B
Pno.
Lo
Lo
yad n'-vi - o ne - e - man bei - to
Lo
yad n'-vi - o ne - e - man bei - to
Lo

39
C
S
A
T
B
Pno.
ya - cha-lif ha - El v' - lo ya - mir da - to, l' - o - la - mim l' - zu - la - to, tzo -
ya - cha-lif ha - El v' - lo ya - mir da - to, l' - o - la - mim l' - zu - la - to, tzo -
ya - cha-lif ha - El v' - lo ya - mir da - to, l' - o - la - mim l' - zu - la - to
ya - cha-lif ha - El v' - lo ya - mir da - to, l' - o - la - mim l' - zu - la - to

43
C
S
fe v'-yo-de-a s'-ta-rei-nu, ma-bit l'-sof da-var b'-kad-ma-to
A
fe v'-yo-de-a s'-ta-rei-nu, ma-bit l'-sof da-var b'-kad-ma-to
T
tzo-fe v'-yo-de-a s'-ta-rei-nu, ma-bit l'-sof da-var b'-kad-ma-to
B
tzo-fe v'-yo-de-a s'-ta-rei-nu, ma-bit l'-sof da-var b'-kad-ma-to
Pno.
47
C
Go-mel l'ish che-sed k'-mif-a-lo, no-
S
A
T
B
Pno.

51
C
ten l'-ra-sha ra k'-rish-a-to
S
yish-lach l'-ketz ya-min m'-shi-che-nu lif-
A
yish-lach l'-ketz ya-min m'-shi-che-nu lif-
T
yish-lach l'-ketz ya-min m'-shi-che-nu lif-
B
yish-lach l'-ketz ya-min m'-shi-che-nu lif-
Pno.
55
C
S
rit.
Meno Mosso
mp
dot m'-cha-kei ketz y'-shu-a-to Me-tim y'-cha-ye El b'-rov chas-do, ba-
A
mp
dot m'-cha-kei ketz y'-shu-a-to Me-tim y'-cha-ye El b'-rov chas-do, ba-
T
mp
dot m'-cha-kei ketz y'-shu-a-to Me-tim y'-cha-ye El b'-rov chas-do, ba-
B
mp
dot m'-cha-kei ketz y'-shu-a-to Me-tim y'-cha-ye El b'-rov chas-do, ba-
Meno Mosso
Pno.
legato
rit.

59
C
S
ruch a-dei ad shem t'-hi-la-to. me-tim y'-cha-ye El b'-
A
ruch a-dei ad shem t'-hi-la-to. me-tim y'-cha-ye El b'-
T
ruch a-dei ad shem t'-hi-la-to. me-tim y'-cha-ye b'-
B
ruch a-dei ad shem t'-hi-la-to. me-tim y'-cha-ye b'-
Pno.
62
C
ba-ruch a-dei ad shem t'-hi-la-to.
mf
S
rov chas-do, ba-ruch a-dei ad shem t'-hi-la-to.
mf
A
rov chas-do, ba-ruch a-dei ad shem t'-hi-la-to.
mf
T
rov chas-do, ba-ruch a-dei ad shem t'-hi-la-to.
mf
B
rov chas-do, ba-ruch a-dei ad shem t'-hi-la-to.
Pno.
mf

Leib Glantz in New York, 1927

6. *Ein Ke'er'ke'cha*

THE ARRANGEMENT FOR THIS COMPOSITION WAS COMMISSIONED BY CANTOR JACOB MENDELSON OF TEMPLE ISRAEL CENTER, NY, IN MEMORY OF DR. FREEMAN RAKUSIN, LOUIS AND TIBBY MENDELSON – OUR DEAR PARENTS, AND LOVERS OF *CHAZZANUT.*

About *Ein Ke'er'ke'cha*:

Leib Glantz was widely acclaimed for his Chassidic interpretations of the prayer texts.

In this incredible composition he displays a scholarly approach to the interpretations and offers varying commentaries to the same text.

Glantz's astonishing mystical opening to the words *Ein Ke'er'ke'cha Ve'ein Zu'lat'cha* (There is no comparison to You, there is nothing except You), is sung by him as if he is saying, "Who am I to even imagine Your greatness, and who is comparable to You?" Again, Glantz resorts to self-persuasion concerning the Almighty's greatness compared to the insignificance of man.

Then Glantz switches to a supplication mode, addressing He who has the power to act not only in this world but in the world to come as well. Glantz addresses God in a very direct manner: *E'fes Bil'te'cha Go'a'lei'nu Li'mot Ha'Ma'shiach* (there is nothing without You, our savior in this world and in the life of the world to come, when the Messiah will appear).

This represents Leib Glantz's strong belief that redemption is near, and he urges the King of the Universe to bring His people salvation as swiftly as possible.

Finally, Glantz ends his composition by retreating back to Chassidic yearning, gently singing *Ve'Ein Do'meh Le'cha Mo'shi'ei'nu Li'Tchi'yat Ha'Mei'tim* (There is no one like You, our savior, Who will raise the dead back to life).

—*Cantor Naftali Herstik*

Score - A
(orig. in C)

אין כערכך

Ein Ke'er'ke'cha

Leib Glantz
Arr: Raymond Goldstein

14
ein ein ein k'-er-k'-cha v'-ein v'-ein v'-ein zu-la-t'-cha
p
mf
18
e-fes e-fes bil-t'-cha u-mi u-mi u-
mp
Ped.
23
mi do-me lach ein k'-er k'-cha ein
fp

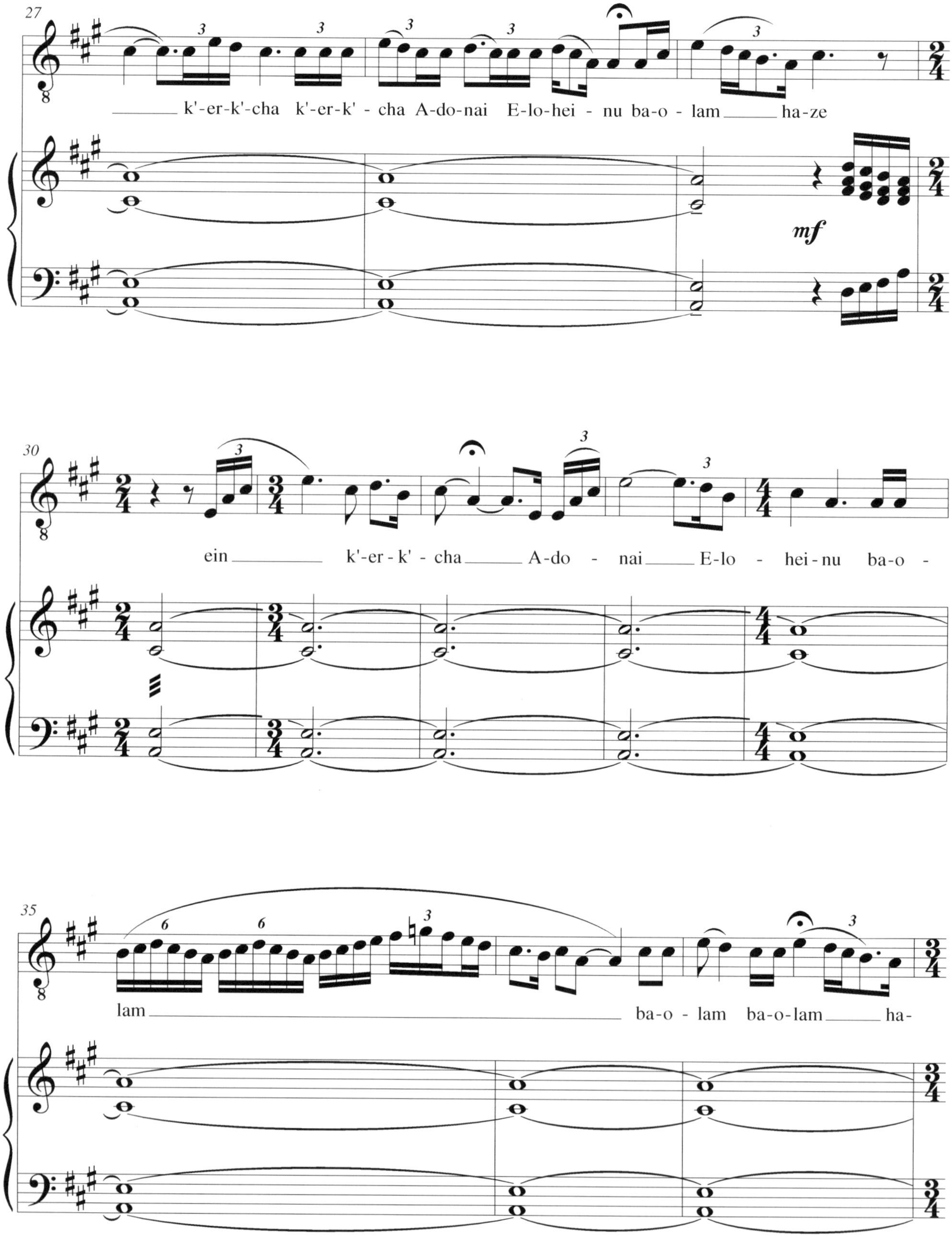
27
k'-er-k'-cha k'-er-k'-cha A-do-nai E-lo-hei-nu ba-o-lam ha-ze
mf
30
ein k'-er-k'-cha A-do-nai E-lo-hei-nu ba-o-
35
lam ba-o-lam ba-o-lam ha-

38
ze v' - ein v'-ein zu-la-t'-
41
cha v'-ein zu - la - t'-cha mal-ke-nu l'-cha - yei ha - o -
43
lam ha-o-lam ha - ba
Ped.

47
e - fes bil-t'-cha
51
e - fes bil-t'-cha go-a - le-nu, go-a - le-nu go-a - le-nu, go-a-
56
ff
le - nu li - mot li - mot ha-ma-shi-ach

60
f
e - fes e-fes bil-t'-cha go-a-le-nu, go-a-le-nu, li - mot li - mot ha-ma-
63
shi - ach v'-ein do - me l' - cha mo-shi-
65
e - - - nu lit-chi - yat
Ped.

67
ha - me - tim
69

7. *Az Be'kol*

THE ARRANGEMENT FOR THIS COMPOSITION WAS COMMISSIONED BY
CANTOR SIDNEY S. DWORKIN, CANTOR EMERITUS OF CONGREGATION SHAAR HASHOMAYIM,
MONTREAL, CANADA,
IN MEMORY OF HIS MENTOR CANTOR JOSHUA H. ROSENSWEIG Z"L.

About *Az Be'kol*:

When I first heard Leib Glantz's *Az Be'kol*, I was mesmerized by the refreshing sound of this beautiful narrative describing the singing of the angels.

To say that his style was unique is an understatement. Glantz employs techniques and musical ideas, which enhance the *Nusach* Prayer Mode in a way that I would describe as "Progressive Variations."

He took this fourteen-word verse from the Sabbath and Holiday *Shach'rit Ke'du'sha* prayer service, and using several repetitions expressed a series of novel statements. Each word or phrase repeated, builds on the previous one until a lavish climax is achieved. This is followed by a surprisingly engaging rhythmical melody, which serves to set up a grand conclusion of the composition.

The *Nusach* typically begins in Major and bridges into the *Fraigish* scale. Glantz takes these prayer modes and literally flirts between the two, occasionally switching within the same phrase. This, along with his characteristic melismatic runs, his extensive use of the chromatic idiom, trills, and even a "high C" towards the ending of the rendition, offer a complex challenge to the singer.

Glantz's creativity and interpretation are so captivating that I continually listened to this *Az Be'kol* over and over again.

—*Cantor Sid Dworkin*

Score

אז בקול

Az Be'kol

Leib Glantz
Arr: Raymond Goldstein

im l'-u-mat s'-ra-fim
az
az b' - kol ra-ash ga-dol a-dir v'-cha-zak mash-mi-
- im kol mit-na-s'-im mit-na-s' - im l'-u - mat l'-u-mat s'-ra - fim

16
17
l'-u-mat
s'-ra-fim
18
az b'-kol ra-ash ga-dol az b'-kol ra-ash ga-dol a - dir v'-cha-zak

20
10
10
az
az
b'-kol
fp
23
5
3
3
ra - ash
ga-dol
ga - dol
25
3
a - dir
v' - cha - zak
mash - mi - im
kol

26
mit-nas'-im
27
mit-na-s'-im
28
l' - u - mat
s' - ra - fim

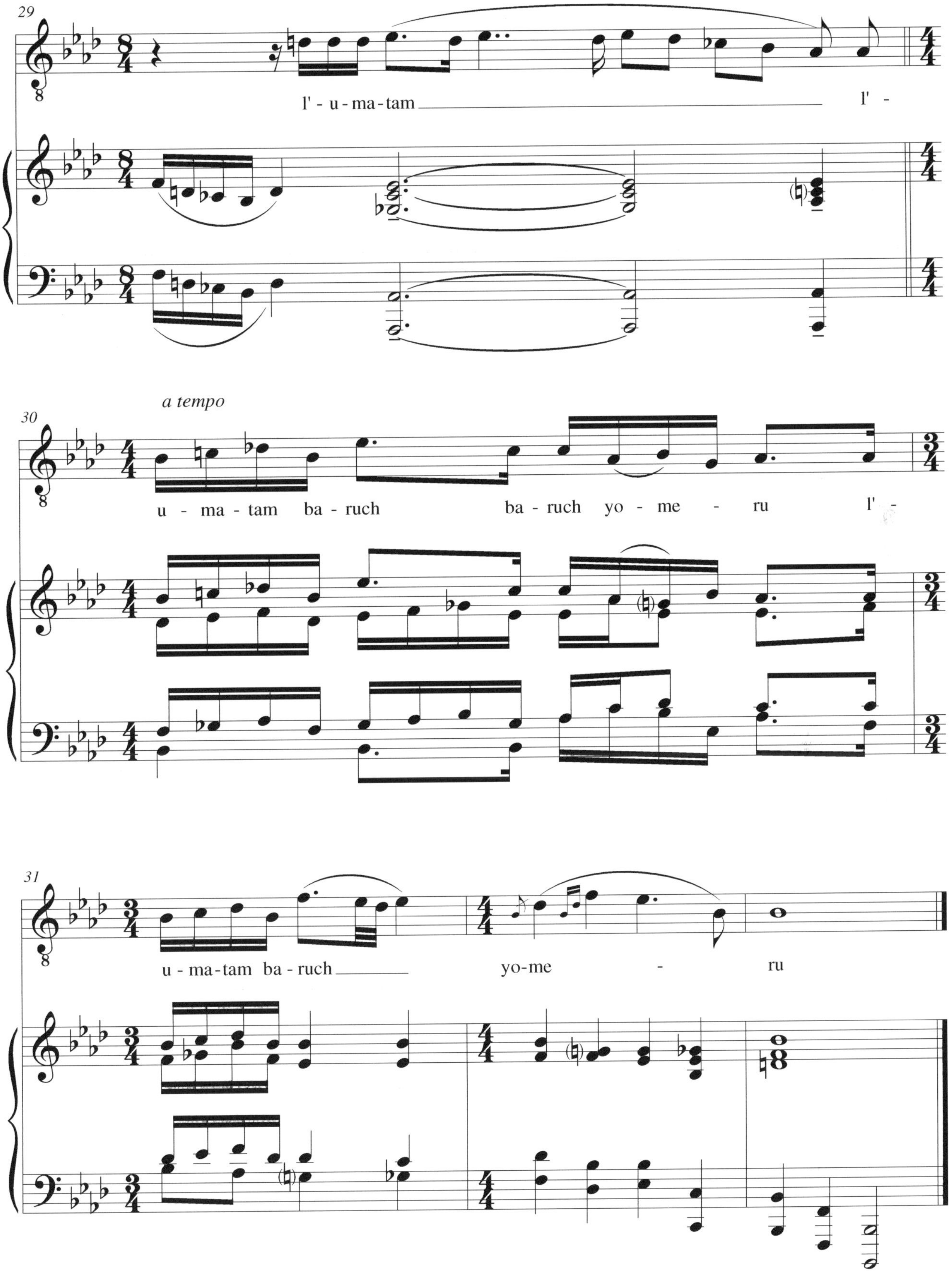
29
l' - u - ma - tam l' -
a tempo
30
u - ma - tam ba - ruch ba - ruch yo - me - ru l' -
31
u - ma - tam ba - ruch yo-me - ru

Leib Glantz in New York, 1929

8. *B'rich Sh'mei*

The arrangement for this composition was commissioned by
Cantor Mikhail Manevich
in honor of his parents Lazar and Regina Manevich.

About *B'rich Sh'mei*:

Leib Glantz proves how skillfully he can construct a simple sounding melody around a seemingly endless barrage of Aramaic words.

Here he appears to *B'rich Sh'mei* to bless God's Name, almost magically with the same levels of enthusiasm found in his most robust pieces. However, loyal to the theme, Glantz chose to bless his Maker's Name through *Kol D'ma'mah Da'kah* ("a still, small voice").

—*Cantor Emanuel C. Perlman*

Score

בריך שמיה

B'rich Sh'mei

Leib Glantz

Arr: Chanan Winternitz

Originally composed in Los Angeles in 1952.

12
ya d' - hu E-la-ha k'shot v'-o-rai-te k'shot u-n'-vi-o-hi
3
3
16
k'shot u-mas-ge l'-me-bad ta-v' - van ta-v' - van uk-shot
20
be be a-na ra-chitz

בריך שמיה

25
v'-li - sh'-me ka - di-sha ya-ki - ra a - na e - mar a -
30
na e-mar e - mar tush-b' - chan a - na e - mar a - na e - mar e -
35
mar tush - b' - chan be a - na ra - chitz v'-lish -

39
me ka-di-sha ya-ki - ra a - na e-mar tush-b'-chan e - mar tush - b'-
44
chan y' - he ra-a-va ko-da - mach d'-tif - tach li-ba-i b'-o-rai -
48
ta d'-tif - tach li - ba - i b'- o - rai - ta b' - o - rai -

52
recit.
ta y'he ra-a-va ko-da-mach d'-tif-
ff
Ped.
55
tach li-ba-i b'-o-rai-ta y'-he ra-a-va ko-da-
p
58
3
mach d'-tif-tach li-ba-i b'-o-rai-ta v'-ta-sh'-
Ped.

61
ff
lim mish-a-lin
mish-a - lin d'-li-ba-i
v'-li-
ff
65
ba d'-chol a-mach Yis-ra - el
l' - tav ul-cha-yin
v'-tash-
69
lim mish-a-lin
mish-a - lin d'-li-ba-i
v'-li-
ff
mf

73
ba d'-chol a-mach Yis-ra - el Yis-ra-el l' - tav ul-cha-yin y' -
77
he ra-a-va ko-da - mach d'-tif-tach li-ba-i b'-o - rai - ta d'-tif-
LH
RH
81
tach li-ba-i b'- o - rai - ta b' - o - rai -

84
ta v' - ta - sh' - lim mish - a - lin d' - li - ba - i v' - li -
87
ba d'-chol a-machYis-ra - el l' - tav l' - tav ul-cha - yin v'-
dim.
Ped.
Ped.
91
li - sh' - lam v' - li - sh' - lam a - men
sffz
8vb

Leib Glantz singing with choir in prayer service in New York, 1936

9. *Ve'nomar Le'fanav*

The arrangement for this composition was commissioned by
Hazzan Leon and Judge Michal Lissek
in memory of their beloved parents –
Rabbi Pinchos Chazin, Beatrice Pugatsky Chazin,
Max Shmuel Lissek, Hanna Greenberg Lissek and Jack Greenberg.

About *Ve'nomar Le'fanav*:

Ve'nomar Le'fanav Shir Cha'dash (And we shall sing a new song before Him) is part of a prayer sung while the Torah scroll is transferred from the Holy Ark to the pulpit from where the Torah is read. The prayer opens with the words *Al Ha'Kol Yit'ga'dal Ve'Yit'ka'dash* (May the Name of the Holy One, blessed be He, be magnified and hallowed). This very ancient prayer underwent several transformations throughout the generations.

Originally, in ancient prayer books we find that it is connected to the prayer *Av Ha'Ra'cha'mim,* which follows immediately afterwards, but ends with the words *Vi'ma'leh Mish'a'lo'tei'nu Be'Mi'dah To'vah Ye'shu'ah Ve'Ra'cha'mim Ve'Ya'a'zor Ve'Ya'gen Ve'Yo'shi'a Le'Chol Ha'Cho'sim Bo Ve'No'mar A'men* (May He graciously grant us eternal survival and fulfill our wishes in ample measure for salvation and mercy. And may He help, shield and deliver all who trust in Him, and let us say, Amen). After that text, a *Siddur* (prayer book) such as this contains an instruction that the cantor is to set down the Torah scroll and recite *Ha'Kol Ha'vu Go'del Le'lo'hei'nu U'Tnu Cha'vod La'To'rah* (Let all render glory to our God and give honor to the Torah).

Siddurim like this can be found in the collection of the *Yad Ha'Rav Nissim* Library in Jerusalem, but were definitely not available to Leib Glantz at the time. However, I have no doubt that Glantz speculated about this interesting order of the words, and after he made *A'li'ya* to Israel in 1954, realizing that his followers implored him to sing his originally recorded *Av Ha'Ra'cha'mim,* he decided to add the words that preceded *Av Ha'Ra'cha'mim,* which contained the ideas of redemption and longing for the land of Israel – *Ve'Nir'e'hu, A'yin Be'A'yin Be'Shu'vo El Na've'hu, Ka'Ka'tuv: Ki A'yin Be'A'yin Yir'u Be'Shuv Ha'Shem Zion* (May every eye see His return to His abode, as it is written: "For every eye shall behold the Lord's return to Zion").

The totally different subject matter, as well as the timing of which Glantz composed this work, inspired Glantz to alter the original style, but Glantz, the genius, found a way to devise a unique connection to the following older and beloved *Av Ha'Ra'cha'mim* prayer without creating a contradiction between the two.

—Cantor Naftali Herstik

Score

ונאמר לפניו

Ve'nomar Le'fanav

Leib Glantz
Arr: Raymond Goldstein

9
mo v'-il - zu l'-fa-nav v'-nir-e - hu a - yin b'-
7
mp
11
a - yin b'-shu - vo el na-ve-hu el na-ve-hu ka-ka-tuv ka-a-tuv ki
mp
14
a-yin b'-a-yin yir - u b'-shuv Ha-shem Tzi-yon Tzi-yon v'-ne-e-
3
mf

17
mar v'-ne-e-mar v'-ne-e-mar v'-ne-e - mar v'-nig-
Ped.
20
la v'-nig-la k' - vod Ha - shem v'-ra-
mf
22
u chol ba-sar yach - dav yach -

24
dav yach - dav yach - dav ki
26
pi Ha - shem di - ber di - ber
3
7

Leib Glantz singing at a concert in Tel Aviv, accompanied by pianist and composer Nachum Nardi, 1947

10. *Av Ha'rachamim Hu Ye'rachem*

THE ARRANGEMENT FOR THIS COMPOSITION WAS COMMISSIONED BY CANTOR MOSHE HASCHEL OF ST. JOHN'S WOOD SYNAGOGUE, LONDON, ENGLAND, WHO WILL ALWAYS BE INSPIRED BY CANTOR LEIB GLANTZ – "THE MAN WHO SPOKE TO GOD."

About *Av Ha'rachamim Hu Ye'rachem*:

Av Ha'ra'cha'mim Hu Ye'ra'chem Am A'mu'sim is one of Leib Glantz's early compositions. It was recorded in 1932. His innovativeness and unique genius as a young composer are clearly evident, often leaving the listener astounded by his dramatic rendition.

However, at this stage Glantz was still conforming to the "conventional" style of *Chazzanut,* and he remains consistent with the styles of cantors that both preceded him and those of his peers in his own generation.

There is a childhood photo of Glantz and Pinchas Segal Pinchik (that appears in the book about Glantz "The Man Who Spoke To God") where both children appear singing in their cantor's choir. Evidently, this experience created a strong influence on both of their styles. Regardless of the immense differences between these two geniuses of *Chazzanut,* there is great similarity in their cantorial expression and their use of *parlando* and irregular motifs.

In this composition, Glantz widely utilizes raised semi-tones and variations within the scale with hints of the open possibilities inside the mode that have become so typical of Leib Glantz's music.

There is no doubt that when he composed this *Av Ha'Ra'cha'mim,* Glantz lived under the intense impact of the Kishinev Pogroms (1903 and 1905) that erupted during his childhood. The burning hatred toward *Am A'mu'sim* (The people borne by Him), widely inflicted on the Jews of the regions where he grew up, led his outraged soul to cry out to the heavens *Ve'Yig'ar Be'Yei'tzer Ha'Ra Min Han'su'im* (and banish the evil impulse from the ones carried by Him). He continues to plead and demand of *Av Ha'Ra'cha'mim* (the All-Merciful Father): "*Ta'teh! Ta'teh!"* (Yiddish for *"Papa! Papa!"*), like a child hugging his father and pleading for the life of His people, His children, to the point where he, Glantz, at the end of the prayer is almost without breath as he cries out *Ye'shu'ah, Ye'shu'ah, Ye'shu'ah, Ve'Ra'cha'mim* (Salvation, salvation, salvation and mercy)!

It is almost impossible to imagine a more suitable emissary, *Do'resh Tov Le'A'mo* ("demanding the good of his people" – Esther 10:3) to Israel's divine Father than Leib Glantz. Only someone with such a burning Chassidic soul, reminding us of the great *Ad'mo'rim* (Chassidic masters) standing before the Almighty, could possibly pray like this.

—Cantor Naftali Herstik

Score

אב הרחמים הוא ירחם

Av Ha'rachamim Hu Ye'rachem

Leib Glantz
Arr: Raymond Goldstein

4
kor v'-yiz-kor b'-rit b'-rit ei-ta-nim ei-ta-nim v'-ya-
mp
6
tzil v'-ya-tzil naf-sho-
mf
f
8
tei - nu min ha-sha-ot ha-ra-ot naf-sho-tei - nu min ha-sha-ot ha-ra-ot naf-sho-

9
te - nu min ha-sha-ot ha-ra-ot min
10
min, min, min ha-sha - ot ha-sha - ot ha-ra-ot v'-yig-
fp
12
ar v'-yig-ar
mf

14
b'-ye-tzer ha-
16
ra
min, min, min, min,
mp
17
min ha-n'-su-im
v'-ya-
marcato

Adagio
chon o-ta-nu lif-lei-tat lif-lei - tat o-la-mim o-la-mim o - la - mim av
a tempo
ha - ra - cha - mim hu y' - ra - chem hu y' - ra - chem
av ha-ra-cha-mim hu y'-ra-chem am a-mu-sim am a-mu-sim v'-

25
yiz - kor b'-rit ei-ta-nim v'-ya-tzil naf-sho-tei - nu min, min, min, min ha-sha-
27
ot ha-ra-ot hasha-ot ha-ra-ot v'-yig-
29
ar b'-ye-tzer ha-
mf

31
ra v'-yig-
33
ar b' - ye-tzer ha-ra min ha-n'-su-im b'-ye-tzer ha-ra min ha-n'-su-im v'-ya-
35
chon o - ta - nu lif - lei - tat

36
lif - lei - tat
37
lif - lei - tat o - la - mim vi - ma - le vi - ma - le vi - ma - le vi -
39
ma - le, vi - ma - le mish - alo - tei - nu b' - mi - da b' - mi -

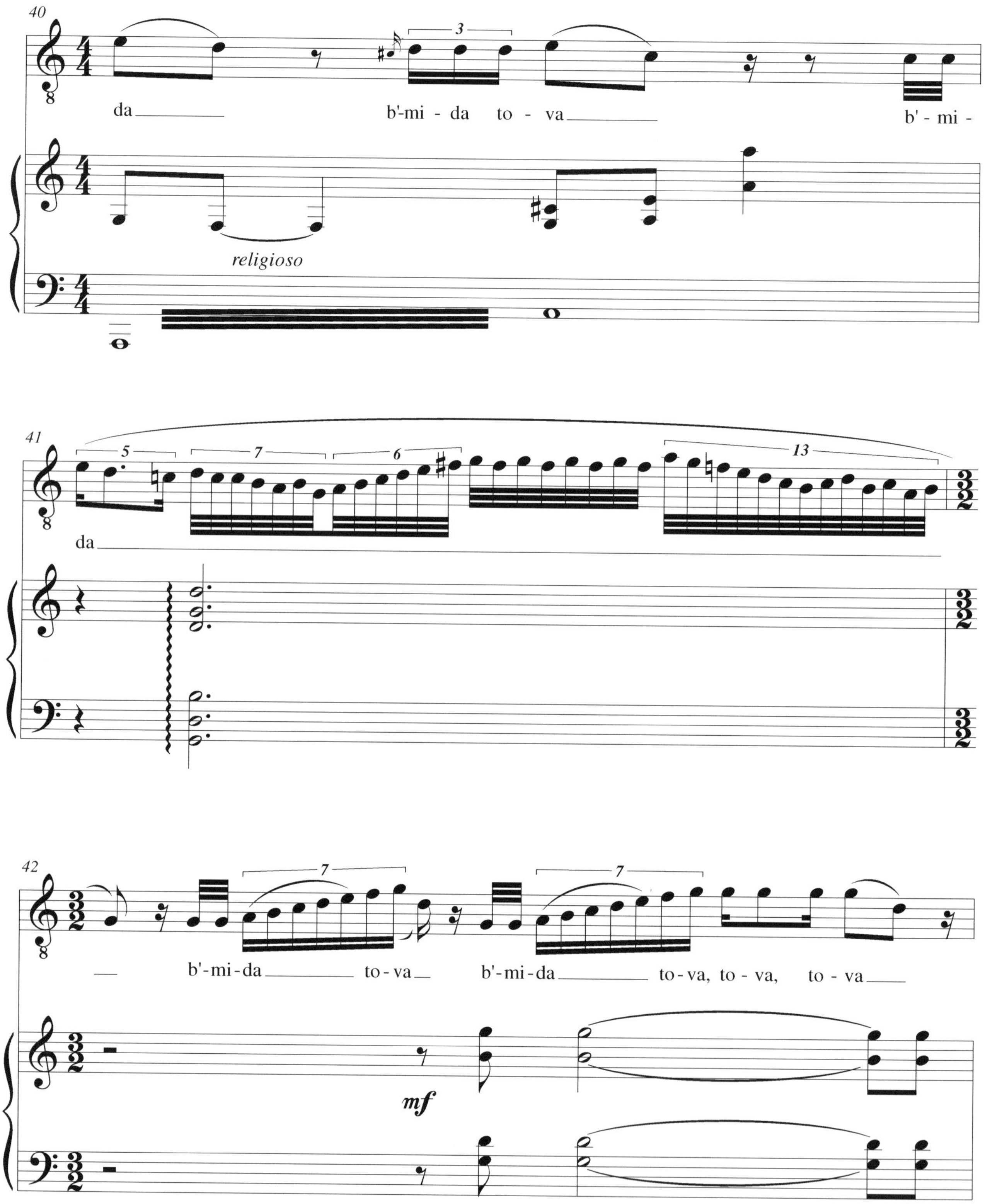
40
da b'-mi - da to - va b'-mi -
religioso
41
da
42
b'-mi-da to-va b'-mi-da to-va, to - va, to - va
mf

43
y' - shu - a y' - shu - - - - -
44
- a y'-shu - - - a, y' -
45
shu - a v' - ra - cha - mim
mp
f

Sinai Temple, Los Angeles, California, 1942. Leib Glantz officiated as chief cantor at Sinai Temple from 1941 till 1946.

11. *Av Ha'rachamim Shochen Meromim*

THE ARRANGEMENT FOR THIS COMPOSITION WAS COMMISSIONED BY CANTOR JOEL CAPLAN OF CONGREGATION AGUDATH ISRAEL, CALDWELL, NEW JERSEY, IN HONOR OF RAYMOND GOLDSTEIN.

About *Av Ha'rachamim Shochen Meromim*:

Similar to his composition *El Ma'leh Ra'cha'mim* for the murdered martyrs of the Holocaust, in this prayer that commemorates *Ke'hi'lot Ha'Ko'desh She'Mas'ru Naf'sham Al Ke'du'shat Ha'Shem* (The holy communities who gave their lives for the sanctification of the Divine Name), Leib Glantz maintains the framework of the composition by adhering to traditional cantorial convention. Glantz always sounds distinctly original in every phrase of his music, but this structural convention creates an instant association between the worshipers and the prayer itself.

The fundamental arrangement for this composition was set for an accompanying choir in a synagogue setting, whose role was to serve as a background for the cantor's chant, and without drawing too much attention. Having said that, both the composer and the arranger created harmonic moments that remind us of the music of the requiems of the great classical composers. These succeed in creating for the listener an ambiance of sacredness, sadness and grief.

I heard this composition at the *Tif'e'ret Zvi* synagogue in Tel Aviv during the *S'fi'rat Ha'O'mer* period. Glantz hummed an introduction melody in unison with the choir, a mysterious melody that awakened hidden emotions in the hearts of his listeners even before he uttered the first words of the prayer.

Glantz remarkably utilizes a soft and almost introverted speaking tone, from where he bursts out an octave higher in a heart-wrenching cry that repeats again and again, almost causing the audience to become breathless.

Towards the end of the composition Glantz returns to the traditional Eastern and Central European cantorial genre, singing a victory march-like song, with the words *Mi'Na'chal Ba'De'rech Yish'teh Al Ken Ya'rim Rosh* (He will drink from the stream on the way; therefore [Israel] will hold its head high).

—*Cantor Naftali Herstik*

Score

אב הרחמים שוכן מרומים

Av Ha'rachamim Shochen Me'romim

Leib Glantz
Arr: Raymond Goldstein

15
C
kod b'-ra-cha-mim k'-hi - lot ___ ha-ko-desh hu yif -
T1
T2
Oo ___
mp
k'-hi - lot ha-ko-desh
B1
B2
18
C
kod b'-ra-cha-mim ha-cha-si-dim v'-ha-y'-sha - rim ha-cha-si-dim v'-ha-y'-sha-
T1
T2
Oo ___
B1
B2
20
C
rim ___ v'-ha-t'-mi - mim ___ hu yif-kod b'-ra-cha-mim ___
T1
T2
Oo ___
B1
B2

23
C
k'-hi-lot ha-ko-desh she-ma-s'-ru naf-sham al k'-du-
T1
T2
Oo
B1
B2
26
C
shat Ha-shem ha-ne-e-ha-
T1
T2
mf
al k'du-shat Ha-shem
B1
B2
28
C
vim v'-ha-n'-i-mim b'-cha-yei-hem u-v'-mo-tam lo lo nif-
T1
T2
Oo Oo Oo
B1
B2

31
C
ra - du
u-v'-mo - tam lo lo nif-
T1
T2
mf
lo nif-ra - du
pp
Oo
B1
B2
34
ra - du mi-n'-sha-rim
ka-lu u-me-a-ra-yot ga-ve-ru ga-
Oo
37
ve-ru la-a-sot r'-tzon ko - nam
ga - ve-ru la-a-sot r'-tzon ko - nam
a2
r'-
a2

41
C
v' - che - fetz v' - che - fetz v' - che - fetz tzu - ram yiz - k'-
T1
T2
tzon ko - nam
pp
Oo
B1
B2
44
rem yiz - k' - rem yiz - k'-rem yiz - k' - rem yiz - k'-
48
rem E - lo - hei - nu l' - to - va im sh' - ar tza - di - kei o-
Oo

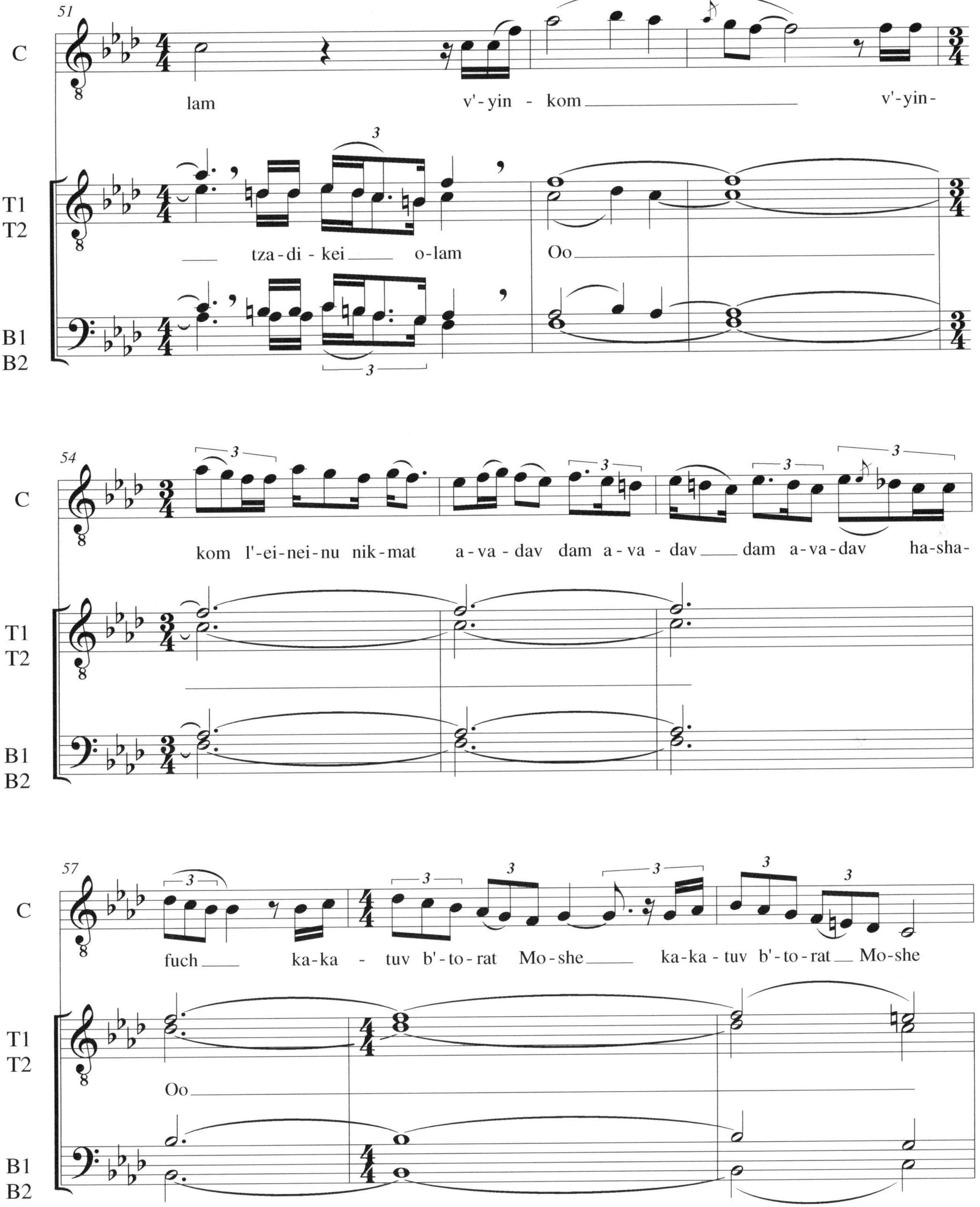
51
C
T1
T2
B1
B2
lam v'-yin - kom v'-yin-
tza-di-kei o-lam
Oo
54
kom l'-ei-nei-nu nik-mat a-va-dav dam a-va-dav dam a-va-dav ha-sha-
57
fuch ka-ka - tuv b'-to-rat Mo-she ka-ka-tuv b'-to-rat Mo-she
Oo

60
C
ish ha-E-lo-him har - ni-nu go-yim a-mo
T1
T2
ish ha-E-lo-him
Oo
B1
B2
63
har - ni-nu go-yim a-mo ki-dam dam dam dam a-va-dav yi-kom v'-na-
dam, dam, dam, dam yi-kom
66
kam ya-shiv ya-shiv l'-tza-rav v'-chi-per ad-ma-to a-
Oo

C
T1
T2
B1
B2
69
mo
v'-al y'-
v'-chi - per ad-ma-to a - mo
f
71
dei a-va-de-cha ha-n'-vi-im v' - al v'-al y'-dei a-va - de-cha ha-n'-vi-im ka-tuv le-
Oo
fp
74
mor ka-tuv le-mor v'-ni-kei-ti da-mam da - mam da-mam da-

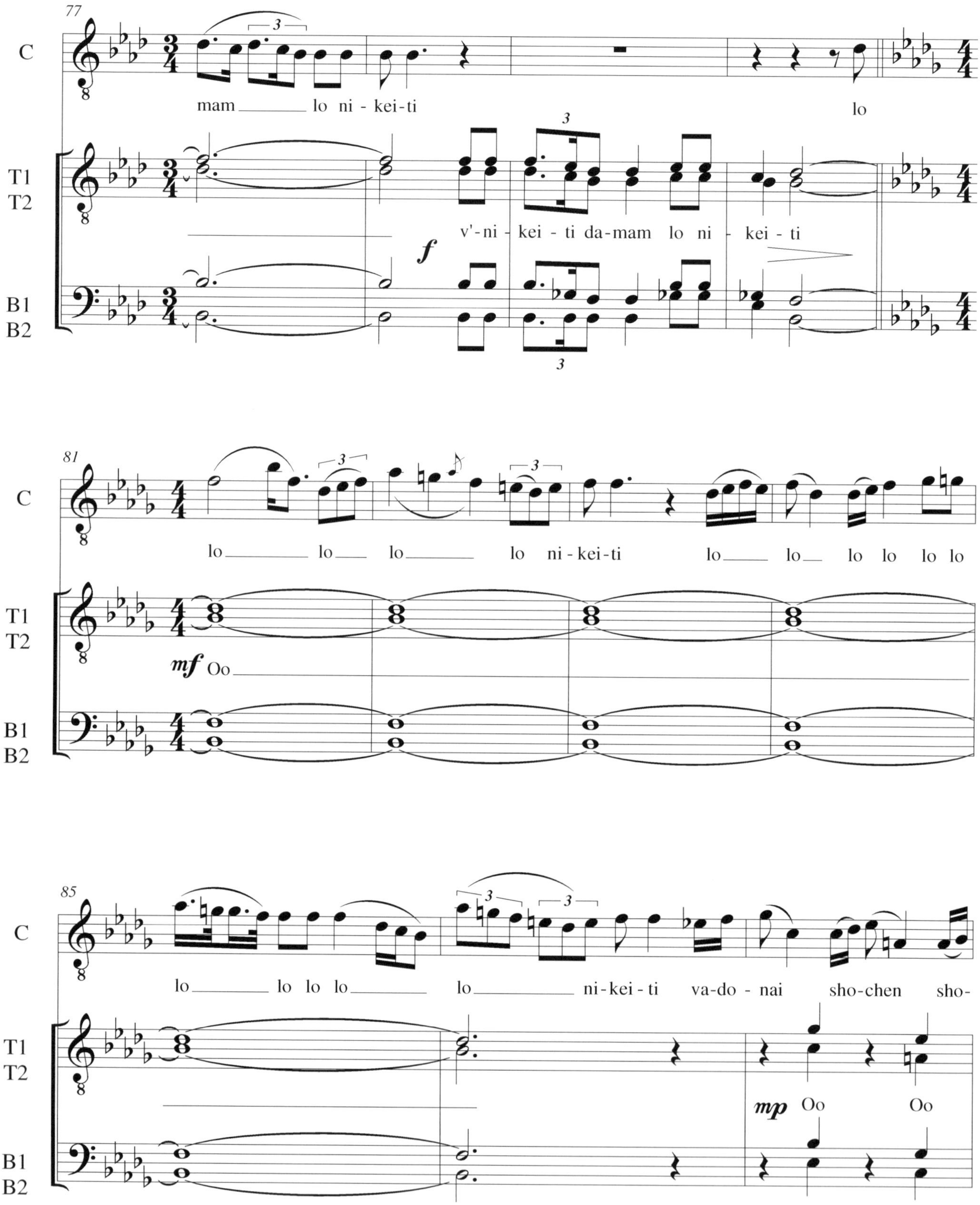

אב הרחמים שוכן מרומים

88
C
chen sho-chen sho - chen b'-Tzi-yon u-v'-chi-t'-
T1
T2
Oo b'-Tzi-yon
B1
B2
91
C
vei ha - ko - desh ne - e - mar u - v'-chi - t' - vei ha - ko - desh ne - e - mar u - v'-chi-t'-
T1
T2
Oo ha - ko - desh ne - e - mar
B1
B2
93
C
vei ha - ko-desh n-e-mar la-ma la-ma la-ma la - ma yo-m'-ru ha-go-yim
T1
T2
B1
B2

96
C
la-ma la-ma la-ma la - ma la-ma yo-m'-ru ha-go-yim
T1
T2
la-ma yo-m'-ru ha-go-
mf
B1
B2
la-ma yo-m'-ru ha-go-
99
la-ma la - ma la - ma oy vei la-ma yo-m'-ru a-ye a-
yim
mf
Oo
p
Oo a-ye, a-
yim
103
ye a-ye e-lo-hei-hem yi-va-da ba-go-yim yi-va-da ba-go-yim l'-ei-nei - nu l'-ei-
ye

106
C
nei - nu l'-ei-nei-nu ni-k'-mat dam dam dam dam
T1
T2
dam, dam, dam,
B1
B2
109
C
dam a-va-de-cha ha-sha-fuch v'-o-
T1
T2
dam
dam a-va-de-cha ha-sha-fuch
B1
B2
111
a tempo
C
mer ki do-resh da - mim ki do-resh da - mim
T1
T2
f ki do-resh da-mim mf ki do-resh da-mim
B1
B2

114
C
T1
T2
B1
B2
o-tam za-char lo sha-chach lo sha-chach lo sha-chach tza-a-kat tza-a-kat lo sha-
116
chach lo sha-chach tza-a-kat a-na-vim v'-o-
lo sha-chach
Oo
118
mer ya-din ba-go-yim ma-le g'-vi-yot ya-
v'-o-mer

אב הרחמים שוכן מרומים

אב הרחמים שוכן מרומים

12. *Sh'ma Yisrael*

IN D [C+TTBB]

THE ARRANGEMENT FOR THIS COMPOSITION WAS COMMISSIONED BY
CANTOR DOV KEREN OF SUTTON PLACE SYNAGOGUE, NEW YORK CITY,
IN MEMORY OF HIS PARENTS MICHAL AND MENACHEM KRANZLER (KEREN) Z"L,
AND THE PARENTS OF HIS WIFE ZILA – STELLA AND GERSHON MALINKER Z"L.

About *Sh'ma Yisrael*:

Any person that ever heard the composition *Sh'ma Yisrael* for the very first time sensed the revolution that Leib Glantz initiated into the world of *Chazzanut.* It represents a marker for new horizons and the broadening of the trajectory in which cantorial music can maneuver within its boundaries.

This immortal *Sh'ma Yisrael* has been analyzed and interpreted by numerous musicologists and cantors worldwide. By virtue of the fact that it represents a starting point for a unique new direction, I would like to emphasize the importance of the mathematical precision and the balanced distribution of each and every *melisma* and every movement or nuance in Glantz's rendition.

It has been said of Glantz that he was the "poet of the pulpit," and as such he religiously concentrated on balance and timing, on dynamic ascending and descending intonation, as well as precisely targeted tonal structures that lead to variation within the mode and open possibilities for amazing improvisations.

As opposed to the many intensely powerful and ostentatious renditions that we sometimes witness in synagogue and concert performances, there was nothing farther than that in Glantz's mind. In his live and recorded renditions he never employed vocal jugglery or arrogant showmanship.

Glantz displayed throughout his career a phenomenal Chassidic ability to study and interpret the prayer texts. This quality is clearly displayed in this composition, which creates a most appropriate atmosphere for the holy *Ke'du'sha* portion of the *Mu'saf* prayer service and appropriately defines the cantor's devout role in the service of the Almighty.

—*Cantor Naftali Herstik*

The composition Sh'ma Yisrael *was dedicated by Leib Glantz to Cantor David Chasman.*

Score

שמע ישראל

Sh'ma Yisrael

Leib Glantz
Arr: Raymond Goldstein

9
C
T1
T2
B1
B2
-nu
hu
hu
hu
nu hu
hu
hu
12
hu a-vi - nu
hu hu
hu
hu a-vi - nu Oo
ppp
sfp
ossia
16
hu
hu
hu

18
C
hu mal - ke - nu
T1
T2
B1
B2
20
hu
hu mal - ke - nu
23
hu
hu
hu mal - ke - nu
Oo
pp
tr

27
C
hu mo-shi-e - nu v'-hu
T1
T2
pp
Oo
sfp
Oo
B1
B2
31
yash-mi-e-nu b'-ra-cha-mav she - nit v'-
she - nit Oo
fp
33
hu yash-mi-e-nu b'-ra-cha-mav she-nit she-

35
C
nit l'-ei-nei kol chai
lih - yot lih - yot la -
T1
T2
she-nit l'-ei-nei kol chai
Oo
f
pp
B1
B2
39
chem lih - yot la - chem
Oo
41
tr
[ossia]
la - chem le - lo - him.
le - lo - him

13. *Sh'ma Yisrael*

IN E♭ [C+SATB]

THE ARRANGEMENT FOR THIS COMPOSITION WAS COMMISSIONED BY RABBI MOSHE MEIROVICH AND DR. JUDITH WEINROTH IN HONOR OF THEIR PARENTS LOUIS AND SALLY MEIROVICH AND RABBI ERWIN AND LAURA SCHILD.

About *Sh'ma Yisrael*:

Any person that ever heard the composition *Sh'ma Yisrael* for the very first time sensed the revolution that Leib Glantz initiated into the world of *Chazzanut.* It represents a marker for new horizons and the broadening of the trajectory in which cantorial music can maneuver within its boundaries.

This immortal *Sh'ma Yisrael* has been analyzed and interpreted by numerous musicologists and cantors worldwide. By virtue of the fact that it represents a starting point for a unique new direction, I would like to emphasize the importance of the mathematical precision and the balanced distribution of each and every *melisma* and every movement or nuance in Glantz's rendition.

It has been said of Glantz that he was the "poet of the pulpit," and as such he religiously concentrated on balance and timing, on dynamic ascending and descending intonation, as well as precisely targeted tonal structures that lead to variation within the mode and open possibilities for amazing improvisations.

As opposed to the many intensely powerful and ostentatious renditions that we sometimes witness in synagogue and concert performances, there was nothing farther than that in Glantz's mind. In his live and recorded renditions he never employed vocal jugglery or arrogant showmanship.

Glantz displayed throughout his career a phenomenal Chassidic ability to study and interpret the prayer texts. This quality is clearly displayed in this composition, which creates a most appropriate atmosphere for the holy *Ke'du'sha* portion of the *Mu'saf* prayer service and appropriately defines the cantor's devout role in the service of the Almighty.

—*Cantor Naftali Herstik*

The composition Sh'ma Yisrael *was dedicated by Leib Glantz to Cantor David Chasman.*

Score

שמע ישראל

Sh'ma Yisrael

Leib Glantz

Arr: Raymond Goldstein

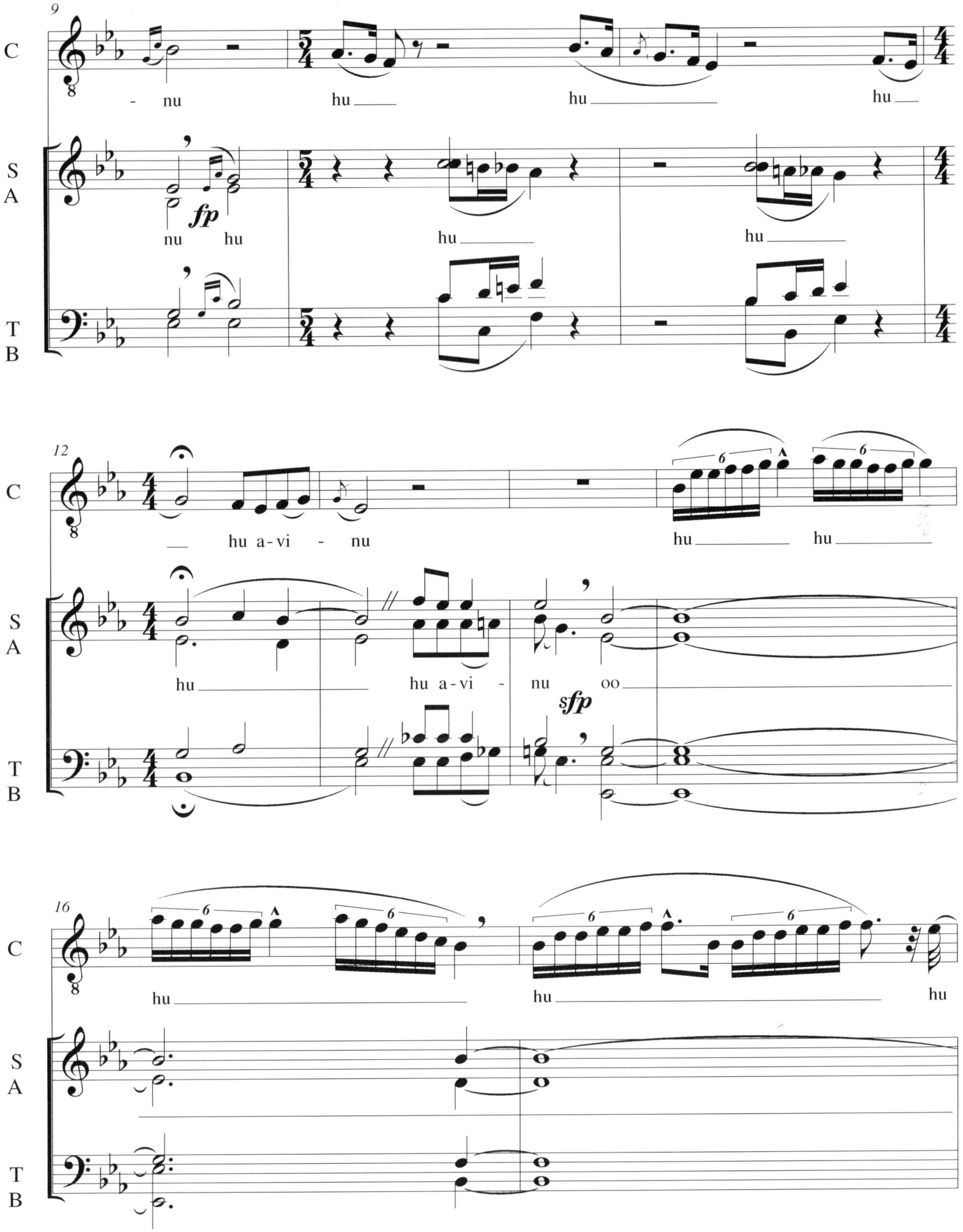
9
C
- nu
hu
hu
hu
S
A
fp
nu hu
hu
hu
T
B
12
C
hu a-vi - nu
hu
hu
S
A
hu
hu a-vi - nu oo
sfp
T
B
16
C
hu
hu
hu
S
A
T
B

18
C
hu mal-ke - nu
S
A
hu mal-ke - nu
T
B
21
C
hu
hu mal-ke - nu
S
A
T
B
24
C
hu
hu
S
A
hu mal-ke - nu
oo
H
T
B

28
C
hu mo-shi-e - nu v' - hu
S
A
oo
pp
sfp
oo
T
B
32
C
yash-mi - e - nu b' - ra - cha - mav she - nit v' -
S
A
she - nit oo
fp
T
B
34
C
hu yash-mi-e-nu b'-ra-cha-mav she-nit she-
S
A
T
B

36
C
S
A
T
B
nit l'-ei-nei kol chai
lih - yot lih - yot la -
con calore
f
she-nit l'-ei-nei kol chai
pp
oo
40
chem lih - yot
la - chem
oo
42
tr
[ossia]
la - chem
le - lo - him.
la - - - chem
le-lo - him.

14. *Sh'ma Yisrael*

[VSC]

THE ARRANGEMENT FOR THIS COMPOSITION WAS COMMISSIONED BY CANTOR NEIL MICHAELS OF TEMPLE ISRAEL, WEST BLOOMFIELD, MI, IN MEMORY OF CANTOR LOUIS DANTO Z"L.

About *Sh'ma Yisrael*:

Any person that ever heard the composition *Sh'ma Yisrael* for the very first time sensed the revolution that Leib Glantz initiated into the world of *Chazzanut.* It represents a marker for new horizons and the broadening of the trajectory in which cantorial music can maneuver within its boundaries.

This immortal *Sh'ma Yisrael* has been analyzed and interpreted by numerous musicologists and cantors worldwide. By virtue of the fact that it represents a starting point for a unique new direction, I would like to emphasize the importance of the mathematical precision and the balanced distribution of each and every *melisma* and every movement or nuance in Glantz's rendition.

It has been said of Glantz that he was the "poet of the pulpit," and as such he religiously concentrated on balance and timing, on dynamic ascending and descending intonation, as well as precisely targeted tonal structures that lead to variation within the mode and open possibilities for amazing improvisations.

As opposed to the many intensely powerful and ostentatious renditions that we sometimes witness in synagogue and concert performances, there was nothing farther than that in Glantz's mind. In his live and recorded renditions he never employed vocal jugglery or arrogant showmanship.

Glantz displayed throughout his career a phenomenal Chassidic ability to study and interpret the prayer texts. This quality is clearly displayed in this composition, which creates a most appropriate atmosphere for the holy *Ke'du'sha* portion of the *Mu'saf* prayer service and appropriately defines the cantor's devout role in the service of the Almighty.

—*Cantor Naftali Herstik*

The composition Sh'ma Yisrael *was dedicated by Leib Glantz to Cantor David Chasman.*

Score

שמע ישראל

Sh'ma Yisrael

Leib Glantz
Arr: Raymond Goldstein

hu
(in 3)
hu hu E - lo - hei - nu
hu hu hu hu a - vi -

15
nu
mp
mf
Ped.
18
hu
hu
fp
21
hu
hu
hu

23
6
hu mal - ke - nu
25
6
6
6
3
hu
hu mal - ke - nu
3
28
hu
hu
tr
pp
legato

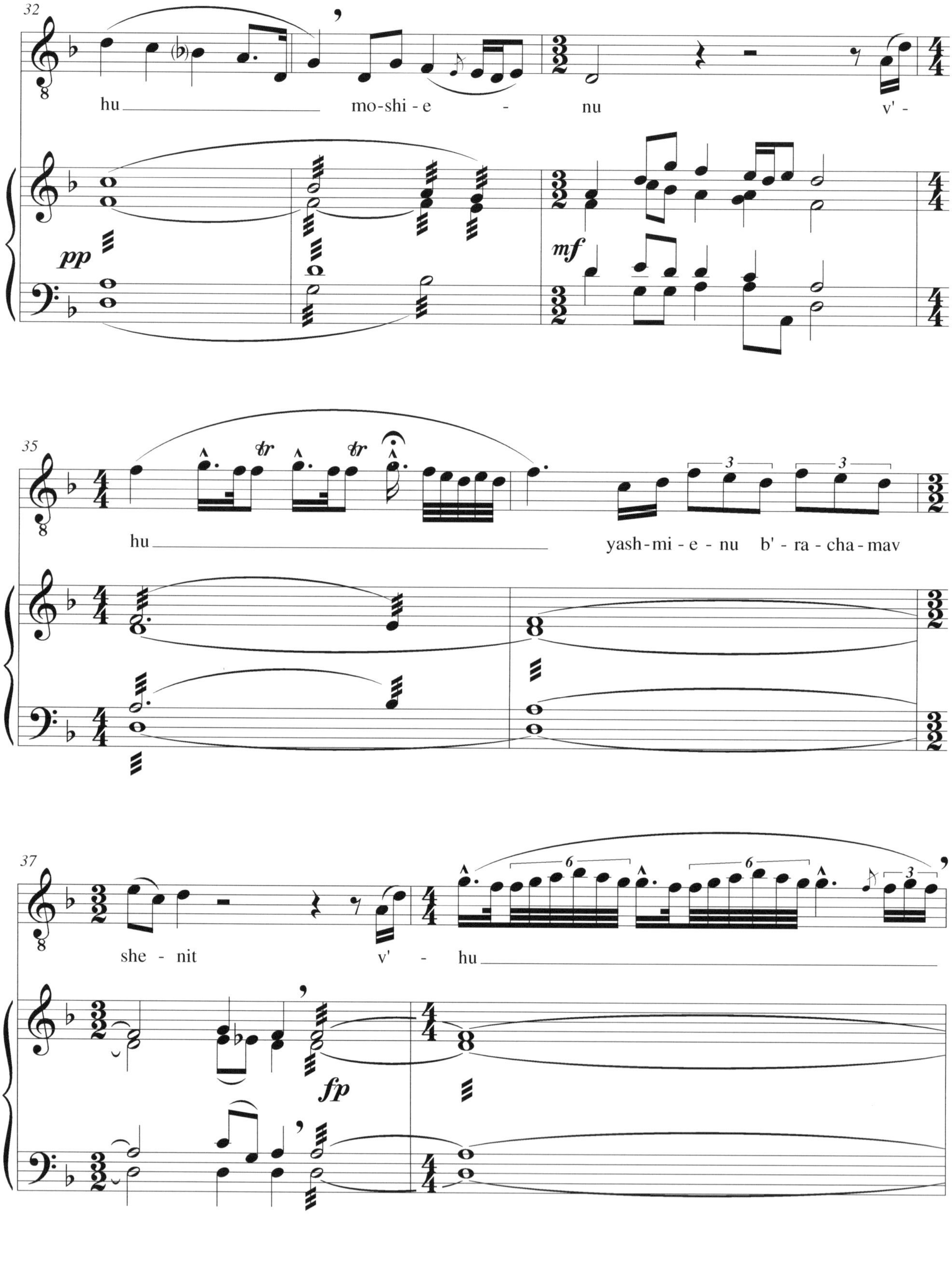
32
hu
mo-shi-e - nu v'-
pp
mf
35
hu
yash-mi-e-nu b'-ra-cha-mav
3
tr
37
she - nit v' - hu
6
fp

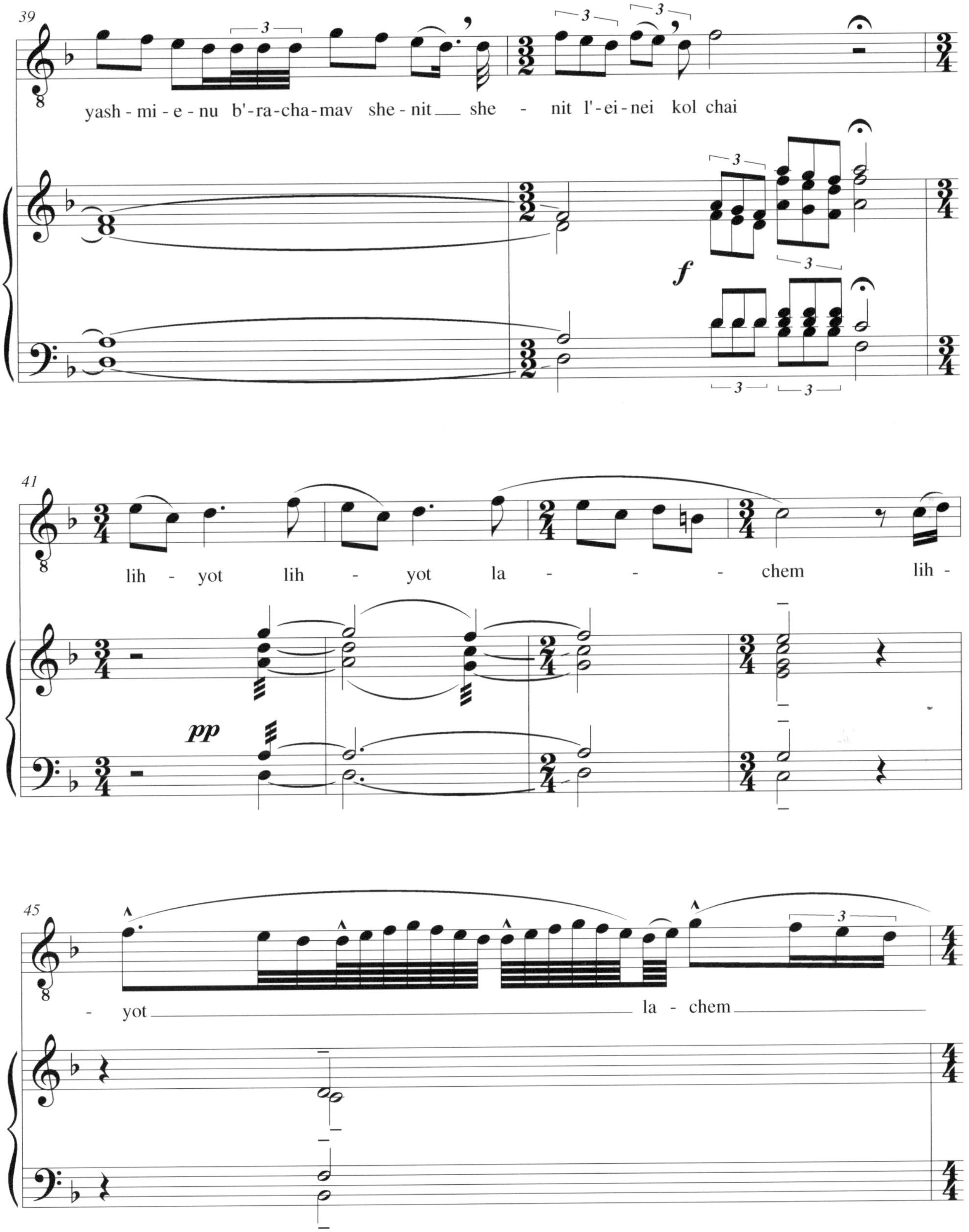
39
yash-mi-e-nu b'-ra-cha-mav she-nit she - nit l'-ei-nei kol chai
f
41
lih - yot lih - yot la - - - - chem lih -
pp
45
- yot la - chem

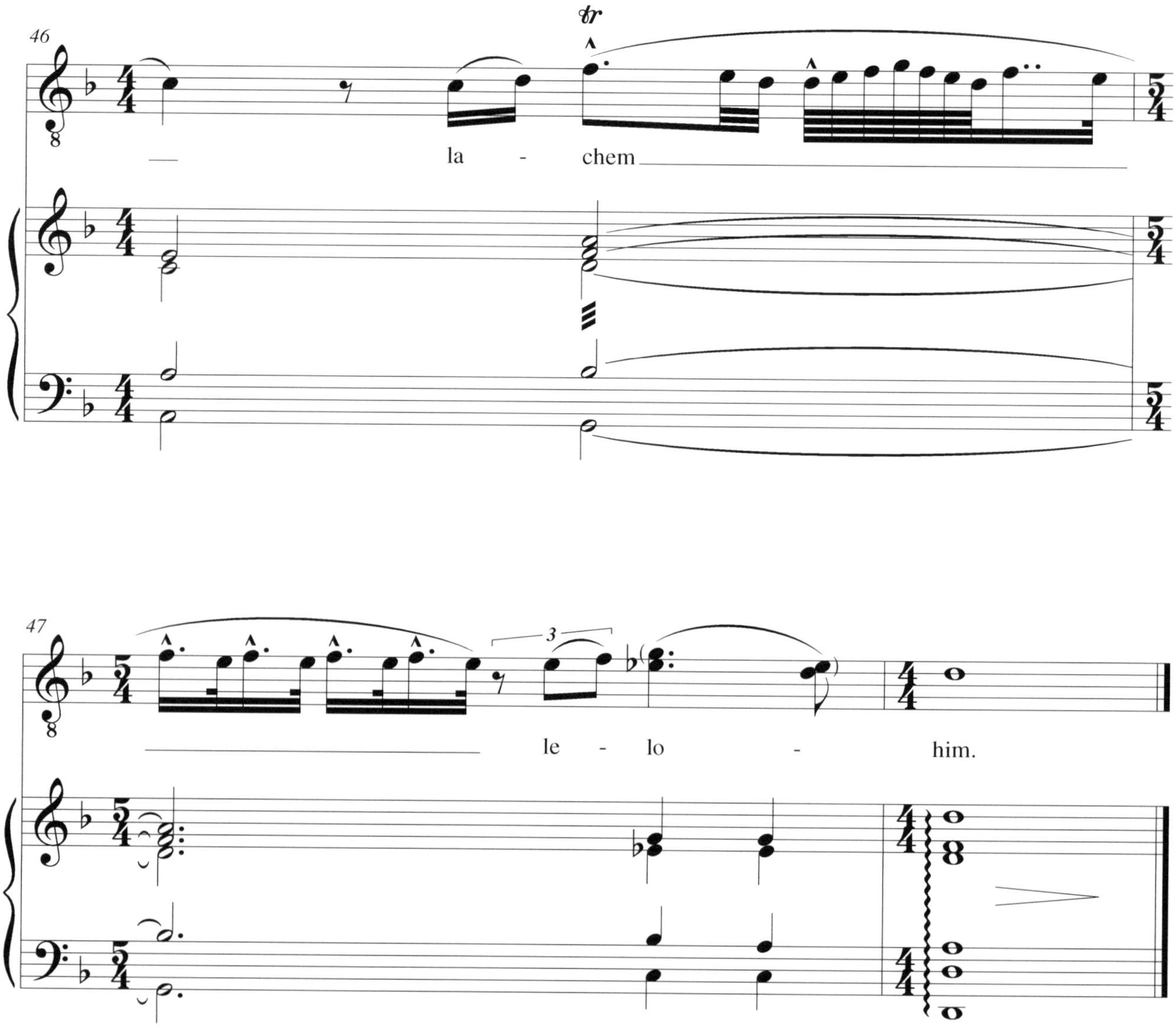
46
tr
la - chem
47
3
le - lo - him.

15. *Uv'yom Ha'shabbat*

THE ARRANGEMENT FOR THIS COMPOSITION WAS COMMISSIONED BY
KATTY COHEN AND JERRY GLANTZ
IN MEMORY OF BERNAT K. WEINER AND LIDIA B. WEINER Z"L
AND IN HONOR OF MIMI KAHN AND PEDRO WEINER

About *Uv'yom Ha'shabbat*:

One listens with awe to Glantz's genius in writing a patter song, characterized by a moderately fast to very fast tempo with a rapid succession of rhythmic patterns, particularly regarding the opening of *Uv'Yom Ha'Shabbat.*

One can but marvel at Glantz's use of the Hebrew language. The entire work is propelled by the incessant motoric rhythm that characterizes the work throughout, and before you know what has happened, the work is at its end!

Beginning in the standard *A'ha'va Ra'bah* mode, it modulates to the sub-dominant major (*U'Va'Yom Ha'Shvi'i*), giving light relief, albeit temporary, before returning back to *A'ha'va Ra'bah* at the words *Chem'dat Ya'mim.*

My particular setting, originally part of the "Chassidic Suite" (for TTBB and piano) was reworked here for Cantor and TTBB *a cappella* – according to the orthodox mode.

The work starts off homophonically, but already by bar #5 (*O'lat Shabbat*), contrapuntal elements are added to the work with the rhythmic use of the words creating their own natural counterpoint.

Am Me'ka'de'shei and *Ku'lam Yis'be'u* are each treated tonally in third relationships to the original E *A'ha'va Ra'bah* key, giving the work the extra harmonic impulses needed at those points. This is normal in classical music but quite novel in synagogue choral writing.

At bar #9, the accompanying words *Yis'me'chu till Ve'Kor'ei O'neg* are divided between the choir, with the basses pitted against the rest of the choir in an *ostinato* fashion – a continually repeated musical phrase or rhythm.

This particular setting has proved to be a *"tour de force"* at and with the Jerusalem Great Synagogue choir and has been in their standard liturgical repertoire since 1990.

—*Raymond Goldstein*

Score

ובים השבת

Uv'yom Ha'shabbat

Leib Glantz

Arr: Raymond Goldstein

7
T1
T2
lat sha - bat b' - sha - ba - to al o - lat ha - ta - mid v' - nis - ka
B1
B2
o - lat sha - bat b' - sha - ba - to al o - lat ha - ta - mid v' - nis - ka
9
(sim...)
Cantor
Yis - m' - chu v' - mal - chut - cha shom - rei shom - rei sha - bat v' - kor - ei v' - kor - ei
Tenor 1
Tenor 2
sm' v' - chu sho - sha v' - ko - rei o - neg kor ei kor ei
Baritone
Bass
Yi chu mal t'cha m'rei bat ko - rei o - neg v' ei v' ei
12
C
v' - kor - ei o - neg
T1
T2
v' - kor - ei o - neg am m' - ka - d' - shei am m' - ka - d' - shei sh'vi - i sha - bat
p
B1
B2
v' - kor - ei o - neg am m' - kad - shei sh'vi - i sha - bat

15
T1
T2
kulam yis-b'-u v'-yit-a-n'-gu mi-tu-ve-cha sha-bat am m'-ka-d'-shei am m'-ka-d'-shei
B1
B2
ku-lam v'-yit-a-n'-gu mi-tu-ve-cha sha-bat am m'-kad-shei
18
T1
T2
sh'vi-i sha-bat ku-lam yis-b'-u v'-yit-a-n'-gu mi-tu-ve-cha sha-bat
B1
B2
sh'vi-i sha-bat ku-lam yis-b'u v'-yit-an'-gu mi-tu-ve-cha sha-bat
21
mf
(sim...)
C
u-va-sh'vi-i ra-tzi-ta bo v'-ki-dash-to u-va-sh'vi-i ra-tzi-ta bo
T1
T2
mp
u-va-shi-i v'-ki-dash-to sha-bat v'-ki-dash-to
B1
B2
mp
u-va-sh'vi-i ra-tzi-ta bo v'-ki-dash-to sha-bat u-va-sh'vi-i ra-tzi-ta bo

24
C
v' - ki - dash - to
T1
T2
v' - ki - dash - to sha - bat
f
chem - dat ya - mim chem - dat ya - mim
B1
B2
v' - ki - dash - to sha - bat
26
o - to ka - ra - ta sha - bat
mp
in 8
rall.
ze - cher ze - cher ze - cher ze - cher
Allargando
28
l' - ma-a - se v' - re - shit sha - bat

Leib Glantz praying at *"O'hel Shem"* concert hall in Tel Aviv in January, 1947.

16. *Birkat Kohanim*

THE ARRANGEMENT FOR THIS COMPOSITION WAS COMMISSIONED BY
PENNY S. MYERS,
DEDICATED WITH AN UNENDING LOVE TO BENNETT, HUNTER, SAUL AND CORRINNE.

About *Birkat Kohanim*:

It is customary that during the blessing of the congregation in the synagogue by the priestly *Ko'ha'nim,* the congregants utter a silent prayer. The priests hum a specific tune for each festival. Leib Glantz uses a mellifluous melody for *"Ye'va're'che'cha Ha'Shem Ve'Yish'me're'cha"* and *"Ya'er Ha'Shem,"* and constructs the whole composition around this melody.

It is fascinating to hear how Glantz creates an "ancient" atmosphere, from the very first words of this recitative, and repeats the motive in *"Ve'Ya'sem Le'cha."* At this point he sounds more like a *Ba'al Te'fi'lah* reading it out for the *Ko'ha'nim* from the *Du'chan* (pulpit).

—*Cantor Naftali Herstik*

Among the giants of modern *Cha'za'nut,* Leib Glantz still stands out as a unique phenomenon; a synthesis of scholar, theoretician, composer and performer. This incredible coexistence of so many virtues in one individual is even more amazing if we understand that some of these virtues actually stood in opposition to each other. The image of the composer and performer is the image of the artist: creative, imaginative, burning with desire to spread out his virtuosity. The image of the scholar is that of the sage: venerable, moderate, wary of foreign influences and innovation. Holding fast to established traditions, while at the same time looking forward for growth and progress of *Cha'za'nut* as an artistic and religious endeavor, typified Glantz's career. He was the brilliant innovator and the formidable conservative.

Glantz repeatedly stressed the importance of the restoration and revival of the musical *Nu'sach* – the traditional Jewish musical formats of prayers – after a period perceived as decadent. He resolutely required that the synagogue be kept clear of foreign and assimilationist influences. He protested against alien influences on the prayer tunes and insisted upon cleansing *Nu'sach* from such tendencies and upon preserving the time-honored melodies that had been passed down through the generations.

Despite this conservatism, Glantz pursued innovation and musical creativity, which constitute his second principle of *Cha'za'nut.*

The verses of *Bir'kat Ko'ha'nim* are among the oldest in continuous liturgical use. Archaeologists have found the words etched on silver scrolls on an amulet from the seventh century BCE.

This interpretation illustrates the inter-connectedness of the musical structure and the textual structure and the intra-connectedness of the musical design in the Priestly Blessing by Glantz. The unity of text and music is a focal point of Glantz's philosophy and in this manner we should interpret the structure of this unique cantorial composition.

—*Dr. Amit Klein, Prof. Eliyahu Schleifer, and Professor Edwin Seroussi*

Score

ברכת כהנים

Birkat Kohanim

Leib Glantz

Arr: Raymond Goldstein

8
ba - r'- che - nu vab'- ra - cha ham'- shu - le - shet vab'- ra - cha ha - m'- shu - le - shet ba - to - ra
3
11
ba - to - ra ha - k'- tu - va al y'- dei Mo - she ha - k'- tu - va al y'- dei Mo - she av -
5
3
mp
14
- de - cha av - de - cha ha - k'- tu -
3
3

17
va al y'-dei Mo-she av - de - cha ha-a-mu-
19
ra mi-pi A-ha-ron u-va-nav A-ha - ron u-va-nav A-ha - ron
21
u-va - nav ko-ha-nim

24
am
25
am k'-do-she-cha ka-a - - - mur
27
y' - va - re - ch'-cha
mf
mp

30
Ah, Ah, Ah, A - do - nai v' -
mf
33
yish - - - m' - re - cha
3
p
35
ya - er A - do - nai oy! pa-nav e-le-cha pa-nav e-le-cha
3

pa - nav e-le-cha vi-chu -
mf
ne - ka
yi -

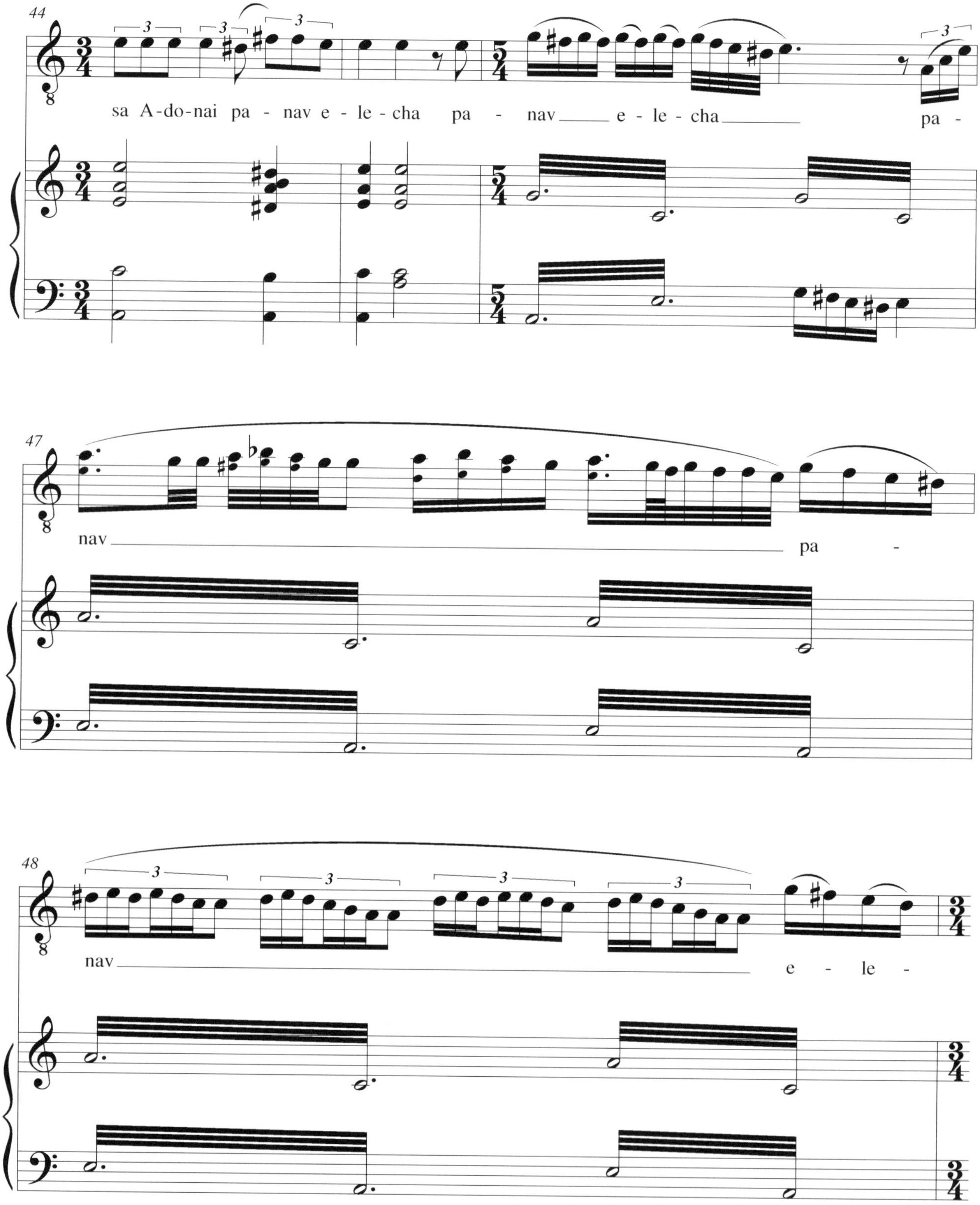
44
sa A-do-nai pa - nav e - le - cha pa - nav e - le - cha pa -
47
nav pa -
48
nav e - le -

49
cha e - le - cha v'-ya - sem l' -
mf
52
cha v'-ya-
54
sem l' - cha

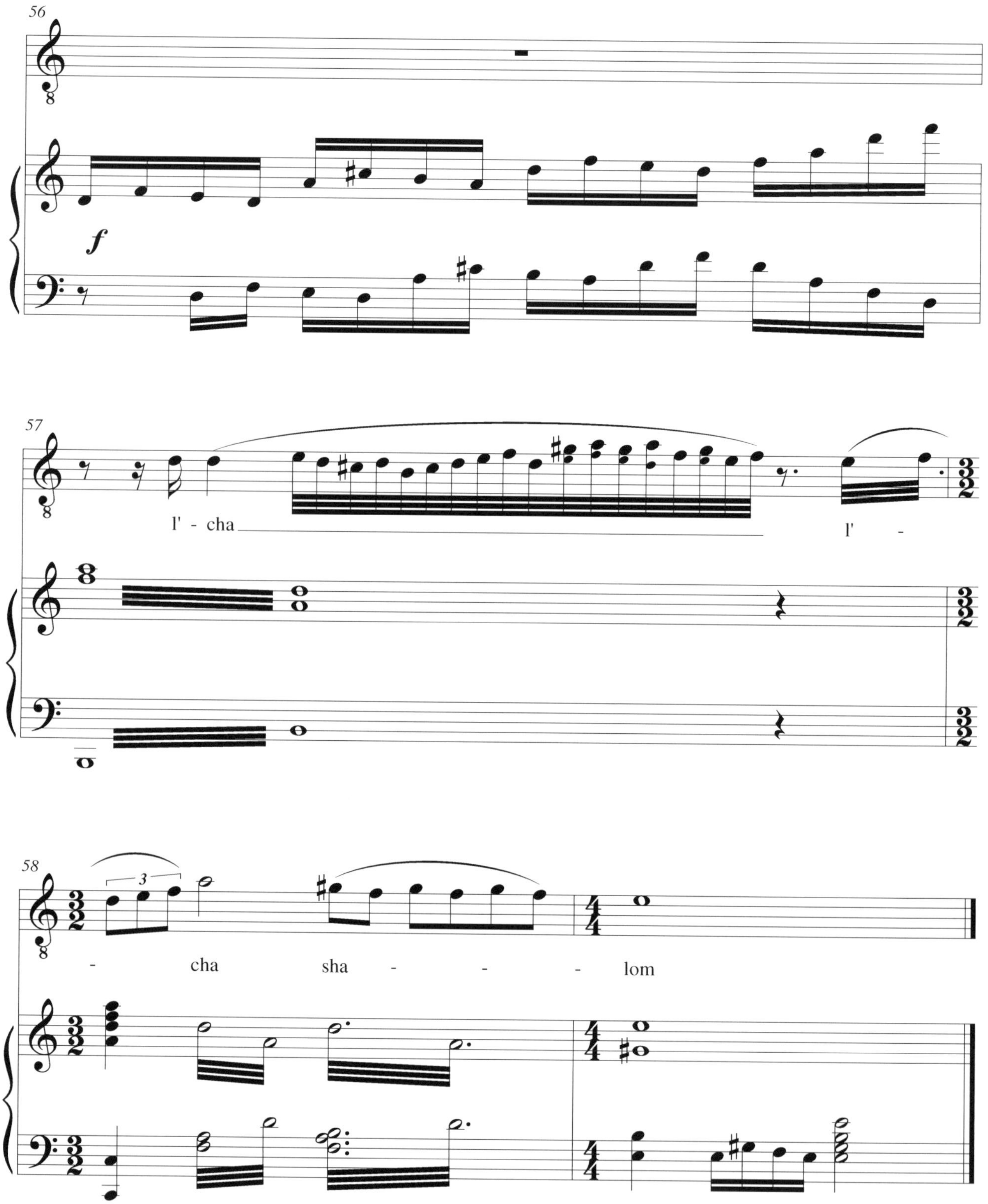
56
f
57
l' - cha
l' -
58
3
- cha sha - - - lom

17. *Sim Shalom*

The arrangement for this composition was commissioned by
Hazzan Emanuel Perlman
in memory of his paternal grandmother Katherine Glantz Perlman
and in honor of cousin Leib Glantz.

About *Sim Shalom*:

This composition was written by Leib Glantz at a time when he was engaged and enveloped by a new Israeli spirit that was influenced by the rhythms, melodic lines, and use of the musical variations of the *Ki'bbutz Ga'lu'yot* (ingathering of the exiles) from the Caucasus, Yemen, Persia, Babylonia, the Magreb countries of North Africa, as well as the music of the Jews of Greece and Turkey. Glantz joined the trend of his fellow secular composers and musicians, such as Marc Lavry, Paul Ben-Haim, and Alexander Boskovich, who strived to connect with these fresh new sounds.

Another aspect was Glantz's Chassidic affinity. He employs the "repeated refrain" of the Chassidic style, using the *A'ha'va Ra'bah* prayer mode, from which he builds a series of colorful adornments around the basic theme. He was one of the first composers to discover that audiences preferred light melodic tunes from time to time, and many of the cantors of those times followed his example. Among them – Moshe Taube, Moshe Stern and Moshe Kraus.

Glantz had an interesting way of dealing with this prayer. As long as he was appealing and praying *Sim Sha'lom* and *Bar'chei'nu A'vi'nu* (Bless us our Father), he remains in the *A'ha'va Ra'bah* prayer mode. But when he arrives at the part where we thank God, *Ki Ve'Or Pa'ne'cha Na'ta'ta La'nu Ha'Shem E'lo'kei'nu To'rat Cha'yim Ve'A'ha'vat Che'sed* (for by the light of Your countenance, You gave us, Lord our God, the Torah of life and loving-kindness), he changes to major in a musical method specifically his own. Then, after a few bars he returns to a mood that suggests pleading – so appropriate for the words *U'Tzda'ka U'Vra'cha Ve'Ra'cha'mim Ve'Cha'yim Ve'Sha'lom* (righteousness, blessing, mercy, life and peace). Just like his typical method in prayer services, Glantz ventures away to realms in which the "regular worshiper" finds difficulty in following, and the listeners are amazed and mesmerized by these interpretations which seem "beyond human comprehension." However, Glantz always seemed to find the road back home to the classical *Nu'sach* (prayer mode) and to more traditional *Chazzanut,* as in *Ve'Tov Be'Ei'ne'cha Le'var'che'nu* (May it be favorable in Your eyes to bless us). This was the kind of adventurous excitement that one would experience at a Leib Glantz prayer service.

It is interesting to point out that when he arrived in Israel in 1954, Glantz switched from *Nu'sach Ashkenaz* to *Nu'sach S'fard,* as was practiced in many of the large synagogues in the country, and he prayed from a Chassidic prayer book.

Listen carefully to Raymond Goldstein's arrangement. Note his use of "hints" of musical motifs that are interwoven into the choral and piano accompaniments.

—*Cantor Naftali Herstik*

Score

שים שלום

Sim Shalom

Leib Glantz

Arr: Raymond Goldstein

9
Cantor
bar - che - nu a - vi - nu ku - la - nu k'-e - chad ku - la - nu k'e - chad ya - chad b'-
legato
Tenor 1
Tenor 2
p
Oo
Oo
Baritone
Bass
Piano
13
C
or pa - ne - cha ki v' - or pa - ne - cha na - ta - ta la - nu Ha - shem E - lo - hei - nu to -
T1
T2
Oo
B1
B2
Pno.

16
p
ff
C
rat cha - yim v'-a-ha-vat che - sed bar - che-nu a-vi-nu ku - la-nu k'-e-chad k'-e-
T1
T2
che - sed bar - che-nu a-vi-nu ku - la-nu k'-e-chad k'-e-
f
B1
B2
Pno.
20
(ad lib - next four bars for cantor)
p
C
chad ya-chad b'-or pa-ne-cha ki v'-or pa-ne - cha na-
a2
T1
T2
chad ya-chad b'-or pa-ne-cha ki v'-or pa-ne - cha na-
p
a2
B1
B2
(these 4 bars could be sung "a capella")
Pno.

24
C
ta - ta la - nu Ha - shem E - lo - hei - nu to - rat cha - yim to - rat cha - yim
T1
T2
ta - ta la - nu Ha - shem E - lo - hei - nu Oo
pp
B1
B2
Pno.
28
v' - a - ha - vat che - sed
Oo to - rat cha - yim to - rat cha - yim

32
C
T1
T2
B1
B2
Pno.
pp
utz-da-ka uv-ra-cha v'-ra-cha-
v'a-ha-vat che - sed che - sed utz - da - ka uv - ra - cha
che - sed
36
p
mim v'-cha-yim v'-sha-lom v'-chol tov sim sha-lom to-
v' - sha - lom v'-chol tov sim sha - lom
pp

39
C
va uv-ra-cha chen va-che-sed v'-ra-cha-mim a-lei-nu v'-al kol
T1
T2
a2
sim sha-lom Oo b'-ra-cha-mim sim sha-lom
B1
B2
Pno.
43
pp
recit.
Yis-ra-el Yis-ra-el a-me-cha v'-
Yis-ra-el a-me-cha a-me-cha
a-me-cha

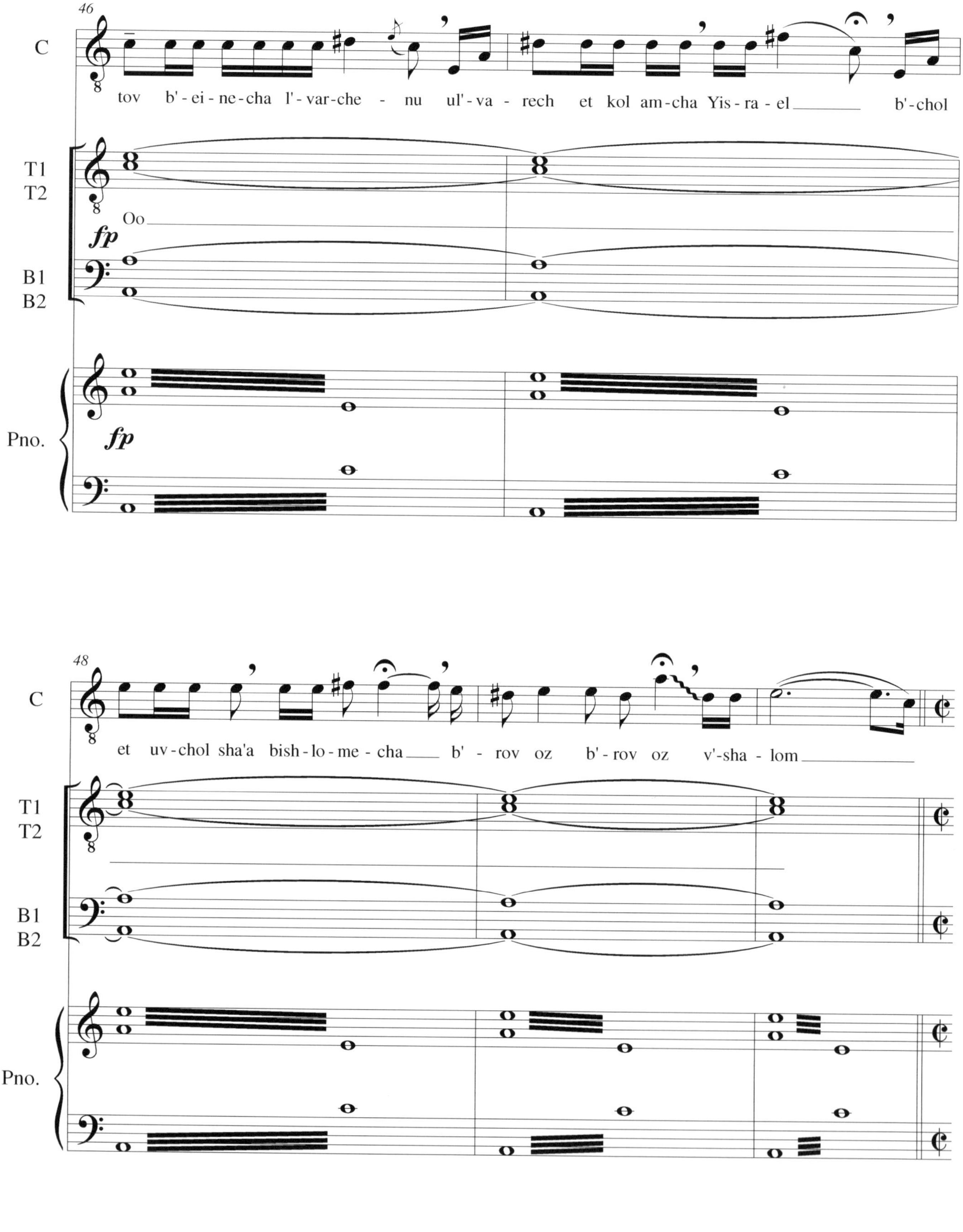
46
C
tov b'-ei-ne-cha l'-var-che - nu ul'-va - rech et kol am-cha Yis-ra-el b'-chol
T1
T2
Oo
fp
B1
B2
Pno.
fp
48
C
et uv-chol sha'a bish-lo-me-cha b' - rov oz b'-rov oz v'-sha - lom
T1
T2
B1
B2
Pno.

a tempo in 2 (piu mosso)
51
C
sim shalom shalom to-va uv-ra-cha chen va-che-sed v'-ra-cha-
Pno.
p marcato
delicato
54
mim a-lei-nu v'-al kol Yis-ra-el Yis-ra-el a-
58
un poco rit.
a tempo
me-cha sim sha-lom to-va uv-ra-cha

62
C
chen va-che-sed v'-ra-cha-mim a-lei-nu v'-al kol Yis-ra-el
Pno.
66
molto rit.
Yis-ra-el a-me-cha bar-
69
tempo primo
mf
che-nu a-vi-nu ku-la-nu k'-e-chad k'-e-chad ya-chad b'-
T1
T2
pp
Oo
Oo
B1
B2

72
pp
C
or pa-ne-cha ki v' - or pa-ne-cha na-ta-ta la-nu Ha-shem E-lo-hei - nu to-
T1
T2
Oo
B1
B2
Pno.
75
C
rat cha-yim v' - a - ha - vat che - sed v' -
T1
T2
Oo che - sed
B1
B2
rall.
Pno.

recit.... ad lib...
77
C
- tov b'-ei-ne-cha l'-var-che - nu v' - tov b'-ei-ne-cha l'-var-che -
Pno.
sfp
sfp
Ped.
79
C
nu u-l' - va - rech
Pno.
mf
81
C
et kol am-cha Yis-ra-el b'-chol et uv-chol
Pno.

82
C
sha - a bish-lo-me - cha, b' - rov oz v'-sha-lom Ba-ruch a - ta A-do-
Pno.
mp
85
C
shem ham'-va - rech et a - mo
T1
T2
ba-ruch hu u-va-ruch sh'-mo
B1
B2
Pno.

87
C
Yis - ra - el___ et a - mo et a - mo Yis - ra - el, Yis - ra -
T1
T2
Yis - ra - el
a - mo___
f
B1
B2
Pno.
90
C
el___ ba - sha - lom___
T1
T2
ba - sha - lom
B1
B2
Pno.

18. *Be'tzeit Yisrael*

THE ARRANGEMENT FOR THIS COMPOSITION WAS COMMISSIONED BY KATTY COHEN AND JERRY GLANTZ IN HONOR OF MIRIAM GLANTZ Z"L, LEIB'S LOVING WIFE AND COMPANION AND LIFETIME PARTNER IN HIS AMAZING CREATIVE CAREER.

About *Be'tzeit Yisrael*:

Be'tzeit Yisrael is one of Leib Glantz's recordings in which he is not speaking to God. He is addressing the listeners, as is the text. His role is that of the storyteller, and his approach is to paint a vivid *picture* of the epic departure of the Israelites from Egypt, using every color and shading of his pallet of sound. My first reaction upon first hearing his recording was that it was like a Chagall painting! I could *see* the Israelites walking in a long column, emerging from the darkness of slavery. I could *see* the mountains, the hills, the Jordan river, the sheep – all seeming to *float about in the air* on the screen of my mind. Such is the power of the art of Leib Glantz.

In composing this arrangement, my objective was to create a choral concept and harmonization that was a natural extension of Glantz's thinking – an expression of what I felt his melody line implied. The vocal line here is a detailed blueprint of how Glantz sang the piece. But we should remember that Glantz composed first and foremost for himself. He was incandescent with the intensity of expressing his *own* religious emotion. I do not think he ever wanted anyone to sing one of his compositions *exactly* the way he did. He was not a teacher interested in manufacturing clones of himself or encouraging imitators. He did, rather, encourage cantors to be creative and innovative, each in his own way. If you are preparing to sing this piece, you are the one who must decide how much of what is notated here is essential to the concept and how much is Glantz's dramatic performance.

Please note the brief reference to the *Ak'da'mut* melody which Glantz included in the piece.

This piece can be performed three different ways: 1. If you observe all the tempo changes, stops and starts, and louds and softs, your rendition will be very dramatic, in the manner of Glantz. In order to avoid the danger of making it sound too chopped up into a collection of separate segments, take care to create some continuity, some unifying element in your performance. Keep in mind at all times that *you are telling a story.* That is what Glantz did, and it works. 2. You can also perform this piece *disregarding* many of the dynamic and tempo indications. *Be'tzeit Yisrael* does work as a more lyrical, smoothly flowing piece. 3. There is also a third way, *modifying and smoothing the degree of the contrast of elements.* Do observe the indications, but in a less extreme, less overstated manner. The result can still retain much of the drama and at the same time flow more smoothly, with a greater sense of continuity.

A pianist or organist can use the choral part as the basis or as a harmonic guide for accompanying either cantor and choir or a solo vocal performance. On the keyboard, chords should be initiated harp-style, arpeggiated rather than initiated by striking all the notes simultaneously. The cantor and choir must rehearse this piece sufficiently that they become *as one* on every detail of tempo, internal rhythm, and dynamics. The choir must follow the cantor like his own shadow.

—*Cantor Ralph Schlossberg*

Score

בצאת ישראל

Be'tzeit Yisrael

Leib Glantz
Arr: Cantor Ralph Schlossberg

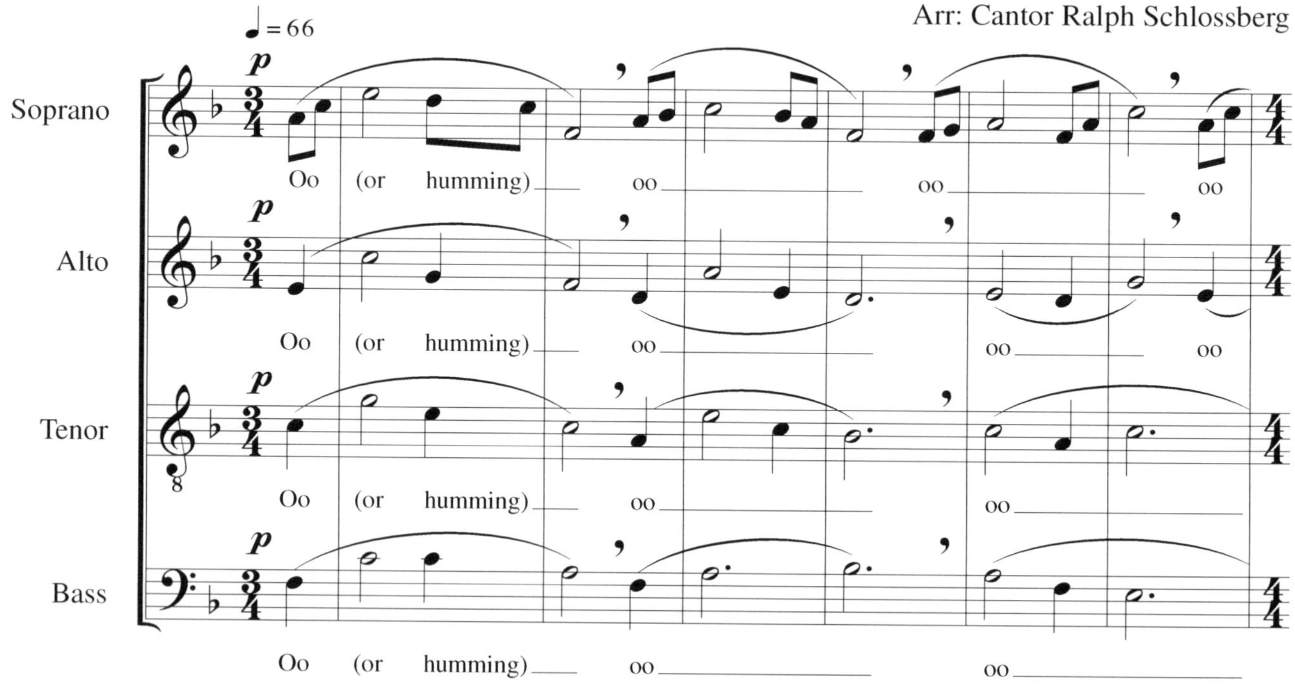

♩ = 69
♩ = 76
12
C
mi-Mitz - ra - yim beit Ya - a - kov me - am lo - ez me-
S
mmm mmm mmm mmm me-
A
mmm mmm mmm mmm me-
T
mmm mmm mmm mmm me-
B
mmm mmm mmm mmm me-
20
♩ = 88
p
C
am lo - ez hai - ta Y'-hu - da Y'-hu -
S
am lo - ez lo - ez mmm
A
am lo - ez lo - ez mmm
T
am lo - ez lo - ez mmm
B
am lo - ez lo - ez

26
♩ = 80
♩ = 72
C
da l'-kod - sho Yis-ra - el mam-sh'-lo - tav hai -
S
mmm mmm mmm
A
mmm mmm mmm
T
mmm mmm mmm
B
mmm
31
♩ = 80
♩ = 60
C
ta Y'-hu - da l'-kod - sho Yis-ra - el mam-sh'-lo - tav mam-sh'-lo-
S
mmm mmm mmm mmm mmm
A
mmm mmm mmm mmm mmm
T
mmm mmm mmm mmm mmm
B

♩. = 58
♩ = 58
♩ = 66
37
C
S
A
T
B
tav
ha - yam ra -
ha - yam
ha - yam
ha - yam
ha - yam
42
♩ = 58
a va - ya - nos ha - Yar -
ra - a va - ya - nos va - ya - nos
ra - a va - ya - nos va - ya - nos
ra - a
ra - a

45
C
S
A
T
B
♩ = 48
den ha-Yar - den yi - sov l'-a-chor
ha-Yar-den ha-Yar-den yi - sov l'-a - chor l'-a-chor
ha-Yar-den ha-Yar-den yi - sov l'-a - chor l'-a-chor
ha-Yar-den ha-Yar-den l'-a - chor l'-a-chor
ha-Yar-den ha-Yar-den l'-a-chor
49
♩ = 60
♩ = 58
he-ha - rim ra-k'-du ch'-ei-lim g'-va-ot
he-ha - rim ra-k'-du ch'-ei-lim ch'-ei-lim mmm g'-va - ot
he-ha - rim ra-k'-du ch'-ei-lim ch'-ei-lim mmm g'-va - ot
he-ha - rim ra-k'-du ch'-ei-lim ch'-ei-lim mmm g'-va - ot
he-ha - rim ra-k'-du ch'-ei-lim ch'-ei-lim mmm g'-va - ot

♩= 60
♩= 58
♩= 60
54
C
S
A
T
B
pp
f
kiv - nei tzon he - ha - rim ra - k'-du ch'-ei-
kiv - nei tzon kiv - nei tzon mmm
kiv - nei tzon kiv - nei tzon mmm
mmm
mmm
57
lim g'- va - ot kiv-nei tzon
ch'-ei - lim g'- va - ot kiv-nei tzon
ch'-ei - lim g'- va - ot kiv-nei tzon
ch'-ei - lim g'- va - ot kiv-nei tzon
ch'-ei - lim g'- va - ot kiv-nei tzon

61
♩ = 58
♩ = 60
C
S
A
T
B
kiv - nei tzon ha-yam ra-
kiv - nei kiv - nei tzon
kiv - nei kiv - nei tzon
kiv - nei tzon
kiv - nei tzon
♩. = 60
♩. = 48
♩. = 60
63
mp
mf
a va-ya - nos va-ya - nos ha-Yar-
mmm mmm mmm

♩. = 48
♩. = 60
65
C
S
A
T
B
pp
mf
den yi-sov l' - a - chor he-ha - rim ra-k'-du ch'-
mmm mmm mmm mmm
pp ♩. = 40
68
ei - lim g'-va - ot kiv'-nei tzon kiv' - nei tzon
mmm mmm mmm mmm

♩. = 58
♩. = 48
♩. = 58
C
ma l' - cha ha-yam ha - yam ki ta - nus ha - Yar -
S
ma l' - cha ha-yam ha - yam ta - nus
A
ma l' - cha ha-yam ha - yam ta - nus
T
ma l' - cha ha-yam ha - yam ta - nus
B
ma l' - cha ha-yam ha - yam ta - nus
73
♩. = 48
♩. = 40
C
den ti - sov l' - a - chor he - ha -
S
ha - Yar - den ti - sov l' - a - chor
A
ha - Yar - den ti - sov l' - a - chor
T
ha - Yar - den ti - sov l' - a - chor
B
ha - Yar - den ti - sov l' - a - chor

♩. = 48
♩. = 40
♩. = 48
75
C
S
A
T
B
rim tir - k'-du ch'-ei - lim g'-va-
he-ha-rim tir-k'-du ch'-ei-lim
he - ha - rim tir - k'-du ch'-ei-lim
77
ot kiv' - nei
g' - va - ot kiv - nei tzon kiv - nei tzon kiv - nei
tzon kiv - nei tzon kiv - nei

♩. = 40
79
C
S
A
T
B
f
ff
♩. = 52
tzon
mi - lif - nei a - don a - don chu -
tzon kiv - nei tzon
mi - lif - nei a - don
81
♩. = 40
- - li a - retz
mi - lif - nei E - lo - a Ya-a-
chu - li a - retz
mi - lif - nei E - lo - a

♩ = 52
83
C
kov
S
Ya - a - kov
A
Ya - a - kov
T
Ya - a - kov
Basses or Cantor
B
Ya - a - kov Ya - a - kov mi - lif - nei a - don a - don a - don chu -
♩. = 48
♩ = 46
85
mmm
li a - retz mi - lif - nei E - lo - a Ya - a -

87
♩ = 40
♩ = 42
ha-hof - chi ha-tzur a-gam ma-yim ha-hof -
mmm
mmm
mmm
kov
mmm
89
chi ha-tzur a - gam ma-yim cha-la -
mmm
mmm
mmm
mmm

Alternative Ending

Tif'e'ret Zvi synagogue in Tel Aviv, Israel, Where Glantz officiated as chief cantor from 1954 till 1963

19. *Ahavti*

[Cantor, Cello, Piano]

The arrangement for this composition was commissioned by
Hazzan Beny Maissner
in memory of his uncle Cantor Israel Alter.

About *Ahavti*:

In his recording of *Ahavti,* Glantz makes great use of contrasts of volume and intensity to convey the emotions of someone in despair.

He begins very quietly with the introspective internal meditation of someone who had been lost in existential angst and who called out to God when all hope was lost. Without actually emitting a sigh, he conveys the idea of the narrator – sighing from the depths of his being. All of this is done within the framework of the appropriate *Nu'sach.* When he cries out to God to be saved, his sudden *forte* is truly a cry from the depths ascending to the heavens.

Once Glantz comes to the words *Ki Chi'latz'ta Naf'shi Mi'Ma'vet* (Thou hast delivered my soul from death), he settles into easily recognizable *Nu'sach,* very intensely *Chazzanic,* beautifully rendered, and unusually dramatic.

Then comes *Et'ha'lech Lif'nei A'do'shem Be'Ar'tzot Ha'Cha'yim* (I shall walk before the Lord in the world of the living) as the narrator realizes he will survive, Glantz goes into a triumphal major before returning to the minor in the traditional signature High Holiday's end-of-section *Nu'sach.*

—*Cantor Ralph Schlossberg*

Score

אהבתי

Ahavti

Leib Glantz
Arr: Raymond Goldstein

Recit. - very slow

10
C
Vc.
Pno.
a - hav - ti a - hav - ti ki hi -
religioso
12
ta oz-no li ki hi - ta oz-no li u-v'-ya - mai ek - ra
16
mf
a-fa - fu-ni chev-lei ma-vet u-m'-tza-rei sh'-ol m'-tza-
mp

C
Pno.
u-ni tza-ra v'-ya-gon tza-ra v'-ya-gon em-tza u-v'-
Vc.
shem A-do-nai ek-ra
pp
a-na a-na a-na a-na
a-na A-do-nai mal-ta
ppp

28
C
mal - ta naf - shi
f
a - na
Pno.
sf
mf
30
a - na a - na A - do - nai mal -
Vc.
f
34
accel.
ta naf - shi
cha -

36
C
nun A-do-nai v'-tza-dik ve-lo - hei-nu m'-ra - chem
p
Vc.
colla parte
p
Pno.
fp
fp
colla parte
39
C
mp
sho-mer p'-ta-im A-do - nai da-lo-ti da - lo-ti v'-li v'-li y'-ho-shi -
Vc.
Pno.

42
C
Vc.
Pno.
f
a
a
fp
44
na a - na a - na mal - ta naf - shi shu - vi naf -
colla parte
colla parte

46
C
shi naf - shi lim'-nu-chai - chi ki A-do - nai ga-mal ga-
Vc.
Pno.

49
C
mal ga-mal a-lai - chi ki
mf
Vc.
Pno.

52
C
ki chi-latz-ta naf - shi naf - shi mi-ma-vet
Vc.
colla parte
Pno.
colla parte
fp

55
C
ki chi-latz-ta naf - shi mi-ma-vet
Vc.
Pno.

58
C
et ei - ni min di-m'-a
et ei-ni
Vc.
Pno.
61
C
min
dim - - - - a
ki chi-
Vc.
Pno.

63
C
latz-ta naf-shi mi-ma-vet et ei-ni ei-ni min dim-a
Vc.
Pno.

66
brighter
C
pp
et rag-li rag-li mi-de - chi
Vc.
f
Pno.

piu mosso
69
C
et - ha - lech lif - nei A-
Vc.
non legato
Pno.
sf
71
C
do-nai b'-ar-tzot ha-cha - yim b'-ar-tzot ha - cha - yim he - e-
Vc.
Pno.

Vivo
74
C
man - ti ki a-da-ber a-ni a - ni____ a-ni-ti m'-od
Vc.
f
Pno.
78
C
a-ni a-
rall.
Vc.
Pno.
legato
82
C
ni a-ni a-ni a-ni a-ni a - mar - ti a - mar - ti b'-chof - zi____ kol ha-a-
3
Pno.
f

86
s.m.
C
dam kol ha-a - dam kol ha-a - dam
Vc.
Pno.
sf
89
C
kol ha-a-dam ko - zev
Vc.
Pno.
sf

CELLO PART

אהבתי

Ahavti

Leib Glantz

Arr: Raymond Goldstein

u - ni tza - ra v' - ya - gon tza - ra v' - ya - gon em - tza u - v' -
shem A - do - nai ek - ra
pp
a - na a - na a - na a - na A - do - nai mal - ta
mal - ta naf - shi
f
a - na
a - na a - na A - do - nai mal -
f
accel.
ta naf - shi cha -

36
p
nun A-do-nai v'-tza-dik ve-lo - hei-nu m'-ra - chem
colla parte
p
39
mp
shomer p'-ta-im A-do - nai da-lo-ti da - lo-ti v'-li v'-li y'-ho-shi -
42
f
- a a - - -
44
na ana ana mal-ta naf - shi shu-vi naf-
colla parte
46
shi naf - shi lim'-nu-chai - chi ki A-do - nai ga-mal ga-

mal ga - mal a - lai - chi
mf
ki
ki chi - latz - ta naf - shi naf - shi mi - ma - vet
colla parte
ki chi - latz - ta naf - shi mi - ma - vet
et ei - ni min di - m'- a et ei - ni
min dim - - - - a ki chi -

63
latz - ta naf - shi mi - ma - vet et ei - ni ei - ni min dim - a
66
brighter
pp
et rag - li rag - li mi - de - chi
f
69
piu mosso
et - ha - lech lif - nei A -
71
do - nai b' - ar - tzot ha - cha - yim b' - ar - tzot ha - cha - yim he - e -
74
Vivo
man - ti ki a - da - ber a - ni a - ni a - ni - ti m' - od
f
78
rall.
a - ni a -

82
ni a - ni a - ni a - ni a - ni a - mar - ti a - mar - ti b' - chof - zi kol ha-a -
86
s.m.
dam kol ha-a - dam kol ha-a - dam
89
kol ha-a - dam ko - zev

20. *Ahavti*

[VSC]

THE ARRANGEMENT FOR THIS COMPOSITION WAS COMMISSIONED BY CANTOR ERIC MOSES OF BETH SHOLOM SYNAGOGUE, TORONTO, CANADA IN MEMORY OF *HAZZANIM* SHMUEL BARUCH TAUBE AND SHLOMO GISSER Z"L – HIS TEACHERS, MENTORS AND FRIENDS.

About *Ahavti*:

In his recording of *Ahavti,* Glantz makes great use of contrasts of volume and intensity to convey the emotions of someone in despair.

He begins very quietly with the introspective internal meditation of someone who had been lost in existential angst and who called out to God when all hope was lost. Without actually emitting a sigh, he conveys the idea of the narrator – sighing from the depths of his being. All of this is done within the framework of the appropriate *Nu'sach.* When he cries out to God to be saved, his sudden *forte* is truly a cry from the depths ascending to the heavens.

Once Glantz comes to the words *Ki Chi'latz'ta Naf'shi Mi'Ma'vet* (Thou hast delivered my soul from death), he settles into easily recognizable *Nu'sach,* very intensely *Chazzanic,* beautifully rendered, and unusually dramatic.

Then comes *Et'ha'lech Lif'nei A'do'shem Be'Ar'tzot Ha'Cha'yim* (I shall walk before the Lord in the world of the living) as the narrator realizes he will survive, Glantz goes into a triumphal major before returning to the minor in the traditional signature High Holiday's end-of-section *Nu'sach.*

—*Cantor Ralph Schlossberg*

Score

אהבתי

Ahavti

Leib Glantz
Arr: Raymond Goldstein

10
a - hav - ti a - hav - ti ki hi-
religioso
12
ta oz-no li ki hi - ta oz-no li u-v'-ya - mai ek - ra
16
mf
a-fa - fu-ni chev-lei ma-vet u-m'-tza-rei sh'-ol m'-tza-
mp

u-ni tza-ra v'-ya-gon tza-ra v'-ya-gon em-tza u-v'-
shem A-do-nai ek-ra
a-na a-na a-na a-na a-na A-do-nai mal-ta
pp
pp
ppp

28
f
mal - ta naf - shi
a - na
sf
mf
30
a - na a - na A - do - nai mal -
f
34
accel.
ta naf - shi
cha -

36
p
nun A-do-nai v'-tza-dik ve-lo - hei-nu m'-ra - chem
fp
fp
colla parte
39
mp
6
sho-mer p'-ta-im A-do - nai da-lo-ti da - lo-ti v'-li v'-li y'-ho-shi -
42
f
- a
a -
fp

44
na a - na a - na mal - ta naf - shi shu - vi naf -
colla parte
46
shi naf - shi lim'-nu-chai - chi ki A-do - nai ga-mal ga-
49
mal ga-mal a - lai - chi ki
mf

52
ki chi-latz-ta naf-shi naf - shi mi-ma - vet
colla parte
fp
55
ki chi-latz-ta naf - shi mi-ma - vet
58
et ei - ni min di-m'-a et ei - ni

min dim - - - - a ki chi-
latz-ta naf-shi mi-ma-vet et ei-ni ei-ni min dim-a
brighter
pp
et rag-li rag-li mi-de - chi

69
piu mosso
et - ha - lech lif - nei A-
sf
non legato
71
do-nai b'-ar-tzot ha-cha - yim b'-ar-tzot ha - cha - yim he - e-
3
Vivo
74
man - ti ki a-da - ber a-ni a - ni a-ni - ti m' - od

rall.
legato
a-ni a-ni a-ni a-ni a-ni a-ni a - mar - ti a-mar-ti b'-chof - zi kol ha-a-
dam kol ha-a - dam kol ha-a - dam
s.m.
kol ha-a-dam ko - zev

Leib Glantz's Hallel & Three Festival Compositions, one of seven music books of the Rinat Ha'Kodesh series, published in the 1960s

21. *Tal*

The arrangement for this composition was commissioned by
***Hazzan* Beny Maissner**
in memory of his uncle David Brenner z"l.

About *Tal*:

The general spirit of this wonderful poem that was written by Rabbi Eliezer Hakalir in the 7th century preserves for eternity a picture of the agricultural way of life in ancient Israel. The prayers for *Ge'shem* (rain) and *Tal* (dew) are about water and dew, about blessed rainfall "that the earth, in pride and glory, may be filled with fruit." It is a poem describing the "precious dew that makes the mountains sweet!"

It is based on an ancient Middle Eastern musical mode and retains the originality and beauty of a Middle Eastern song. The preservation of this composition was most fortunate. Two thousand years have passed since the Jews were exiled and dispersed all over the world. We were subjected to the influences of many nations among whom we lived, yet we continued to pray for dew and rain to fall over the distant lands of Israel! This attests to the eternal bond of the Jewish people with their holy land of Israel.

The original Jewish *Tal* must be garbed in Middle Eastern dress – in other words, in Middle Eastern musical scales. The cantor must do everything he can to divest himself of those ordinary Major and Minor keys. The agricultural village life of our country must be given the proper and true musical expression in our prayers. It is very important that the *"Nu'sach* from Sinai" be revived, perhaps in a modern manner, but in a clear and concrete fashion.

—*Cantor Leib Glantz*

Score

טל

Tal

Leib Glantz

Arr. Raymond Goldstein

12
- - cha b'- di - tzach rov
colla parte
14
dagan v'-ti-rosh b'-haf - ri - tzach ko - mem ir ba ba-chef-
16
tzach chef - tzach b'- tal b'-

19
tal
f colla parte
Ped.
21
tal
tal
tal
24
bo t'-va-rech t'-va - rech ma-zon b'-
pp
mf
Ped.

26
mash - ma-ne-nu al y'-hi ra-zon b' - mash-ma-ne-nu al y'-hi ra-zon al al
29
al y'-hi al y'-hi ra-zon a-yu-
31
ma

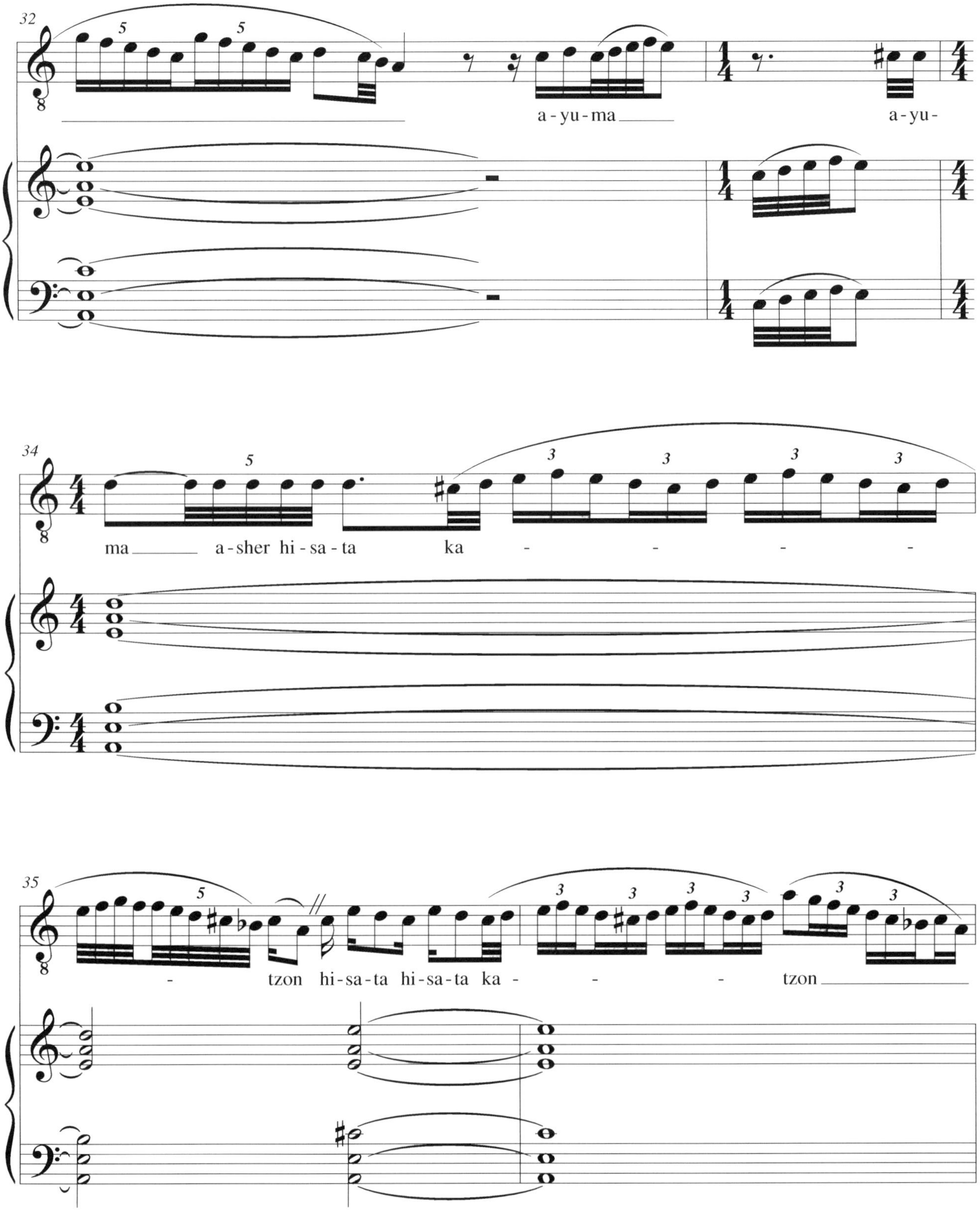
32
a - yu - ma
a - yu -
34
ma a - sher hi - sa - ta ka - - - -
35
- tzon hi - sa - ta hi - sa - ta ka - - - tzon

37
hi - sa - ta hi - sa - ta ka - tzon
a-na ta-fek la ra-
colla parte
40
tzon
a - na ta - fek la ra - tzon
42
a - na ta-fek la ra - tzon

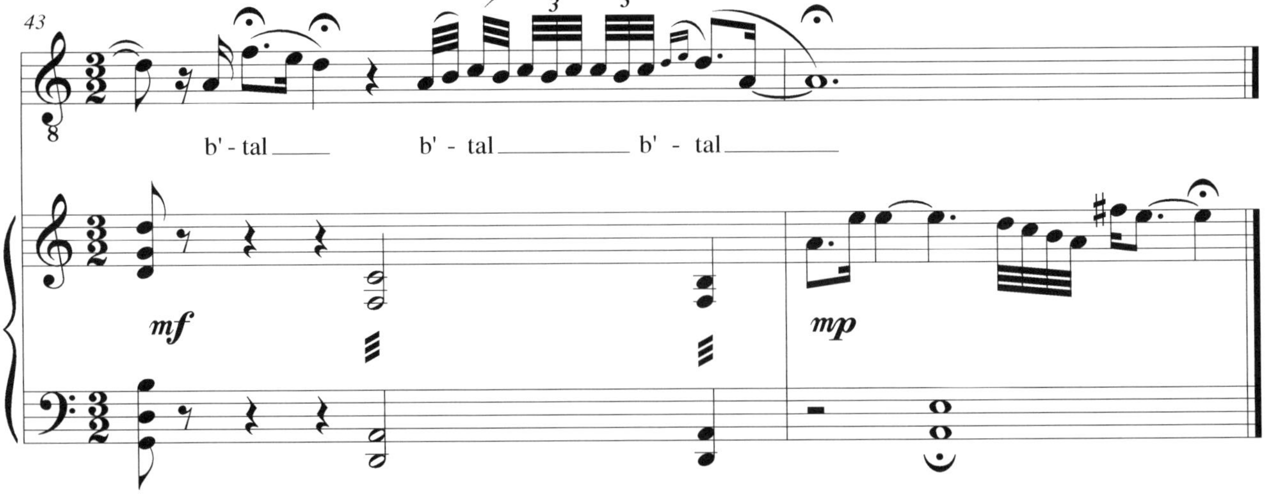
43
b' - tal
b' - tal
b' - tal
mf
mp

22. *Ashrei*

THE ARRANGEMENT FOR THIS COMPOSITION WAS COMMISSIONED BY
HAZZAN ALBERTO MIZRAHI
IN MEMORY OF HIS GREAT TEACHER – CANTOR MOSHE GANCHOFF.

About *Ashrei*:

We must establish from the very beginning that Glantz was a great exponent of *Nu'sach Ha'Te'fi'la.* He was an ardent warrior in the battle to maintain these traditional prayer modes as the basis of all liturgical music. It is therefore even more significant, even astonishing, to realize that Glantz's "revolution" took place *within* the boundaries of traditional *Nu'sach.*

From *Ash'rei* ("Happy are those who dwell in His house"), the very first word of the *Se'li'chot* service, one is impressed by Glantz's penetrating thought and profound original interpretation of the text. Above all, he creates a unique atmosphere that elevates his listeners towards readiness to pray before the Creator during the period of the "Days of Awe." Such is his choral introduction to *Se'li'chot,* which is interwoven with the modes and moods of the High Holiday spirit, encompassing the entirety of prayer from *P'su'kei D'Zim'ra* to *Ne'i'la.* One immediately senses Glantz's clever way of using the Relative Major in order to brighten up the somber mode of the minor chords.

Part of his innovation in the *Nu'sach* of *Se'li'chot* is the use of the aforementioned Relative Major as early as the word *"Od"* in his opening of the *Ash'rei* prayer and in his well-known composition *"L'chu Ne'ra'ne'na."* It would be impossible to analyze here all of Glantz's uses of modes and scales in his *Se'li'chot* service, but I would mention that unlike the limited modes of the "conventional" *Nu'sach* of the *Se'li'chot,* Glantz skillfully maneuvers among a whole range of traditional modes, from what he calls Major and Minor Pentatonic, to *Yish'ta'bach* and *A'do'nai Ma'lach,* to *A'ha'va Ra'bbah* and *Av Ha'Ra'cha'mim,* to Natural Minor and Harmonic Minor.

It is very interesting to follow Glantz's unique use of the choir as an integral part of his service. I firmly believe that on the one hand Glantz wanted to create an effect of *Shi'rat Ha'Le'vi'im* (the Levites singing in the ancient Holy Temple in Jerusalem) – hence the use of minimalist harmony and open fifths, his unusual emphasis of basses over the tenors, and the descending upper line against the ascending lower line. On the other hand Glantz wanted to create *Shi'rat Ka'hal* (congregational singing).

However, the most outstanding feature of Glantz's *Se'li'chot* is his ability to carry the worshipers through every kind of mood and emotion in the liturgy.

—Cantor Naftali Herstik

Score

אשרי

Ashrei

Leib Glantz

Arr: Raymond Goldstein

poco piu mosso
Cantor
Ash - rei yosh - vei vei - te - cha od
Soprano Alto
Tenor Bass
vei - te - cha
C
S A
T B
od
od
rit. e dim.
falsetto
od
od y'-ha-l'-u - cha

22
C
S
A
T
B
ten.
mp
f
od y'-ha-l'-lu - cha se -
25
la
Allegro
dim.
rit.
ash-rei ha-am she-ka-cha lo ash - rei ha-am she-A-do-nai E - lo - hav
dim.

23. *L'chu Ne'rane'na*

The arrangement for this composition was commissioned by
Noam Brown
in memory of his sister Nechama Aviva Brown z"l
and his grandparents Zvi and Malka Braun z"l.

About *L'chu Ne'rane'na*:

Contrary to the traditional *A'ha'va Ra'bah* prayer mode, in which cantors were used to begin this early part of the *Se'li'chot* service, Leib Glantz offers us a lesson regarding the deeper meaning of this prayer and hence opens with a regal and joyous "major."

Ne'ra'ne'na stems from the word *Ri'nah*, which according to our sages means *T'fi'lah* (prayer). However, it also implies joy, as in *"Gi'lah, Ri'nah, Di'tza, Ve'Chedva"* and probably has a dual meaning, as in *"Kol Ri'nah Vi'Yshu'ah."*

The word *Na'ri'ah* also has two possible interpretations: the use of trumpets in the Holy Temple at joyous occasions *("Ha'ri'u La'Ha'shem Be'Kol Sho'far")*, as well as a warning in times of danger or war *("Va'Ha're'o'tem")*.

Glantz calls upon the people to pray to God in a joyous manner and with a sense of gratitude *("Ne'Kad'mah Fa'nav Be'To'da, BiZ'mi'rot Na'ri'a Lo")*, and only at that point does he turn to the *Se'li'chot*/High Holiday mode.

His wholehearted rendition of *"HaN'sha'mah Lach"* and *"Chu'ssah Al A'ma'lach"* are on the verge of *"Me'si'rut Ha'Nefesh"* (sacrificing the soul) by one who speaks and pleads to God!

—*Cantor Naftali Herstik*

Score

לכו נרננה

L'chu Ne'rane'na

Leib Glantz
Arr: Raymond Goldstein

Moderato

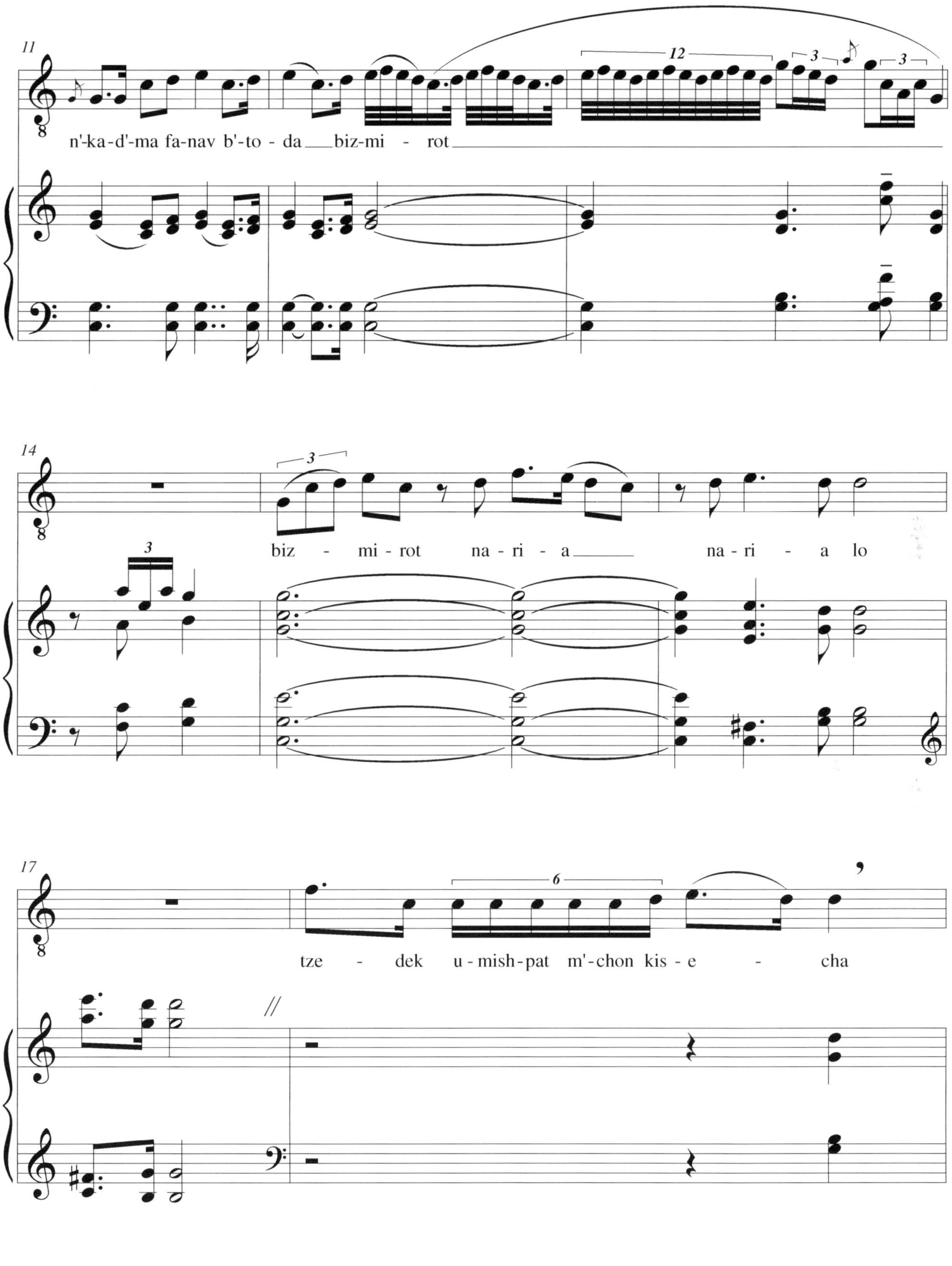
11
n'-ka-d'-ma fa-nav b'-to - da biz-mi - rot
14
biz - mi-rot na-ri - a na-ri - a lo
17
tze - dek u-mish-pat m'-chon kis - e - cha

19
che - sed ve - e - met y' - kad - mu y' - kad-mu fa - ne - cha
20
y' - ka - d'-mu fa - ne - cha
22
a - sher b'-ya-do ne-fesh kol chai v' - ru - ach v'-
fp

26
ru-ach kol b'-sar v'-ru-ach kol b' - sar b'-sar ish
29
religioso
f colla parte
ha-n' - sha-ma n'-sha-ma lach v'-ha - guf v'-ha-guf po - o-lach
32
tr
ha - n' - sha - ma ha-n'-sha - - - ma

35
lach v'-ha-guf v'-ha - guf v'-ha-
39
guf po-o-lach chu-sa chu-sa
mp
43
chu - sa chu-sa chu-sa chu-sa

46
al al a - ma - lach ha-n' - sha - ma lach v'-ha -
mf
48
guf v' - ha -
50
guf v'-ha-guf she-

52
lach
A - do - shem a - se l' -
54
ma-an, l'-ma-an, a - se l'-ma'an, l'-ma-an sh'-me-cha
57
a - ta-nu al shim-cha A - do-shem a - se
7

58
l' - ma - an sh' - me - cha
ba - a - vur k' - vod
3
mp
60
shim - cha
v' - sa - lach - ta la - a - vo - ne - nu v' - sa -
f
62
lach - ta la-a - vo - ne - nu ki rav hu

Leib Glantz singing at a wedding in Tel Aviv, 1955

24. *Machnisei Rachamim*

THE ARRANGEMENT FOR THIS COMPOSITION WAS COMMISSIONED BY
HAZZAN ABRAHAM LUBIN
IN MEMORY OF HIS BROTHERS DAVID AND SHLOMO, *ALEIHEM HA'SHALOM.*

About *Machnisei Rachamim*:

During his Israeli period (1954-1964), Leib Glantz finally found himself in his element – in an environment in which he particularly felt comfortable and where he could perform optimally. In Tel Aviv there existed a compassionate appreciation: From Glantz to his listeners and from them towards him.

The spoken language in the street was Hebrew and the whole congregation comprehended the language of the prayers.

As not only a cantor, but also as a Zionist leader, his ideological partners who served with him in his Zionist journey were now close by. His audiences were packed with sophisticated public figures and important secular musicians. He finally felt unrestricted to compose music that expressed his desire to talk directly to the Almighty (and in this particular case, to the angels as well).

Knowing that his listeners understood the language, he allowed himself to literally cry out, expressing this through extreme musical intervals and sudden dynamic changes, he created a true drama while praying on the synagogue pulpit.

It was not an easy task to harmonically bring about all the above-mentioned effects without deviating from Glantz's unique path and his original intentions. However, the resulting arrangement speaks for itself.

—*Cantor Naftali Herstik*

Score

מכניסי רחמים

Machnisei Rachamim

Leib Glantz
Arr: Raymond Goldstein

7
mim
mash-mi-ei t'-fi - la hash-mi-u t'-fi-la-
9
tei-nu lif-nei sho-me-a lif-nei sho - me-a lif-nei sho - me-a sho-me - a t'-fi-
mp
fp
Ped.
12
- la mash-mi-ei tz'-a - ka mash-mi-ei tz'-a - ka
mf
sf

15
hash-mi-u tza-a-ka-te-nu hash-mi-u tsa-a-ka-te-nu lif-nei lif-nei
17
sho-me-a - sho - me-a sho-me-a tz'-a-ka
20
mach-ni-sei dim - a mach-ni-sei dim-a

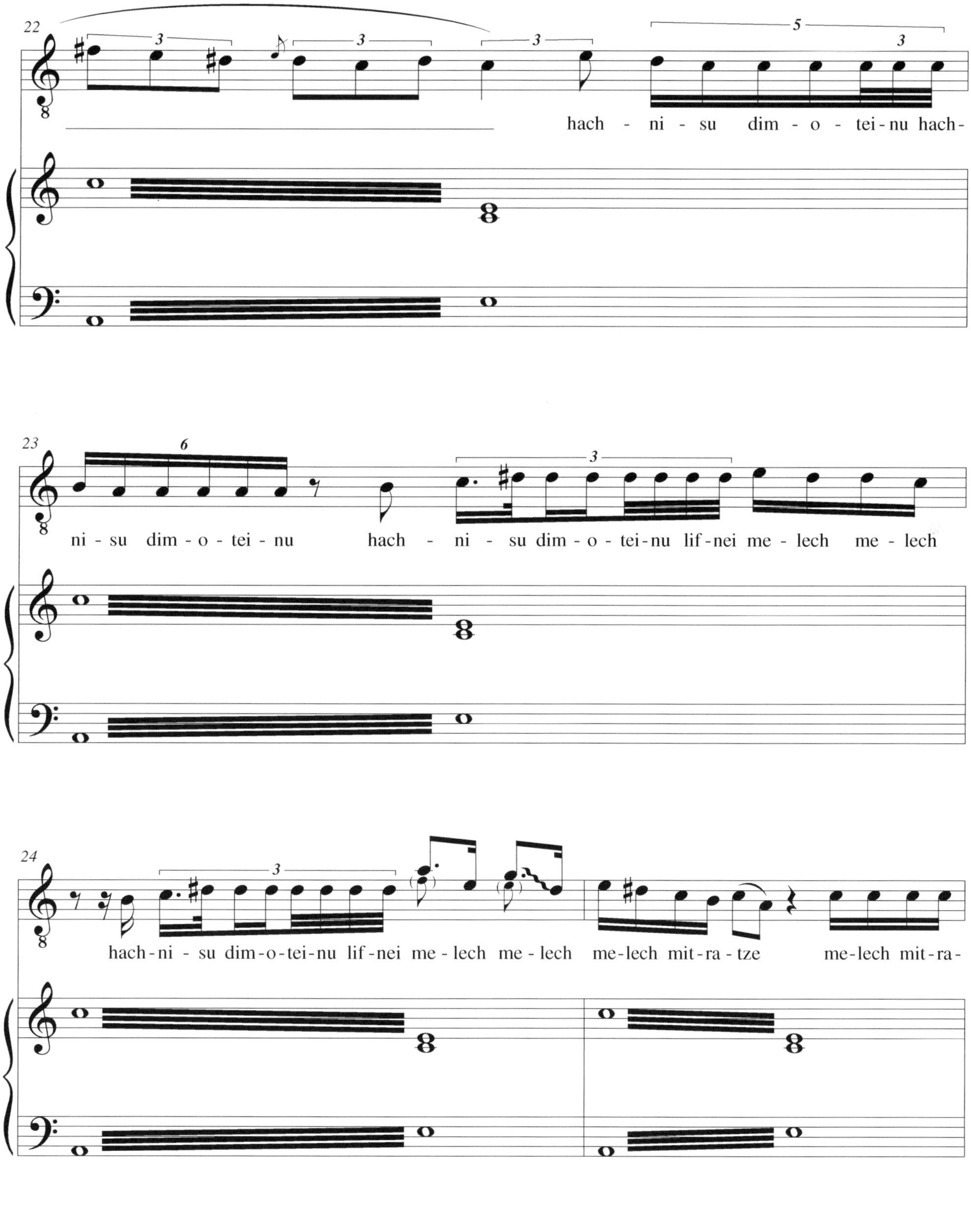
22
hach - ni - su dim - o - tei - nu hach-
23
ni - su dim - o - tei - nu hach - ni - su dim - o - tei - nu lif - nei me - lech me - lech
24
hach - ni - su dim - o - tei - nu lif - nei me - lech me - lech me - lech mit - ra - tze me - lech mit - ra-

26
tze bid-ma-ot hish-tad - lu v'-har-bu t'-chi-na u-va-ka-sha lif-nei
p
29
me-lech me-lech me-lech hish-tad - lu v'-har-bu t'-chi-na u-va-ka-sha lif-nei
31
me-lech El ram v'-ni-sa haz-ki-ru l'-fa - nav hash-mi-u l'-fa-
mf
f
Ped.
Ped.

34
nav to - ra u-ma-a-sim to-vim shel sho-ch' - nei a-far to-
mf
37
ra u-ma-a-sim to-vim shel sho-ch' - nei a-far mach-ni-sei
40
ra-cha-mim mach-ni-sei ra-cha-mim hish-tad - lu v'-har-bu t'-chi-na u-va-ka-sha lif-nei
mp

42
me - lech me - lech hish-tad - lu v'-har-bu t'-chi-na u-va-ka-sha lif-nei
3
44
me-lech me-lech me-lech El ram v'-ni-sa hazki-ru l'-fa-
mf
47
nav hash-mi-u l'-fa - nav to - ra u-ma-a-sim to-vim
6

50
shel sho-ch'-nei a-far
yiz-kor a-ha-va-
52
tam vi-cha-yei zar-am
she-lo she-lo to-vad
mp
54
she-lo to-vad she-e-rit Ya-a-kov
fp

56
ki tzon ro - e ne - e - man ha - ya l'- cher - pa Yis - ra - el goy e - chad l'- ma -
58
shal v' - li - sh' - ni - na ma -
p
60
her ma - her ma - her ma - her ma - her ma - her ma - her a - ne - nu a - ne - nu
mp

63
E-lo-hei yish - e-nu u-f'-de-nu mi-kol g'-ze-
mf
66
- rot g'-ze-rot ka-shot ka - shot u-f'-
68
de-nu mi-kol g'-ze-rot ka - shot v'-ho-shi-a b'-ra-cha - me-cha v'-ho-shi-a b'-ra-cha-
f

71
me - cha b'-ra-cha-me-cha ha-ra - bim m' - shi-ach tzid-ke-cha m'-
74
shi-ach tzid-ke-cha m' - shi-ach tzid-ke - cha v'-a - me - cha

25. *Ki Ke'shimcha*

THE ARRANGEMENT FOR THIS COMPOSITION WAS COMMISSIONED BY THE COUNCIL OF *HAZZANIM* OF GREATER MONTREAL IN HONOR OF THE MEMBERS OF THE COUNCIL.

About *Ki Ke'shimcha*:

Ki Ke'Shimcha was composed by a very young Cantor Glantz in the early 1920s and was recorded by RCA in 1930.

Already in this early recording we witness not only his cantorial genius and his musical innovativeness, but even more so – his sensitivity to every nuance implied by the prayer texts and his profound interpretation of the prayer's deeper meanings.

Glantz's unique approach toward God, one of supplication and penitence when opening with the words: *E'met Ki A'ta Hu Yotz'ram Ve'A'ta Yo'de'a Yitz'ram* ("It is true that You are their Creator and You know their inclination") – is exceptional in its gentleness. Yet at the same time it expresses how he, Glantz, as the advocate of the people before the Almighty, is fully convinced of the strength of his plea.

Just minutes before, we recited *U'Ne'ta'neh To'kef* and *Be'Rosh Ha'Sha'na Yi'ka'tei'vun Uv'Yom Tzom Ki'ppur Yay'cha'tei'mun.* We shudder as we face the Day of Judgment, gripped with fear as we stand before the One who judges, proves, knows and bears witness; who records and inscribes every one of our secret thoughts and acts. This is followed by, as described by the poet of *Ki Ke'Shimcha*, a defense of human beings who are but flesh and blood, motivated mainly by instincts and impulses.

Through his soulful plea to the Creator, the young Glantz illustrates these contradictions one in opposition to the other. He utilizes his exceptional ability to speak, tell a story, debate and appraise – confronting God – using *Chassidic* fervor, both in fearfulness and in reverence, as he presents his case on behalf of his fellow "defendants" in a manner that would be difficult to undermine.

His musical approach manifests itself in a variety of colors, using at his disposal every option embodied within the musical scale, unconventional intervals, and an infinitely dynamic interpretation, which leaves the congregation breathless.

In addition, in this composition Glantz employs his secret of utilizing the Relative Major within passages written in the minor. This is in order to create a release of tension, after which he re-engages the listener by developing it anew. As the years passed, Glantz utilized this even more frequently, always timing it to perfection, as the master musician that he was.

He follows this with a measure of philosophic introspection concerning "man whose origin is dust and whose end is dust." However, Glantz exhibits "second thoughts," as he modulates to *Freygish* to bolster his "legal" argument in defense of man, which "at risk of his life he earns his bread, he is likened to a broken shard." He then illustrates this by offering musical descriptions to images like "a dissipating cloud, a blowing wind, flying dust, and a fleeting dream."

What kind of dream is the prayer talking about? Is it a nightmare in which the soul departs from the dead body or is it a dream of redemption where repentance, prayer and righteousness avert the severe decree – a victory for the defense against the allegations by *Ha'Mas'tin Ha'Ga'dol* – the great Accuser?

I am confident that in the heavens above, God and His angelic entourage convene in full force to listen to this awe-inspiring prayer, and to savor the beautiful renditions conveyed by this brilliant artist of the synagogue.
—Cantor Naftali Herstik

Score

כי כשמך

Ki Ke'shimcha

Leib Glantz

Arr: Raymond Goldstein

Moderato

12
hem ba - sar ba - sar ba-
15
sar va-dam v'-a-ta yo - de - a v'-a-
17
ta yo-de-a yitz-ram ki

19
hem ki hem hem ba - sar va - dam a -
23
dam a-dam y'-so-do me-a - far v'-so-fo v'-so - fo v'-so-
pp
p
26
fo le - a - far a - dam a - dam a -

29
dam a -
mf
31
dam a - dam a - dam y'-so -
3
34
do me - a - far v'-so - fo v'-so - fo v'-so-fo v'-so-

38
fo v'-so - fo le - a - far v'-so-
3
3
4
42
fo le-a - far v' - so - fo
45
le-a - far v' - so - fo le - a -
5
4

47
far
b'-naf - sho ya-vi lach-mo
ma-
mf
50
shul k'-che-res ha-nish - bar k'-cha-tzir ya-vesh
k'-cha-
54
tzir ya - vesh
u-ch'-tzitz no - vel k'-tzel o-ver
u-ch'-a-

nan uch'-a-nan uch'-a-nan ka-
la uch'-ru-ach uch'-ru - ach no - sha - vet uch'-a-
vak po-re - ach v'-cha-cha-lom v'-cha-cha-

65
lom v'-cha-cha - lom
69
v'-cha-cha - lom
ya -
72
rit.
- uf
rit.

Leib Glantz

26. *Haloch Ve'karata*

THE ARRANGEMENT FOR THIS COMPOSITION WAS COMMISSIONED BY PROFESSOR ALAN L. AND NAOMI BERGER IN HONOR OF THEIR GRANDCHILDREN ELIANA ROSE AND JACKSON EZRA BERGER.

About *Haloch Ve'karata*:

This is one of Leib Glantz's compositions in which he is speaking *to* God, but doing so by quoting God's own words as transcribed by the prophets. In the context of the High Holidays he is reminding the worshippers that God has promised to have mercy on the Jewish people and establish an everlasting Covenant.

Glantz's vocal line reflects this hopeful theme. In much of the piece he is telling the story of how God fondly remembers aspects of His early relationship with His chosen people. In Glantz's recording of the composition he *tells* this using a soft, sweet, ethereal voice that evokes the Biblical scenes as though seen through the mysterious mists of time.

In the passage in which God expresses strong emotion Glantz suddenly and dramatically goes full double *forte.* Glantz was not one to musically or vocally smooth over and homogenize differences in meaning and mood. He brought out the contrasts very effectively, and he did all of this within the framework of the traditional *Nu'sach* appropriate for this section of the *Mu'saf* prayer service.

Toward the end, the vocal line becomes very *Chazzanic,* but interestingly he combines some phrases that utilize very complex and rapid *coloratura* which are unusually conventional (for Glantz), with some phrases that utilize some of his characteristic expressive lyrical leaps to unconventional intervals.

—*Cantor Ralph Schlossberg*

Score

הלוך וקראת

Haloch Ve'karata

Leib Glantz
Arr: Raymond Goldstein

Dedicated to the First Prime-Minister of Israel, David Ben Gurion.

le-mor le - mor ha -
loch v'-ka-ra - ta v'-oz - nei Y'-ru-sha-la-yim le - mor
ko

16
a -
f
17
mar a - mar a -
18
Lento
mar A-do-nai za - char - ti lach che - sed n'-u-
pp
misterioso

21
ra - yich a-ha - vat a-ha-
sostenuto
24
vat k'-lu - lo-ta - yich
9
9
5
p
26
a tempo
mp legato

32
38
lech - tech a - cha - rai ba - mid -
43
bar ba - mid - bar be - e - retz

sostenuto
48
lo,
lo,
lo,
pp
51
lo
lo
z'-ru-a
mf
v'-ne-e-
pp
53
mar
v'-za-
pp
mf
molto rall...

Largo
misterioso
sostenuto
char - ti a - ni, a - ni, a - ni, a - ni et b'-ri - ti o -
pp
tach bi - mei n' - u - ra - yich va - ha - ki -
mp
fz
a tempo
accel.
animato
mo - ti lach b'rit b'-rit
f

66
o-
mf
69
lam
v' - ne - e - mar
71
In 8
misterioso
In 4
v' - ne - e - mar
v' - ne-e-mar
ha-

73
ven, ha - ven ha - ven ya - kir li
pp
75
li Ef - ra - yim
fz
tr
f
sfz
misterioso
sostenuto
77
im im
pp

78
ye - led
80
ye - - - led sha-a - shu - im
ppp
Ped.
83
mp

85
a tempo
mp
sostenuto
89
Ped.
Ped.
93
ki mi - dei da - b'ri
mp
sostenuto

97
bo
bo
Ped.
Ped.
101
105
Ped.
Ped.

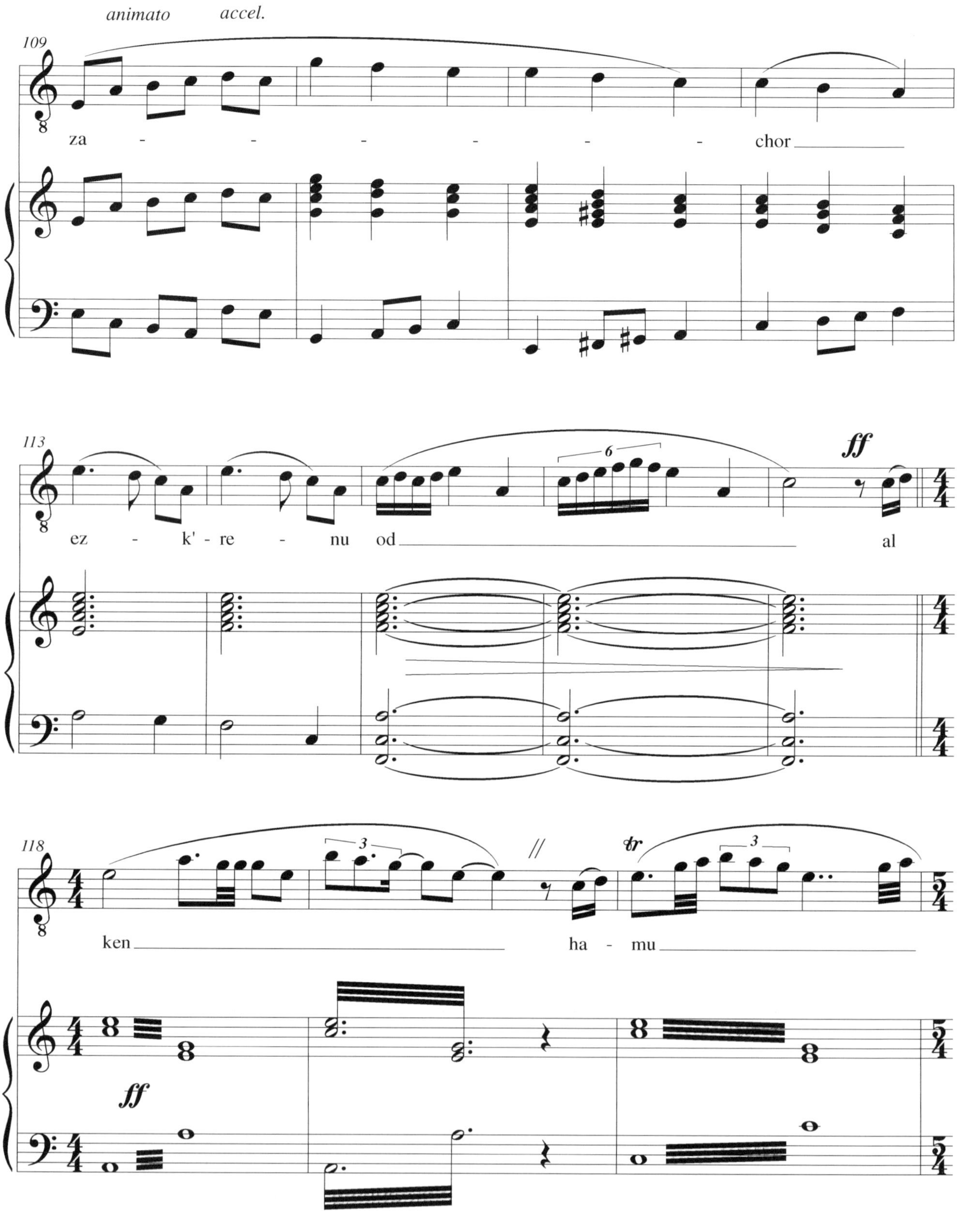
animato
accel.
za - - - - - chor
ez - k're - nu od
ff
al
ken
ha - mu
tr
ff

121
subito p
ha-mu
me - ai
123
me - ai
lo
al
mp
126
ken
ha -
mp

128
tr
6
mu
me-
130
3
ai
lo
ra - chem
ra-
Lento leggiero misterioso
mp
pp
133
chem
a - ra - cha - me - nu

135
ff
n' - um
agitato
cantabile
137
n'-
ff
cantabile
138
um
n'um
A-do - nai

Leib Glantz, Blessing of the wine
in Israel, 1960

27. *Ki Hi'neh Ka'chomer*

THE ARRANGEMENT FOR THIS COMPOSITION WAS COMMISSIONED BY
CANTOR PENNY S. MYERS
WITH DEEP ADMIRATION FOR HER DEAR FRIEND AND MENTOR –
BENJAMIN MAISSNER.

About *Ki Hi'neh Ka'chomer*:

The great Cantor David Roitman defined Leib Glantz as 'the poet of the pulpit.'

In this composition, Glantz exhibits his unique lyrical powers, as he interprets the text as if it were a musical painting.

The harmonic portrayal within the movements of the musical scale amazes the listener in its beauty and reminds us of the Expressionism of the composers Claude Debussy and Maurice Ravel.

In addition, this composition is characterized by the intentional lack of resolution between the different sections that creates a continuity and uniformity.

Glantz reveals the dialogue between the power and greatness of the Almighty as compared to the insignificance of mankind, who capitulates to his impulses and then begs God to remember the Covenant and show His mercy.

On a personal note, I first heard Glantz singing this composition on the radio in Montreal, Canada, in 1963, when I was sixteen years old. It was on the eve of *Yom Kippur.* Hearing Glantz sing this totally mesmerized me and I couldn't get it out of my mind throughout the holy Day of Atonement. Till this day, more than fifty years later – that memory still makes me shudder!

—*Cantor Naftali Herstik*

Score

כי הנה כחומר

Ki Hi'neh Ka'chomer

Leib Glantz

Arr: Raymond Goldstein

11
f
tzo - to m'-ka - tzer___ ken
14
rit.
___ a-nach-nu ken___ a-nach-nu a-nach-nu a-nach-nu b'-yad - cha ken
15
___ a - nach - nu a - nach - nu a -

rit.
16
nach-nu b'-ya-d'-cha
18
che-sed no-tzer che-sed no-tzer che - sed no - - - tzer
20
la-b'-rit ha - bet la-b'-rit ha-bet ha-bet v'-al te - fen v'-
f

rit. Larghetto misterioso
23
al v'-al v'-al te-fen la - ye - tzer
25
ki hi-ne cha-e-ven b'-yad ham - sa-tet ki
27
hi-ne cha-e-ven b'-yad b'- yad ham-sa-tet

29
ki hi-ne cha-e - ven b'-yad b' -
30
yad ham-sa-tet bir - tzo - - - - to
mf
32
o - - - - - - chez u-vir-

rit.
34
tzo - to m' - cha - - - tet
36
ken a-nach-nu b'-yad-cha ken
38
ken a - nach-nu b'-yad-cha m'-cha - ye u - m'-mo - tet

39
ken a-nach-nu b'-yad-cha m'-cha-ye oh u - m'-mo-tet oy
41
ken a-nach-nu b'-yad-cha m'-cha - ye a-
f
43
nach-nu b'-yad-cha m'-cha-ye u-m'-mo-tet u-m'-

44
mo - - - - - tet
Ped.
46
la-b'-rit ha-bet la-b'-rit ha-bet ha-bet v'-al te-fen v'-
49
tr
al v'-al v'-al te - fen v' - al v' - al v'-
mp

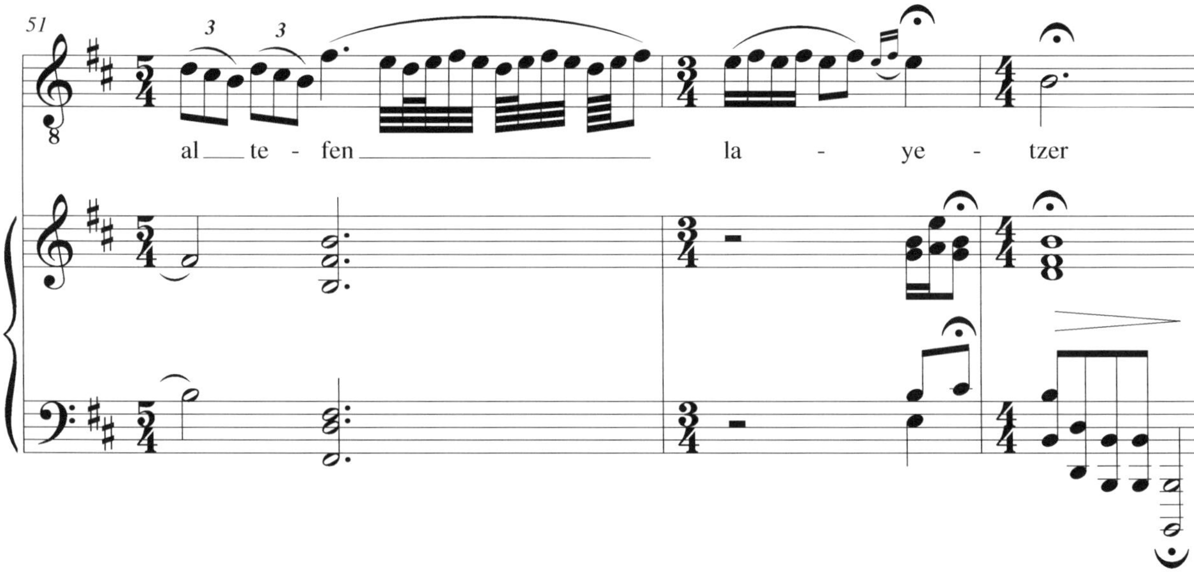
51
al — te - fen — la - ye - tzer

28. *Ezkera Elokim*

THE ARRANGEMENT FOR THIS COMPOSITION WAS COMMISSIONED BY
CANTOR GIDEON ZELERMYER OF CONGREGATION SHAAR HASHOMAYIM,
WESTMOUNT, CANADA,
IN MEMORY OF CANTOR SOLOMON GISSER Z"L.

About *Ezkera Elokim*:

Leib Glantz had the unique talent to turn the simplest rendering of the *Nu'sach* prayer mode into a moving and heartwarming piece of art. And yet, with all his artistry, Glantz never deserted his traditional role at the pulpit as a *Ba'al T'filah* (prayer leader) even for a moment.

When he reaches the part of *Ye'hi Ra'tzon,* he seems to be speaking directly to God. It begins with a whisper into God's ear – a God that listens to His people's sobbing. In his Chasidic way of interpretation (to be found in many of his compositions), Glantz interprets the words *Sho'me'a, Sho'me'a Kol, Sho'me'a Kol Bich'yot,* pairing them in various combinations in a most fascinating manner of expression.

This prayer, being part of the focal *Se'li'cha* in the *Ne'i'lah* service, requires of the cantor the ability to lead the congregation into an exalting and optimistic ending to the Day of Atonement, amidst the anguish and eulogizing of the ill fate of Zion. Glantz poignantly expresses the full rainbow of these feelings in this rendition. Therefore, you have to carefully follow the composer's lead in this maze of thoughts and contemplation.

—*Cantor Naftali Herstik*

Score

אזכרה אלוקים

Ezkera Elokim

Leib Glantz
Arr: Jack Baras

Originally composed in Los Angeles in 1940.

10
ten.
pe-let ad sh'-ol ad sh'-ol tach-ti-ya u-v'-
13
chol zot a-nu l'-Ya v'-ei-nei - - nu v'-ei-
8vb
17
nei-nu l'-Ya mi-dat ha-ra-cha-

21
mim mi-dat ha-ra-cha - mim a - lei-nu hit-gal-g'-li hit-gal-g'-li hit-
25
gal - g'-li a - lei - nu hit-gal - g' - li v'-
28
lif - nei ko - nech t'chi-na - te - nu t'-chi-na - te - nu ha - pi -

31
li
uv-ad a-mech ra-cha - mim sha-a-li uv-ad a-
34
mech ra-cha - mim sha-a-li ki chol le-vav da - vai
38
ki chol le-vav da - vai

41
ki chol le - vav
45
6
3
3
3
da-vai
v'-chol rosh
la-cho - li
49
3
y' - hi
ra-

52
tzon mi-l'-fa-ne-cha sho-me - a y'-hi ra-
55
tzon mi-l'-fa-ne-cha sho-me - a kol y'-
58
hi ra-tzon mi-l'-fa-ne-cha sho - me - a kol kol bich-

60
yot
she-ta-
p
63
sim
dim-o-tei-nu
dim - o-tei-nu dim - o-tei-nu
b'-no-d'-
65
cha
b' - no-d'-cha li-yot

67
she-ta - sim dim-o-tei-nu dim-o-tei-nu dim-o - tei-nu b'-no-d'-
70
cha li-h'-yot v'-ta-tzi - le - nu mi-kol g'-ze-
6
73
rot ka-shot ka-shot ach-za-ri - ot v'-ta -

76
tzi - le - nu mi - kol g'ze -
78
3 3 3 3
rot ach - za - ri - ot
80
ki l' - cha l' - vad ki l' - cha l' -

83
vad ki l' - cha l'-
7
85
vad ei - nei-nu t'-lu-yot El me-lech yo-shev
3
f
88
al ki-se ra - cha - mim
3
8vb

Leib Glantz after a concert at the Tel Aviv Mann Auditorium (*Heichal Ha'Tarbut*), 1957

29. *Sheva P'amim Ata*

THE ARRANGEMENT FOR THIS COMPOSITION WAS COMMISSIONED BY
HAZZAN BENY MAISSNER
IN MEMORY OF HIS PARENTS REGINA AND YITZCHAK MAISSNER,
AND SISTER NAOMI LEHRER Z"L.

About *Sheva P'amim Ata*:

Long before Leib Glantz presented his amazing series of lectures on *Chazzanut* on Israeli radio in the 1960s, he gallantly challenged the trend that had developed in the world of cantorial music, which emphasized trying to satisfy the musical taste of the masses instead of presenting "true" *Chazzanut.* This trend unfortunately led to ignorance about the principles of *Nu'sach,* the ancient Jewish prayer modes.

This composition, which was first presented by Glantz in a concert in New York in 1930, was intended to offer a sophisticated shift between several prayer modes, all connected by the word *"A'ta"* (Thou).

Perhaps Glantz wanted to seize the opportunity to offer a "cantorial medley" as opposed to the Yiddish medleys that characterized the Jewish concerts of that period.

In addition, Glantz might have been interested in offering the masses an educational lesson, in an effort to raise their awareness about the synagogue customs and Jewish life, similar to the Yiddish songs composed for the Yiddish Theatre by the likes of S. Secunda and A. Singer.

—Cantor Naftali Herstik

Score

שבע פעמים אתה

Sheva P'amim Ata

Leib Glantz
Arr: Raymond Goldstein

7
ber i - mam
i - mam
9
min ha - sha - ma - yim nish - ma - tam ko - le - cha v'- nig - lei - ta a - lei - hem b'- ar - p'- lei to -
11
har
gam kol ha - o - lam ku - lo chal mi - pi -
subito p

13
- - - cha uv'-ri-yot b'-re-shit__ char-du__ mi-me-ka__
15
rall.
char-du mi-me-ka a-ta, a-ta, a-ta__ a-ta__ nig - lei - ta.
f
Ata Ritzatzta
18
A-ta__ ri-tzatz-ta ra-shei liv-ya-tan tit - ne-hu ma-a-chal l'-am l'-tzi-yim v'-yo-
mp

20
rit.
rit.
3
du sha-ma - yim pil-a - cha A-do-shem
23
ten.
af e-mu-nat-cha af e-mu-nat-cha bi - k'-hal
26
rit.
k' - do - shim

29
a - sher b'-ya-do ne-fesh kol chai
fp
32
a - sher b'-ya-do ne - fesh, ne - fesh kol chai v'-
f
34
ten.
ru - ach
v'- ru - ach
mf

37
ten.
ten.
ten.
rit.
v' - ru - ach kol b'-sar b'-sar ish
rit.
40
han' - sha-ma, ha-n' - sha-ma lach v'-ha-guf
43
po-o-lach ha-n'-sha-ma, han-sha-ma

46
lach v'-ha - guf v'-ha - guf v'-ha-
49
guf po - o - lach chu - sa, chu -
52
- sa, chu - - - sa,

55
ten.
3
chu - sa, chu - sa
al, al, al a - ma - lach
58
ha - n'-sha - ma, han'-sha - ma lach v' - ha-
f
61
guf
v' - ha-

guf
v' - ha - guf she - lach
a -
ta - nu al shim - cha A - do - shem
a - se l'ma-an sh' - me - cha. A -

Ata Yatzarta

Ata Kadosh
77
ta ka-dosh v'-shim-cha ka-dosh uk-do-shim b'-chol yom y'-ha-l'-lu-cha se-la ki
a tempo
p
79
El me-lech ga-dol v'-ka-dosh a-ta Ba-ruch a-ta A-do-shem
81
ha-El

Ata Zocher

שבע פעמים אתה

91
mon nis-ta-rot
nis-ta - rot
nis-ta-
93
rot
she-mi-b'-re-shit
va-a-ke-
95
dat Yitz-chak l'-zar-o ha-yom, ha - yom,
ha - yom, ha-yom, ha-yom
mp

97
b'-ra-cha-mim, b'-ra-cha - mim tiz - kor
99
Ba - ruch a - ta A-do-shem zo-
mf
102
cher zo-
subito p

104
cher zo - cher zo-cher
Ata Echad
106
ha - brit. A - ta e-chad v'-shim-cha e-chad u-
mf
108
parlando
mi k'-am-cha Yis-ra-el goy e-chad ba - a-retz v'-ya-
mf

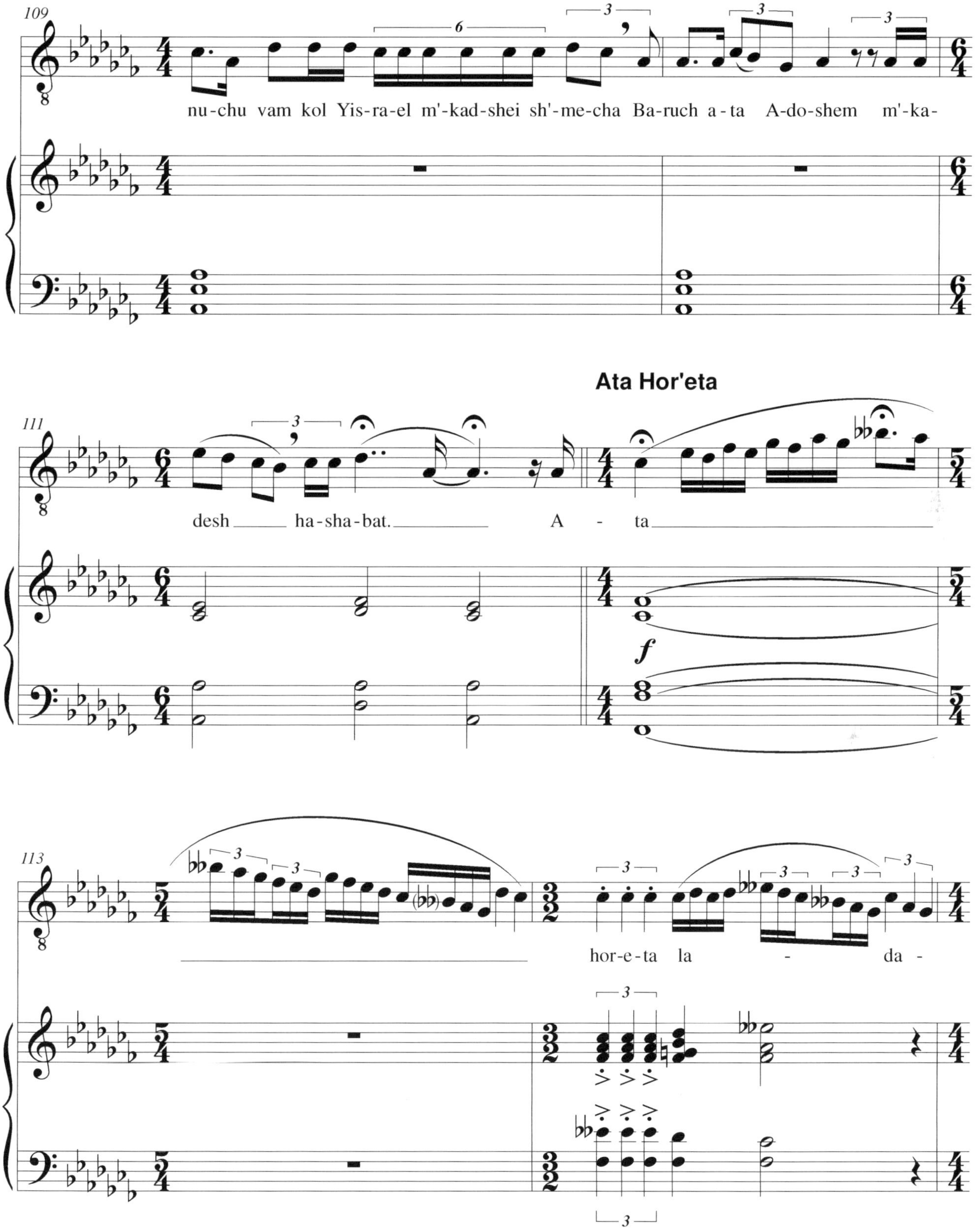
109
nu-chu vam kol Yis-ra-el m'-kad-shei sh'-me-cha Ba-ruch a-ta A-do-shem m'-ka-
Ata Hor'eta
111
desh ha-sha-bat. A - ta
113
hor-e-ta la - da-

115
at ki A - do - shem hu
117
ha - E - lo - him ein od ein
119
od ein od ein od
mp

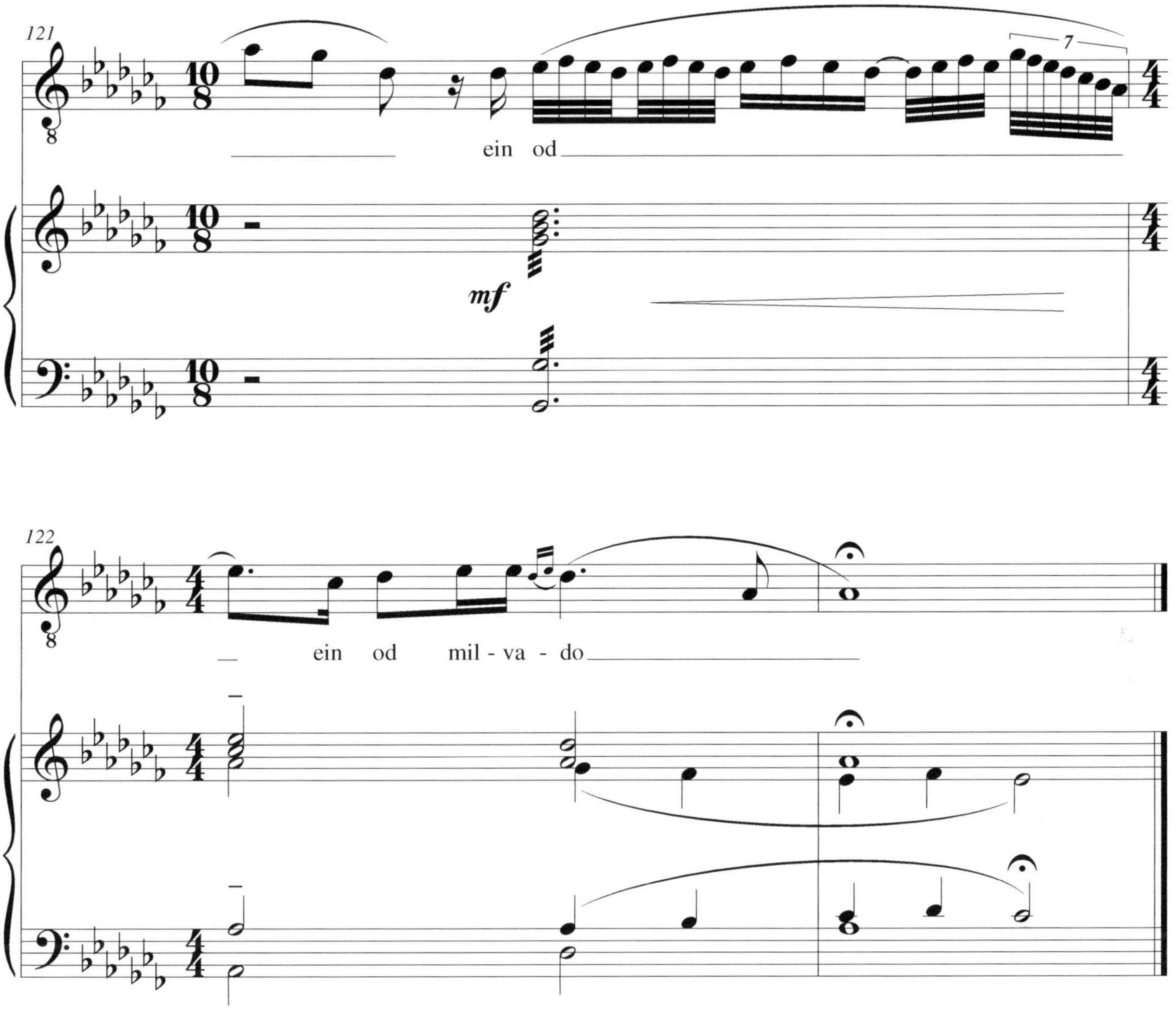
121
ein od
mf
122
ein od mil - va - do

Leib Glantz working on a composition on his piano at home in Tel Aviv, Israel, 1958

30. *El Maleh Rachamim (Shoah)*

THE ARRANGEMENT FOR THIS COMPOSITION WAS COMMISSIONED BY
HARLAN I. COHEN
IN MEMORY OF HIS PARENTS SAMUEL AND EDYTHE B. COHEN Z"L.

About *El Maleh Rachamim (Shoah)*:

Upon looking at the text as well as the musical character of this composition, it is obvious that it was written during the early years of the State of Israel, at a time when *"Mapai"* – the "Workers' Party of the Land of Israel" was the dominant political power of the country.

This specific prayer text carefully avoids mentioning "Germany" in the context of the Holocaust. This unjustifiable logic, which is employed to this very day, exemplifies Leib Glantz's effort to refrain from jeopardizing Prime Minister David Ben Gurion's endeavor to bring about a Reparations Agreement* between Israel and West Germany.

Ben Gurion was accused by certain segments of the Israeli population of behaving in a shameful manner, betraying the memory of the victims of the Holocaust in exchange for financial assistance. He defended his policy arguing that achieving the agreement was the only way to sustain the nation's failing economy and strengthening Israel's military power in the face of the Arab threat.

Glantz, who was close to Ben Gurion and to the *"Mapai"* party leadership, wisely formulated a Holocaust prayer text that satisfied the "diplomatic" requirements of the State of Israel and at the same time expressed his own flow of emotions and deep anguish in regard to the atrocious extermination of the Jews by the Nazis.

I am positive that Glantz himself composed and edited the text of this composition in addition to the musical score. During the many years that I officiated as chief cantor, I wrote texts and prayers for several national holidays and they were always approved by the religious and legal authorities.

In regard to the music, which is typically "Glantz style," it is based on the simple *Nu'sach* that is fluent among our people. It is this *Nu'sach* that warms the hearts of our people and guides their emotions to imagine the wailing of the slaughtered martyrs. This gives some consolation to the tormented souls of a people captivated in this awful dispute (regarding the reparations agreement) that is still extremely painful.

I believe it is justifiable to adjust the text properly for each event where this prayer is conducted.

—*Cantor Naftali Herstik*

* The Reparations Agreement between Israel and West Germany (*Hes'kem Ha'Shi'llu'mim*) was signed on September 10, 1952, and entered in force on March 27, 1953. According to the Agreement, West Germany was to pay Israel for the slave labor and persecution of Jews during the Holocaust, and to compensate for Jewish property that was stolen by the Nazis.

Score

אל מלא רחמים - לקדושי השואה

El Male Rachamim - for Marytrs of the Shoah

Leib Glantz

Arr: Raymond Goldstein

b'-ma-a - lot k'-do - shim k'-do - shim u-t'-ho - rim k'-
zo - har ha-ra - ki - a m'-i - rim u-maz-hi-
rim l'-nish - mot ha-k'-do-
mf
fp

20
3
shim v'-ha-t'-ho-rim she-ne-her-gu v'-nish-cha-tu she-nech-n'-
22
5
ku v'-she-nit-b'-u she-nis-r'-fu v'-she-nik-b'-ru cha-yim b'-
24
3
chol ar-tzot Ei-ro-pa bi-dei r'-sha - im v'-a-ri-tzim she-naf-lu cha-lal al ki-
mf

26
dush ha-shem ba - a - vur she-kol am Yis-ra-el ba-m'-di-
29
na u - va - go - la mit - ya - cha - dim im zich-ram ha - ka - dosh u-mit-pa-l'-
sotto voce
31
- lim l'-i-lu-i nish-mo-tei-hem ha-za-kot b'-gan e - den t'-he m'-nu-cha-tam

33
la - chen
f
Ped.
35
ba-al ha - ra - cha - mim yas - ti - rem b'-se-ter k'-na-fav l' - o - la -
36
mim v'-yitz-ror bitz - ror ha - cha - yim et nish - mo - tei -

38
hem
A - do - nai
40
hu na-cha-la-tam v'-ya-nu-chu b' - sha-lom al mish-k'-vo-tam yin-
43
kom E-lo-him et nik-mat da-mam ha-sha - fuch v'-no - mar a - men

Leib Glantz at the Cantors Academy of the Tel Aviv Institute for Jewish Liturgical Music, which he founded in 1959

31. *Maoz Tzur*

THE ARRANGEMENT FOR THIS COMPOSITION WAS COMMISSIONED BY
CANTOR ROSLYN BARAK OF CONGREGATION EMANU-EL, SAN FRANCISCO, CA,
IN MEMORY OF ZELIG AND LEAH YANOWER Z"L.

About *Maoz Tzur*:

The *Channuka* holiday annually reminds us that for centuries the Jewish people lived as minorities among other nations, and had to struggle constantly in order to avoid integrating the customs and culture of those among whom they lived.

Among the Jewish people were those who sought to assimilate. There was also what might be described as *unintentional* assimilation.

In our music this assimilation actually occurred. Current "Israeli" songs that are sung in Hebrew are frequently just imitations of Cossack, Gypsy and Wallachian melodies. In our concert halls and on the radio we hear melodies "borrowed" from Russia, Romania and Hungary as well as American Jazz and Arabian Debka melodies.

This in itself is not necessarily a bad thing as long as it does not affect our cantorial tradition, which represents an original cultural treasure of the Jewish people. Lately, we find ourselves praying in the synagogue or listening to cantorial music on the radio, as if we are listening to an aria from an opera.

One of the most popular Jewish holiday melodies, a tune sung throughout the Jewish world, is *"Ma'oz Tzur,"* (O mighty rock of my salvation, to praise Thee is a delight), which accompanies the blessings of the *Channuka* candles on the eight nights of the holiday. Shocking as it may sound, the origins of this traditional "Jewish" holiday song are three famous German melodies:

- A German Lutheran Choral hymn from the fifteenth century: an adaptation of an old German folk song *"So weiss ich eins, das mich erfreut, das pluemlein auff preiter heyde"*, also adapted by Martin Luther for the opening of his church chorale *"Nun freut euch, lieben Christen g'mein"* (Now rejoice, all you dear Christians, together).
- A German song from the sixteenth century: a popular German battle song, *"Benzenauer,"* which was originally sung in 1504.
- The cantionales from Magenza and other cantionales (fifteenth and sixteenth century). Especially Protestant chorales in Central Europe.

Can this really be our "national" *Channuka* song?

In order to correct this "sin" I have composed a melody for *Ma'oz Tzur* that is based on the original *Nu'sach* prayer mode of the traditional blessings of the *Channuka* candles. This *Nu'sach* has been a Jewish legacy for generations. The melodic composition of the music and its rhythm strictly adhere to the special spirit of the *Channuka Nu'sach* – free of foreign influence or imitation. Hopefully, this *Ma'oz Tzur* will capture the hearts of those who yearn for true authentic culture in Israel.

—*Cantor Leib Glantz* – translated from the Israeli daily newspaper *"Da'var,"* 1956.

Score

מעוז צור

Maoz Tzur

Leib Glantz
Arr: Raymond Goldstein

14
fi-la-ti v'-sham to-da n'-za-be - ach l'-et ta-chin mat-be - ach
19
mi - tzar ha - m'-na-be - ach az egmor b' -
22
rit.
shir miz - mor cha - nu-kat ha - miz - be - ach

Leib Glantz lighting the *Cha'nu'ka* candles in a Jerusalem concert, 1956

32. *Acharei Moti*

THE PRINTING OF THIS COMPOSITION AS ARRANGED BY RAYMOND GOLDSTEIN
WAS COMMISSIONED BY
THE GLIED FAMILY OF SUBOTICA, SERBIA
IN HONOR OF THE WEINER FAMILY OF SUBOTICA, SERBIA.

About *Acharei Moti*:

I first heard *A'cha'rei Mo'ti* on the radio in January 1964, soon after Leib Glantz's untimely passing was announced. The song left me with tears in my eyes. A month earlier I had attended a concert and lecture by Glantz in Montreal, Canada. This song was the truest eulogy for Glantz. The lyrics broke my heart, as it sounded like a man eulogizing *himself* – as if it was a prophesy becoming a reality! I truly believed that the composition was written only a few years earlier, even though Chaim Nachman Bialik, Israel's 'National Poet', wrote the poem in 1914.

Leib Glantz and Bialik developed a very warm friendship. Bialik famously complimented Glantz for his extremely fluent Hebrew and his mastery of Hebrew grammar and syntax. So, I was sure that Glantz composed *A'cha'rei Mo'ti* soon after Bialik passed away in 1934, saddened at the loss of a friend and one of the great cultural icons of his time.

I researched the historiography of this composition, only to discover that it was composed in Kishinev, Bessarabia in the early 1920s. This was very surprising. The very young Glantz, in his early twenties, was so deeply moved by Bialik's lyrics that he composed this song.

I would frequently find myself listening to the recording and find myself shedding tears when Glantz uttered the words *A'cha'rei Mo'ti Sif'du Ka'cha Li: Ha'ya Ish – U'Re'u: Ei'ne'nu Od. Ko'dem Zma'no Meit Ha'Ish Ha'Ze, Ve'Shi'rat Cha'yav Nif'se'ka. Ve'Tzar Me'od! Od Miz'mor E'chad Ha'yah Lo, Ve'Hi'nei A'vad Ha'Miz'mor La'Ad, A'vad La'Ad!* (After My death, say this eulogy for me: 'there was a man who died before his time, leaving his poetry, the song of his life, unfinished. And what a shame! He had one more song to sing, and now it's gone. That song is lost, lost forever').

What caused these youngsters to deal with the subject of death? It is difficult to gauge the depth of compassion and sensitivity that these giants shared – one with his poetry, the other with his music.

Bialik's tender and heartening eulogy together with Glantz's appropriate melancholic music is set to a sensitive arrangement by Raymond Goldstein in honor and in memory of these two great men.

—*Cantor Naftali Herstik*

Score

אחרי מותי

Acharei Moti

Leib Glantz
Arr: Raymond Goldstein
Words: Chaim Nachman Bialik

9
Ha - ya ish ur'-u
11
Ei - ne - nu, ei - ne - nu od
mf
13
poco rall.....
ko - dem z'ma - no met ha - ish ha - ze

15
a tempo
v'shi - rat cha - yav b'em - tza b' - em - tza
ten.
subito p
ten.
rit.
17
nif - s' - ka
rit.
a tempo
19
V'-tzar od miz - mor e - chad,
mp

21
od miz - mor - e - chad ha-ya lo
rit.
24
v'hi - ne a - vad ha - miz-mor la - ad a - vad
un poco rall.....
27
meno mosso
la - ad
pp

Leib Glantz

33. *Ashreinu*

The arrangement for this composition was commissioned by Eviatar Feldman in memory of his father and Leib Glantz's nephew – Yitzchak Feldman z"l.

About *Ashreinu*:

Ashreinu is an Israeli song in Chassidic style, influenced by the modern songs of the *Cha'lu'tzim* (Jewish pioneers in *E'retz Yis'ra'el*).

Leib Glantz was an active leader in the Labor Zionist *"He'Cha'lutz"* movement from a very young age.

Here he expresses the happiness of the pioneers: *Ash'rei'nu, Ma Tov Chel'kei'nu, U'Ma Na'im Go'ra'lei'nu, Ma Ya'fa Ye'ru'sha'tei'nu!* (How fortunate we are; how good is our situation; how pleasant our fortune; how beautiful our legacy).

—*Jerry Glantz*

Leib Glantz playfully paints with melody and rhythm with an understated imbued "happiness" that expresses how substantial is our lot in life, how pleasant is our good fortune and sings with unbridled pride how beautiful is our lineage and heritage. He uses his voice with great skill bringing to life the inherent meaning of the words like a highly trained ventriloquist makes a puppet appear that it is doing the talking...

—*Cantor Emanuel C. Perlman*

As a young cantor I encountered Leib Glantz's music and was instantly captivated by his artistic qualities. I discovered that Glantz not only composed liturgical music, but also *Chassidic* melodies and folk songs. These were art songs that fused Eastern and Western musical themes that I, as a Yemenite, grew up listening to in Jerusalem.

Like many of Glantz's songs, *Ashreinu* exhibits changing dynamics and momentum, with colors that merge musical sounds of East and West. Singing *Ashreinu* is a challenge that demands musical and vocal precision.

—*Cantor Avshalom Zfira*

Score

אשרינו

Ashreinu

Leib Glantz
Arr: Raymond Goldstein

Originally composed in Los Angeles in 1947.

13
1.
2.
ma ya-fa u-ma ya-fa y' - ru-sha-te-nu y' - ru-sha-te-nu ash-
16
re - nu ma tov ma tov chel-ke-nu u-ma ya-fa u-ma ya-fa y'-
mf
p
19
rit.
ru-sha-te - nu u - ma ya-fa u - ma ya-fa ya-fa u-
3
fp

rit.
Marziale in 2
ma u-ma u-ma ya-fa y' - ru-sha-te - nu ash - rei - nu ash - rei - nu ma
un poco marcato
mp
tov chel - ke - nu u - ma na-im u - ma na-im na - im go-ra - le - nu u-
col 8
rit.
ma ya - fa u - ma ya - fa y' - ru-sha - te - nu u - ma ya - fa u - ma ya - fa

38
ad lib.
y' - ru - sha - te - nu ash - rei - nu
come prima
mp
42
a tempo
ma tov chel-ke - nu u - ma na-im u - ma na-im u - ma u-ma u-ma na-im na-
p
47
allargando
Moderato
im go - ra - le - nu u - ma ya - fa u - ma ya - fa y' - ru-sha - te - nu
mf
Ped.

Leib Glantz lecturing on Jewish music in Montreal, Canada, November, 1963

34. *Be'shuv Ha'shem*

The arrangement for this composition was commissioned by Cantor Raphael M. A. Frieder, Great Neck, NY.

About *Be'shuv Ha'shem*:

This composition by Glantz represents a musical implementation of the exciting experience of the beginning of *the* redemption *(At'chal'ta De'Ge'u'lah)* and the realization of the vision of the prophets as sensed by the pioneering Jews in *Eretz Yisrael.* This redemption was achieved with the blood, sweat and tears of the generation of the Holocaust and the establishment of the State of Israel.

What could be more appropriate in a period "When the Lord will return the exiles of Zion, we will have been **like dreamers**" *(Be'Shuv Ado'shem Et Shi'vat Zion Ha'yi'nu Ke'Chol'mim)* than the 126th psalm of King David?

Glantz's unique composition offers a wide spectrum of interpretations from a *cantata* to a ballad, and from a liturgical poetic song to a victory march with a choral *finale,* reminding us of the music of George Handel and Felix Mendelssohn.

Typical of Glantz, he uses unusual and surprising intervals to create both tension and beauty. He also wisely tosses in majors within minor phrases, bringing *"Ri'na"* (joy) to *"Ha'Zor'im Be'Dim'ah"* (those who sow in tears): to all those who sacrificed their lives through redeeming the malaria infested land and fighting to establish an independent Jewish state.

This use of modal music was fashionable for Israeli composers as well, being introduced to them by the ingathering of the exiles from all corners of the world. However, Glantz surpassed them all.

I see here an attempt by Glantz to compose an anthem-like piece, which would enter the Jewish musical canon and be sung by the "assemblies of the myriads of the House of Israel" (*Mak'ha'lot Re'va'vot Beit Yis'ra'el)* as a thanksgiving hymn for the land and its fruits. The music is dance-like, creating the image of a processional to mark the bringing the first fruits and the proud waving of *"P'ri Ha'A'retz Le'Ga'on Ul'Tif'e'ret"* (the fruit of the earth — proud and splendrous).

Unlike many of Glantz's other works, however, the tonal range of the piece is quite limited. This is in order to assist the listener in imagining the people *themselves* singing as they return from exile to Zion.

Any sensitive ear will also notice the allusions to the melody of Israel's national anthem, *Ha'Tik'va.* Even earlier, Glantz offers musical hints to emphasize the redemption as we discern in the background a musical quote from the Song of Songs (2:9) – *Hi'neh Zeh, Hi'neh Zeh, O'med A'char Kot'lei'nu* – from David Nowakowsky's *"Kol Do'di,"* that proclaims the Redeemer gazing in at the windows, looking through the lattice.

Lastly, let us hope that the new harmonies composed by Raymond Goldstein for this arrangement will make it easier for this composition to be received and accepted by the whole Jewish community.

—Cantor Naftali Herstik

Score

בשוב ה' - מזמור קכ"ו

Be'shuv Ha'shem - Psalm 126

(in Oratorio Style)

Leib Glantz
Arr: Raymond Goldstein

8
3
yi - nu ha-yi - nu k' - cho - l'-mim b'-shuv A - do-nai
cresc.
mf
11
rit. dim.
3
et shi-vat Tzi-yon ha - yi - nu ha-yi - nu k'-cho - l'-mim
cresc.
f
14
a tempo animato grazioso rit.
az

animato grazioso
16
yi-ma-le s'-chok pi-nu ul-sho-ne-nu ri-na
a tempo
18
az yi-ma-le s'-chok pi-nu ul-sho-ne-nu ri-na az
3
a tempo agitato
20
yo-m'-ru yo-m'-ru va-go-yim hi-g'-dil A-do-nai

la - a - sot la - a - sot im e - le im e - le hi - g'-
dil A - do - nai la - a - sot i - ma - nu
ha - yi - nu ha - yi - nu s'- me - chim

Maestoso
28
shu-va A-do-nai
31
et sh'vi-te - nu ka - a - fi - kim ba - ne - gev
34
ka - a - fi - kim ba - ne - gev

a tempo
marcato
36
ha - zo - r'-im b' - di - m' - a b' - ri - na
39
p
yik - tzo - ru ha - loch ye - lech u -
p
41
va - cho no - se no - se
mf

43
rit.
me - shech ha - za - ra bo
dim.
a tempo
44
yo - vo v' - ri - na no -
mf animato grazioso
46
se no - se a - lu - mo - tav bo

[Piu Mosso - Allegro Moderato]
48
ya-vo bo ya-vo v'-ri - na no - se no-se a-lu-mo-tav a-
cresc.
51
lu - mo - tav a - lu - mo-
53
rit.
ff
tav bo ya - vo v'-ri-
rit.
ff
3

55
mf
grazioso
na no - se a -
espress.
57
lu - mo - tav a - lu - mo - tav
59
ff
animato e marcato
a - lu - mo - tav a - lu - mo - tav
ff
marcato

35. *Chassidic Medley*

The arrangement for this composition was commissioned by Cantor Azi Schwartz of Park Avenue Synagogue, New York.

About the *Chassidic Medley*:

In 1988, I had the privilege to perform as musical accompanist and arranger for an International Cantorial Concert devoted to the music of Leib Glantz. The concert took place at the Mann Auditorium in Tel Aviv under the auspices of the Tel Aviv Municipality.

In addition to a host of famous cantors, the Jerusalem Great Synagogue Choir, under the baton of Elli Jaffe, performed a number of interesting Glantz works for the occasion.

We worked from sheet music that we had at our disposal, as well as cantorial transcriptions set down by Cantor Shmuel Baruch Taube *z"l*.

In order to perform a wide variety of works, I devised this "potpourri" for virtuoso male choir and piano. Later I re-adapted the *Ashreinu* as a solo concert piece, and subsequently made an *a capella* version of *Uv'yom Ha'Shabbat* for cantor and male choir. Both items appear elsewhere in this volume. The *Uv'yom Ha'Shabbat* thus became part of the core repertoire of the Jerusalem Great Synagogue Choir. The *"Hit'la'ha'vut"* (fervor) and natural musical pacing of the various Chassidic sects manifest themselves in this selection, making the work irresistible to the listener and performer alike.

—*Raymond Goldstein*

Score

Chassidic Medley

Ashreinu/Uv'yom Hashabbat/Le'cha Dodi

Leib Glantz

Arr: Raymond Goldstein

Molto rall.
Slow, in 8
T1
T2
B1
B2
Pno.
ma ya-fa u-ma ya-fa
y' - ru-sha - te - nu
u-ma ya-fa
u -
ma ya-fa
y' - ru - sha - te - nu

Andantino
in 2, un poco piu mosso
cantando
rit.
Adagio (in 8)
12
a2
T1
T2
ash - rei-nu ma tov ma tov chel-ke-nu u - ma na-im u-
H
mp
B1
B2
Pno.
sf mf
sempre Ped.
16
Vivo in 4 marcato
rit.
ma na-im
u-ma na-im u-ma na-im na - im go-ra-le-nu

Adagio (in 8) (come prima)
legato
19
a2
T1
T2
ma ya-fa ma ya-fa
(♮)
y' - ru-sha-te-nu
mp
f
a2
B1
B2
p
Pno.

Allegro ma non troppo
21
T1
T2
mp U-v'-
B1
B2
f
Pno.

23
T1
T2
yom u - v'- yom u - v'- yom ha - sha - bat sh'nei k'va - sim b'- nei sha - na t'mi - mim ush -
B1
B2
sub. p
Pno.
p
col 8 (four bars)
25
T1
T2
nei ush - nei ush - nei es - ro - nim so - let mi - n'- cha b'- lu - la va - she - men v'- nis - ko o -
f
sub. p
pp
B1
B2
Pno.
Ped.

27
T1
T2
lat sha - bat b' - sha - ba - to al o - lat ha-ta-mid v'-nis-ka o -
B1
B2
sha - bat sha-ba-to ha-ta-mid v'-nis - ka
Pno.
29
T1
T2
lat sha-bat b' - sha - ba - to o - lat ha-ta-mid v'-nis-ka
f
B1
B2
o-lat sha - bat b'-sha-ba-to o - lat ha-ta-mid v'-nis-ka
Pno.

31
a2
T1
T2
yis-m'-chu b'-mal-chut-cha
shom-rei shom-rei sha-bat
v'-kor-ei v'-kor-ei
a2
B1
B2
a2
(sim)
Pno.
mf
34
o-neg o - neg sha-bat
am m'-ka-d'-shei am m'-ka-d'-shei
sh'vi - i sha - bat
am m'-kad-shei
mp
tr

37
T1
T2
kulam yis-b'-u v'-yit-a-n'-gu mi-tu-ve-cha sha-bat
B1
B2
8va
tr
Pno.

39
T1
T2
am m'-ka-d'-shei am m'-ka-d'-shei sh'vi-i___ sha-bat
B1
B2
am m'-kad'-shei sh'vi-i___ sha-bat
tr
Pno.

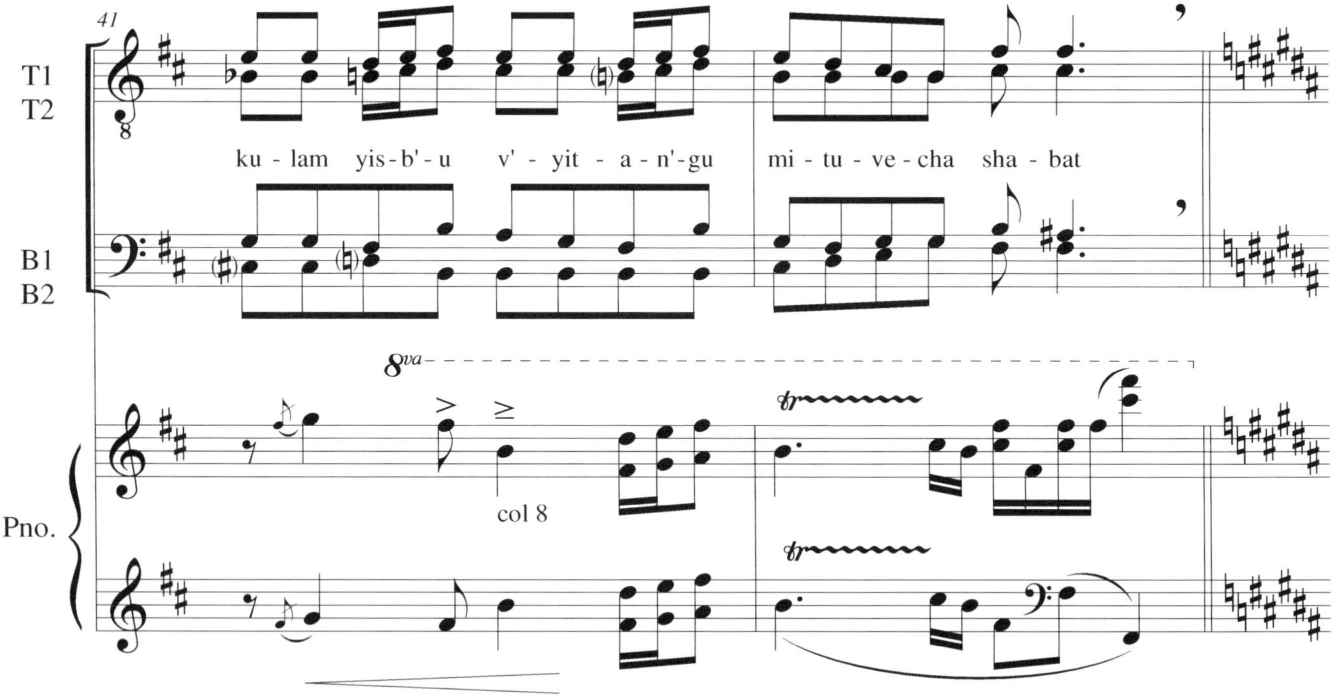
41
T1
T2
kulam yis-b'-u v'-yit-a-n'-gu mi-tu-ve-cha sha-bat
B1
B2
8va
tr
col 8
Pno.

43
a2
(un poco maestoso)
sha - - - bat
T1
T2
u-va-sh'vi-i ra-tzi-ta bo v'-ki-dash-to sha-bat
a2
B1
B2
Pno.

rit.
45
a2
T1
T2
u - va - sh'vi - i ra - tzi - ta bo v' - ki - dash - to sha - bat
pp
a2
B1
B2
8va
Pno.
a tempo un poco meno
47
T1
T2
f
chem - dat ya - mim chem - dat ya - mim o - to ka - ra - ta sha - bat
B1
B2
Pno.
(mp_mf)

rall.
allargando
a tempo
49
pp
T1
T2
ze - cher ze - cher ze - cher ze - cher
l'-ma'a-se v'-re - shit sha - bat
p
B1
B2
allargando
Pno.
pp
[l'istesso tempo]
51
a2
T1
T2
L' - cha do - di lik - rat ka - la p' - nei sha - bat n' - kab - la l'-
p
pp
B1
B2
Pno.
non leg.
legato

56
a2
1.
T1
T2
cha do-di lik-rat ka-la p'-nei sha-bat n'-kab-la l'-
B1
B2
Pno.
p

60
2.
T1
T2
kab-la
f
sha-mor v'-za-chor b'-di-
B1
B2
Pno.
p

64
T1
T2
bur e - chad hish-mi - a - nu el ha -
B1
B2
Pno.
legato
68
T1
T2
- m'-yu-chad A-do - nai e - chad u - sh' - mo e - chad u - sh'-
pp
B1
B2
Pno.
staccato
Ped.
sempre p

72
T1
T2
B1
B2
Pno.
mo e - chad l' - shem ul-tif - e - ret v' -
76
li - t'-hi-la
l'-cha do - di lik - rat ka - la p' -

80
T1
T2
nei sha - bat n' - kab - la l' - cha do - di lik - rat ka - la p' -
B1
B2
Pno.
molto rall
1.
2.
84
T1
T2
nei sha - bat n' - kab - la
nei sha - bat n' -
B1
B2
Pno.

a tempo
87
T1
T2
kab - la
B1
B2
Pno.
f

The cover of the book *"Zeharim"* – In Memory of Leib Glantz, edited by Eliezer Steinman and David Vinitzky (published in Tel Aviv in 1965)

36. *D'ror Yikra*

The arrangement for this composition was commissioned by Cantor Efraim Sapir of Temple Anshei Shalom, Delray Beach, FL, in memory of his parents Dov and Yehudit Sapir *z"l*.

About *D'ror Yikra*:

Most of us have heard some version of this melody at a Sabbath table in a variety of Jewish communities. This is the original version composed by Leib Glantz.

The familiar, catchy melody has a charming, hopeful character, and it should be noted that in his recording of this piece Glantz applied this musical setting only to two verses, whose subject matter is cheerful and optimistic.

The poem was written by Donash ben Labrat, from Baghdad, 920-990 C.E. Some of the other verses express such sentiments as "Smash my foes with wrathful anger!" and "Crush my foes O jealous God, with melting heart and grief!" Glantz was surely aware that his charming melody would be sung at many Sabbath tables and applied to *all* the verses, and surely intended that it would serve to keep the mood light even when covering those vengeful sentiments in the poem.

—*Cantor Ralph Schlossberg*

Score

דרור יקרא

D'ror Yikra

Leib Glantz
Arr: Raymond Goldstein

14
u - la - mi v' - ot ye - sha a - se i - mi n' - ta so - rek b' - toch kar - mi sh'-
19
e shav-at b'-nei a - mi d'rosh na - vi v' - u - la - mi v'-
23
ot ye - sha a - se i - mi n' - ta so - rek b' - toch kar - mi sh'-

27
e shav-at b'-nei a - mi ba-
31
bam ba - bam ai di di di ai di di di ai
f
35
ai di di di ai di di di ai di di di ai di di di ai

39
ai ai di di di ai di di di ai ai di di di ai di di di
mf
44
ai di di di ai di di di ai d'rosh na-vi v'-
48
u-la-mi v'-ot ye-sha a-se i-mi n'-ta so-rek b'-toch kar-mi sh'-
mp

e shav - at b'-nei a - mi
e shav - at b'-nei a - mi
d'ror yik - ra l' - ven im bat v' - yin - tzor - chem k' - mo ba - vat n' - im shim - chem v'-
lo yush - bat sh' - vu v' - nu - chu b' - yom sha - bat d'ror yik - ra l'-
mp

66
ven im bat v'-yin-tzor-chem k'-mo ba-vat n'-im shim-chem v'-lo yush-bat
mf
rall.
meno mosso
71
sh'-vu v'-nu-chu b'-yom sha-bat
f
75

Leib Glantz singing in Tel Aviv, Israel, in 1955

37. *D'voirele*

The arrangement for this composition was commissioned by JuMu (Nu Juwish Music) in memory of the great Leib Glantz.

About *D'voirele*:

Whispers and secretive gazes have always accompanied the lyrics of this moving Yiddish song. Who was this *D'voirele* that Glantz sung so passionately about?

The solution to this spicy topic is connected to the author of the lyrics – Shneur Zalman Rubashov (Shazar), a close teenage friend of Glantz from their Labor Zionist days in Europe, who, as Zalman Shazar, became the third President of the State of Israel.

D'voirele is a story about a *Ye'shi'va* student who fell in love with the Rabbi's beautiful daughter, but had no chance of fulfilling his dream because the Rabbi had promised his daughter to another.

A full array of feelings and sentiments are unveiled in this song, and Glantz, Shazar's friend and confidant, conveys them with astounding emotion, effectively expressing the anguish of the rebellious student against his Rabbi, the emotions of the poet's yearnings, and perhaps the image of the beautiful maiden, which is burning in the student's **and** the poet's mind.

Before engaging in performing this song it is very important to listen to the Glantz recording and take into account the subtle musical interpretations he displays.

—Cantor Naftali Herstik

דבורה׳לה

D'voirele

Leib Glantz
Arr: Chanan Winternitz
with additional changes by Raymond Goldstein

Yiddish transliteration- following YIVO romanization.

8
bam, bam, bam, bam, bam, bam, bam, bam, bam, bam, ba ba-bam, bam, bam, bam, bam, bam, ba,
10
rit.
in tempo
ay, yai, yai, yai yai, yai, yai yai, D'voi-re - le ba-bam, bam, bam, bam, bam, ba, ba-
dolce, meno mosso
p
13
bam, bam, bam, bam, bam, ba ba - bam ay D'voi-oi, oi, oi-re-le

ossia
16
ba-bam ba-bam ba-bam ay D'voi-re-le ay ay
[as before!]
ppp
19
rit.
meno mosso
ay sheyn vi-zi-bn vel-tn iz meyn D'voi-re-le
22
p
piu mosso
ba meyn re-bins m'la - ve mal-ka shpet ba-nakht
p
3
5

25
tif far-trakht iz ge-ze - sn in dem tsvey-tn khe-der Dvoi - re-le
misterioso
29
D'voi-re-le un fun ye-ner m'la - ve mal-ka Got meyn Got
5
poco piu f
33
nakht nokh nakht hot ge - fan-gen meyn ne - shu-me D'voi - re-le
5
meno f
p

37
D'voi - re-le oy - gn vi di him - len bloy un
40
lo-kn hel vi mor-gn - toy oy - gn vos der - mo - nen oft k'hob ge-
44
benkt ge - vart ge - hoft oy bam ba - bam

46
k'hob dem re - bin nit ge-folgt hot mikh got ge -
espress.
49
shtroft k'hob dem re - bin nit ge - folgt oy
52
nit ge - folgt hot mich Got ge - shtroft na
espress.

Moderato
55
na, na, na, na, na, na, na, na, na, ba, ba, ba, bam, bam, ba, ba, ba, ba,
p
58
bam la, la, la, la, la, la, la, la, la, la, la, la, la,
61
la - la, la, la, la, la la, la, la, la, la, la, la, la, la, la, la, la, la, la,
rall.
p

meno mosso
la, la, la, la, la, la.
ay ay ay ay yay yay yay
ay ay ay a yay yay yay
LH
ppp
Lento
p
sheyn vi zi - bn vel - ten iz meyn D'voi - re - le
ten.
p
ten.
8va

Leib Glantz

38. *Elokeinu Kadsheinu*

THE ARRANGEMENT FOR THIS COMPOSITION WAS COMMISSIONED BY THE CANTOR LIPPS DISCRETIONARY FUND OF CONGREGATION ADATH JESHURUN, LOUISVILLE, KY.

About *Elokeinu Kadsheinu*:

This melody is in the style of the *Bratzlaver Chassidim.* The *Bratzlavers* were unique even among *Chassidim.* In their synagogues they actually danced in a circle while performing the prayer services. Song and dance was part of the prayer. Although their music was not as deep and meaningful as the intense meditation of the *Cha'bad Chassidim,* it was so full of mounting excitement and overwhelming enthusiasm that onlookers as well as participants were often caught up into religious ecstasy – *D'vei'kut.*

—*Jerry Glantz*

Leib Glantz conveys the subtle nuances he skillfully discovers in the traditional *Nu'sach* and liturgy with a controlled Glantzlike precision in his lyric tenor voice that lands on a trampoline of rapidly changing vocal dynamics. He fuses together a pensive, elegant *sotto voce* opening phrase into a melodramatic elocutionary, booming musical "lecture."

—*Cantor Emanuel C. Perlman*

Score

אלוקינו קדשנו

Elokeinu Kadsheinu

Leib Glantz

Arr: Raymond Goldstein

A Chassidic spiritual in the style of the "Bratzlaver".

8
rit.
tze vim-nu-cha-te-nu ka-d'-she-nu b'mitz-vo-te-cha v'ten chel - ke-nu b' - to - ra - te-cha ka-d'-
10
1.
she-nu b'mitz-vo - te-cha v'ten chel-ke-nu b'to-ra-te-cha v'ten chel - ke - nu b'-to - ra - te - cha ka-d'-
mp
marcato
12
2.
ke - nu b'-to-ra-te - cha v'-ta - her li - be - nu l' - ov - d'-cha be-e - met v'-ta-
3

15
rit.
a tempo
her li - be - nu l' - ov - d' - cha be - e - met v' - ta - her li - be - nu l' -
mf
Ped.
Ped.
18
ov - d' - cha be - e - met v' - ta - her li - be - nu l' -
marcato
20
rit.
a tempo
ov - d' - cha be - e - met v' - ta - her li - be - nu l' -

22
ov - d' - cha be - e - met v' - ta - her li - be - nu l' -
24
3
ov - d' - cha be - e - met v' - han - chi - le - nu v' - han - chi - le - nu Ado - nai E -
26
lo - hei - nu b' - a - ha - va u - v' - ra - tzon sha - bat sha -
mp

bat kod - she - cha b'-a-ha - va u - v'-ra - tzon sha-bat sha-
mp
Ped.
bat kod - she - cha v'-ya-nu - chu va Yis - ra - el m'-ka - d'-
mp
shei sh' - me - cha b'-a-ha - va u - v'-ra - tzon sha-bat sha-
mf

ff
34
bat kod - she - cha v'-ya - nu - chu va
ff
Yis - ra - el m' - ka - d' -
f
rit.
36
3
shei sh' - me - - cha

Leib Glantz

39. *Hu Yiftach Libeinu*

THE ARRANGEMENT FOR THIS COMPOSITION WAS COMMISSIONED BY
THE FARKAS-GEIGES FAMILY OF HANNOVER, GERMANY,
IN MEMORY OF THE GREAT *HAZZAN* ISRAEL ALTER.

About *Hu Yiftach Libeinu*:

This Glantz composition begins in a subdued manner, sweetly and subtly repeating the opening phrase – *Hu Yif'tach Li'bei'nu Be'To'ra'to* (He will open our heart to His Torah).

Then, he continues with pure gentleness in his interpretation – *Ve'Ya'sem Be'Li'bei'nu A'ha'va'to Be'Li'bei'nu Ve'Yir'a'to* (to put the love and fear of Him into our hearts). At that point Glantz authoritatively crescendos with the full richness of his voice – *Ve'La'a'sot Re'tzo'no Ul'Ov'd'cha Be'Lei'vav Sha'lem* (to do His will and to serve Him with a whole heart).

After that Glantz pleads to embrace the Messiah, after which he brings the "tenor" of the piece back to its initial volume. He playfully uses the built in rhythms in words like *Be'Li'bei'nu* (in our heart), and uses his voice like Michelangelo brush stroked the Sistine Chapel, each stroke of repetitive phrases with a fresh palate of melodic colors.

Leib Glantz's family were Tolner *Chassidim.* This Chassidic melody is in the style of the Tolner *Chassidim.* The Tolner dynasty made every effort to make life for its followers as joyful as possible, especially through music and dance.

—*Cantor Emanuel C. Perlman*

Score

הוא יפתח לבנו

Hu Yiftach Libeinu

Leib Glantz
Arr: Raymond Goldstein

a tempo
18
hu yif-tach li-be-nu hu yif-tach li-be-nu b'-to-ra-to li-be-nu
24
b'-to-ra-to v'-ya - sem b'-li-be-nu v'-ya -
29
a tempo
sem b'-li-be-nu a-ha-va-to b'-li-be-nu v'-yi-ra-to v'-la-a-
mf

הוא יפתח לבנו

52
hu — yif - tach li-be-nu b'-to-ra - to li-be-nu b'-to-ra - to
3
58
v' - ya - sem b'-li-be-nu v' - ya - sem b'-li-be-nu a - ha - va - to b'-li-be-nu
64
v' - yir - a - to y' - hi ra - tzon mil - fa - ne-cha y' - hi ra - tzon mil-fa-ne-cha
RH - legato

70
she-nish - mor chu-ke-cha ba-o-lam ha - ze v'-niz - ke v'-nich-ye
3
mf
Ped.
76
v'-niz - ke v'-nich-ye v'-nir - e v'-ni-rash to-va uv-ra - cha lish-nei y'-
3
83
mot ha-ma-shi - ach lish - nei y' - mot ha-ma-shi - ach u - l' - cha -
mf

rall.
a tempo un poco meno
87
yei ha-o-lam o-lam ha-ba lish-nei y'-mot ha-ma-shi-ach
mp
92
lish-nei y'-mot ha-ma-shi-ach u-l'-cha-yei ha-o-lam ha-o-lam ha-
97
ba hu yif-tach li-be-nu hu yif-tach li-be-nu b'-to-ra-
mp

103
to li-be-nu b'-to-ra-to v'-ya - sem b'-li-be-nu
108
v' - ya - sem b' - li - be - nu a - ha - va -
111
to b' - li - be - nu v' - yir - a - to

40. *Kol Me'kadesh*

THE ARRANGEMENT FOR THIS COMPOSITION WAS COMMISSIONED BY
CANTOR MICHAEL SMOLASH
OF TEMPLE ISRAEL, WEST BLOOMFIELD, MI,
IN HONOR OF CANTOR HAROLD ORBACH.

About *Kol Me'kadesh*:

In this composition, it sounds like Leib Glantz returned to his Kiev home, back to his father's Chassidic house. Perhaps he even dropped by to visit Rabbi Dovid'l, the *Ad'mor* (spiritual leader) of the Tolner *Chassidim.*

Although this rendition is sometimes "Glantzy", as a whole it is almost *Ba'la'ba'tish,* with hardly a deviation from the *Nu'sach* of the singing of *Z'mi'rot* (religious songs regularly sung at the Sabbath table).

In the 1949 recording, Glantz is accompanied by the Tel Aviv Chamber Orchestra, conducted by Marc Lavry. It is clearly evident that there was great harmony and understanding between the two. Therefore, in his new arrangement, Raymond Goldstein made a great effort to leave the harmonic and musical structure intact.

—*Cantor Naftali Herstik*

Score

כל מקדש

Kol Me'kadesh

Leib Glantz

Arr: Raymond Goldstein

9
ish al mach-ne - hu v' - ish al dig-lo o-ha-
mf
12
vei A-do-shem ha-m'-cha-kim b'-vin-yan a-ri - el b'yom sha-bat ko-desh
14
In 2 - a tempo
sisu v'-sim-chu kim-kab-lei ma-tan nach - li - el si - su v'-sim-
mp
cantabile

17
rit.
chu kim-kab - lei mat - tan nach-li-el
20
a tempo
gam s'-u y'-dei-chem ko - desh v'-im - ru la - El ba-ruch A-do-shem a-
mf
23
sher na-tan na-tan na - tan m'-nu-cha l'-a-mo

26
l' - a - mo Yis - ra - el na - tan m'- nu - cha
29
l' - a - mo l' - a - mo Yis - ra - el a -
3
32
zor la - shov - tim bash - vi - i be - cha - rish uv - ka - tzir o - la -

35
3
mim posim bo p'-si-ah k'-ta-na so-a-dim
38
bo l'-va-rech sha-losh p'-a-mim tzid-ka-tam tatz-hir k'-
41
or k'-or shiv-at ha-ya-mim A-do-

44
shem E - lo - hei Yis - ra - el a - ha - vat a - ha - vat ta -
47
mim A - do - shem E - lo - hei Yis - ra - el t' - shu -
Ped.
50
3
at t' - shu - at o - la - mim
Ped.

Leib Glantz

41. *Nachpe'sa*

THE ARRANGEMENT FOR THIS COMPOSITION WAS COMMISSIONED BY CANTORIAL SOLOIST LINDI RIVERS OF HOLY BLOSSOM TEMPLE, TORONTO, IN HONOR OF HER HUSBAND, STEPHEN.

About *Nachpe'sa*:

This composition is in the style of the *Cha'bad Chassidim.* The Hebrew meaning of *Cha'bad* is *Choch'ma* (wisdom), *Bi'nah* (insight) and *Da'at* (knowledge). *Cha'bad* singing was individual, mystic and intense – aspiring toward the "higher spheres of spirituality."

Nach'pe'sa has more of a serious philosophical nature. It is not intended to be a literal copy of *Cha'bad* songs, but is an attempt, as Leib Glantz himself stated, to recreate the mood, the rhythm and the typical melodic themes and musical figures of the *Cha'bad* style.

The lyrics are very optimistic: *Nach'pe'sa De'ra'chei'nu, Ve'Na'shuva Ei'le'cha. Ki Ye'min'cha Pe'shu'ta Le'ka'bel Sha'vim. Ma No'mar U'ma Ne'da'ber, U'ma Nitz'ta'dak.* (We shall look for our path to return to You, because Your right hand is open to welcome those who return to your Realm. What can we say, how can we speak, and how can we become righteous).

—*Jerry Glantz*

Here Glantz takes the term "grandiloquent" traditionally applied to speech and elevates it to a musical parlance. He somehow masterfully manages to keep it from sounding garrulous, pompous or bombastic. Glantz must have been influenced by *sprechgesang* and *sprechstimme.* He vacillates in *Nach'pe'sa* between an operatic recitative style of singing to almost approximating speech itself... Berg or Schoenberg (but certainly not Wagner) would have probably been ardent fans!

—*Cantor Emanuel C. Perlman*

Score

נחפשה

Nachpe'sa

Leib Glantz
Arr: Chanan Winternitz

A chassidic spiritual in the style of "Chabad"

Originally composed in Los Angeles in 1947.

13
p
ki y' - mi-n'-cha p' - shu - ta l' - ka - bel sha - vim
p
espress.
17
ki y' - mi-n'-cha p' - shu - ta l' - ka - bel sha - vim
21
ma no - mar u - ma n' - da - ber u - ma nitz - ta - dak

24
ma no - mar u - ma n'-da-ber u - ma nitz-ta-dak ma no - mar u-
28
ma n' - da-ber u - ma nitz - ta - dak ma no - mar u-
31
ma n' - da-ber u - ma nitz - ta - dak

poco piu mosso
33
p
nach-p'-sa d'-ra-chei-nu v'-nach-ko - ra v'-na-shu-va
p
38
v' - na - shu - va e - le - cha
41
f
ki y'-min'-cha p'-shu-ta l'-ka-bel sha-vim ki y'-min'-cha
f

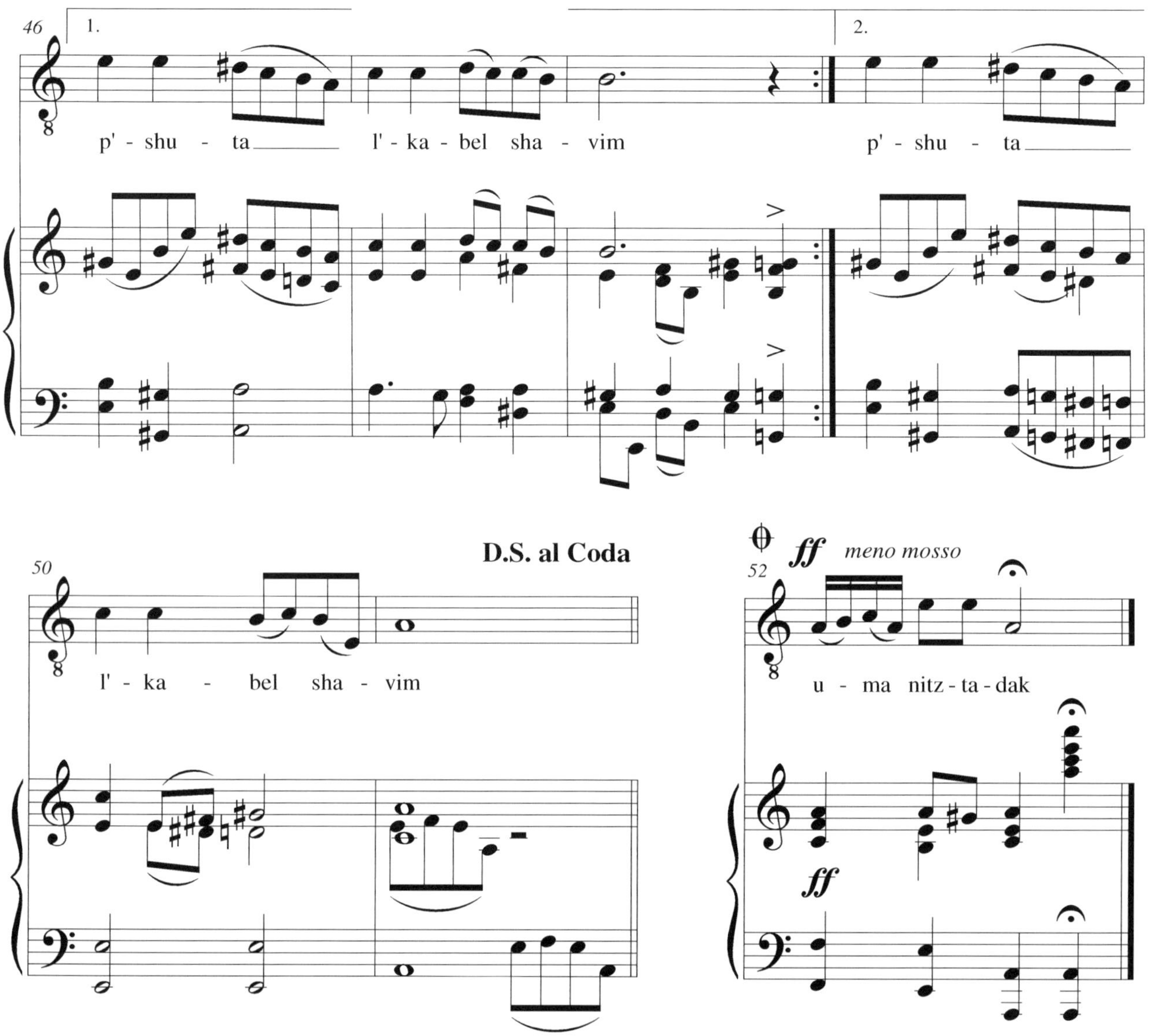
46
1.
2.
p' - shu - ta
l' - ka - bel sha - vim
p' - shu - ta
50
D.S. al Coda
l' - ka - bel sha - vim
52
ff
meno mosso
u - ma nitz - ta - dak
ff

42. *Titgadal Ve'titkadash*

[CHANAN WINTERNITZ ARRANGEMENT – VSC]

THE REPRINT OF CHANAN WINTERNITZ'S ORIGINAL ARRANGEMENT FOR THIS COMPOSITION WAS COMMISSIONED BY EVIATAR FELDMAN IN MEMORY OF HIS MOTHER PNINA FELDMAN Z"L.

About *Titgadal Ve'titkadash*:

When Leib Glantz made *A'li'ya* to Israel in the early 1950s, and settled in Tel Aviv, the whole country was buzzing with excitement. He was the only cantor among the great cantors of his era that immigrated to Israel from one of the prosperous countries of the West.

Glantz, who was already a prominent cantorial legend in his lifetime, brought with him rich musical skills and a multi-faceted personality that generated media attention as well as curiosity in the general public as to who was this newly arrived enigmatic "modern Jew" who was widely proclaimed as the "poet of the pulpit."

What made Glantz approachable and beloved were his Chassidic melodies such as *Tit'ga'dal' Ve'Tit'ka'dash, Nach'pe'sa, Hu Yif'tach Li'bei'nu* and *D'ror Yik'ra.* These songs were broadcast over and over on the radio and proved to be very catchy. Notwithstanding the high level of musical artistry that Glantz employed, they typically resonated like authentic Chassidic dances full of exaltation and joy.

The atmosphere surrounding the building and establishment of a new nation and the absorption of masses of new immigrants, all importing with them new and different musical sounds from far-away lands, proved to be fertile soil for songs filled with hopeful spirit and freedom.

I actually heard this *Tit'ga'dal Ve'Tit'ka'dash* sung by my kindergarten teachers while preparing decorations for the various holiday celebrations. Even my own mother *z"l* used to hum this melody while preparing Sabbath feasts, and the melody became an anthem to the spirit of redemption adopted from the visions of our prophets.

Many of Tel Aviv's cantors strived (and frequently were forced by their congregants…) to deal with the modulations of these seemingly "simple" melodies.

This singing transpired from Glantz's heart, overflowing with a yearning for the redemption of his people. As always, what comes from the heart goes into the hearts of his listeners from all walks of life. These songs naturally became an integral part of the cultural scene of Israel, often performed in many concerts with Glantz and many of the leading Israeli cantors and singers.

The arrangement of this composition by Dr. Chanan Winternitz was executed under the strict supervision of Glantz himself, and it affords us with a truly authentic aroma of the State of Israel in its infancy.

—Cantor Naftali Herstik

Score

תתגדל ותתקדש

Titgadal Ve'titkadash

Leib Glantz
Arr: Chanan Winternitz

Originally composed in Los Angeles in 1947.

21
1.
2.
toch Y'-ru-sha - la-yim i-r' - cha
-cha
27
mf
tit - ga - dal v' - tit - ka - dash b' - toch b' - toch b' -
mf
31
toch Y' - ru - sha - la - yim i - r' - cha
l' -
p

35
dor va-dor l' - dor va-dor ul - ne - tzach ul - ne - tzach n' - tza - chim
41
1.
2.
p
tit - ga - dal v' - tit - ka - dash b' -
p
47
1.
toch b' - toch b' - toch Y'-ru-sha - la-yim i - r' - cha

53
2.
f
-cha
tit - ga - dal v' - tit - ka - dash b' -
f
57
toch b' - toch Y' - ru-sha-la-yim i - r' - cha
l'dor va-dor l'-
64
1.
dor va-dor ul - ne - tzach ul - ne-tzach n'-tza - chim

71
2.
-tzach ul - ne-tzach n'-tza - chim
p
tit-ga-dal v' - tit-ka-dash b'-
78
1.
toch b' - toch b'-toch Y'-ru-sha - la-yim i-r' - cha
rall. e cresc.
meno mosso - maestoso
rall.
84
2.
f
-cha b'-toch Y' - ru - sha - la-yim i - r' - cha

43. *Titgadal Ve'titkadash*

[Raymond Goldstein arrangement – TTBB]

The arrangement for this composition was commissioned by Haim and Gila Wiener of Miami Beach, Florida.

About *Titgadal Ve'titkadash*:

In this rather "free" setting concert version of *Titgadal Ve'titkadash* for male choir, the intervallic relationship of the original melodic line inspired me to write a short contrapuntal series of *fugato*-like variations on a theme with a concluding *coda.*

This version was premiered at a Leib Glantz concert performed at the Tel Aviv Mann Auditorium in 1988 with the Jerusalem Great Synagogue Choir conducted by Elli Jaffe.

Titgadal Ve'titkadash is in the style of the *Bratzlaver Chassidim.* Music played a great part in Chassidism. It was a medium through which the *Chassidim* aspired to embrace God. They believed they could achieve more in the heavens through the power of their songs than through the power of their prayers – for "music is the soul of the universe."

In the language of mysticism, *"D'vei'kut"* represented one of the stages in the "elevation of the soul." To the masses it came to mean a mood of religious ecstasy, in which reality was effaced and spiritual joy prevailed.

—*Raymond Goldstein*

Score

תתגדל ותתקדש

Titgadal Ve'titkadash

Leib Glantz
Arr: Raymond Goldstein

23
T1
T2
B1
B2
toch Y' - ru - sha - la - yim i - r' - cha
ru - sha - la - yim i - r' - cha
toch Y' - ru - sha - la - yim i - r' - cha
meno mosso
27
f
tit - ga - dal v' - tit - ka - dash b' - toch b' - toch b' - toch Y' - ru - sha - la - yim i - r' -
1.
33
2.
cha
toch Y' - ru - sha - la - yim i - r' - cha

tempo primo
39
T1
tit-ga-dal v' - tit-ka-dash b' - toch b' - toch b'-
T2
tit-ga-dal v' - tit-ka-dash b' - toch b' - toch b'-
a2
B1
B2
tit-ga-dal v' - tit-ka-dash b' - toch b' - toch b'-toch Y'-ru-sha - la-yim i-r' -
45
T1
toch Y'-ru-sha - la-yim i-r' - cha tit-ga-dal v' - tit-ka-dash b' -
T2
toch Y'-ru-sha - la-yim i-r' - cha tit-ga-dal v' - tit-ka-dash b' -
B1
B2
cha tit-ga-dal v' - tit-ka-dash b' - toch b' - toch b' -
51
T1
toch b' - toch Y' - ru-sha-la-yim i-r'-cha tit-ga-dal v' - tit-ka-dash b' -
T2
toch b' - toch Y' - ru-sha-la-yim i-r'-cha tit-ga-dal v' - tit-ka-dash b' -
B1
B2
toch b'-toch b'-toch Y'-ru-sha - la - yim ir - cha tit-ga-dal v' - tit-ka-dash b' -

תתגדל ותתקדש

תתגדל ותתקדש

Leib Glantz Published Books

The Man Who Spoke to God

By Jerry Glantz
Published by the Tel Aviv Institute of Jewish Liturgical Music, 2008

"Zeharim — In Memory of Leib Glantz"

[Hebrew and Yiddish]
Edited by Eliezer Steinman; prepared for publication by David Vinitzky.
Published by the Tel Aviv Institute of Jewish Liturgical Music, Tel Aviv, 1965.

Leib Glantz's Selected Works — "Rinat Hakodesh Series"

[English and Hebrew]
Edited by David Loeb; prepared for publication by Yehoshua Zohar.
Published by the Tel Aviv Institute of Jewish Liturgical Music in conjunction with the Israel Music Institute (I.M.I.), Tel Aviv, Israel:

Volume 1: ***Nu'sa'chei Te'fi'la*** (Prayer modes for solo cantor).

Volume 2: ***Te'fi'lot Leil Sha'bbat*** (Friday Evening Service).

Volume 3: ***Te'fi'lot Sha'bbat*** (Sabbath Morning Service).

Volume 4: ***Ha'llel Ve'Sha'losh Re'ga'lim*** (Hallel and Three Festivals).

Volume 5: ***Se'li'chot*** (Penitential prayers).

Volume 6: ***Ya'mim No'ra'im*** (High Holidays).

Volume 7: ***Shi'rim*** (Songs).

***S'lichot Service for Cantor, Chorus and Organ,* by Leib Glantz**

Edited by David Loeb.
Published by the Hallel V'Zimra Association, Montreal, Quebec, Canada, 1965.

Books can be ordered by contacting email address: jgpacific@gmail.com

31927114R00281

Made in the USA
Charleston, SC
04 August 2014